BOOK DESIGN

Design Media Publishing Limited

CONTENTS

PREFACE

Dissimilarity

One of the principles of human nature is to impose one's will, as well as transformation of the world according to his/her own necessities. A designer who aspires to gain designated model, proceeds similarly – abides by the rules or breaks them intentionally. When creating a layout, a designer makes use of graphic elements, images and typography, arranging them in a controlled manner on pages of a publication coming into existence. In spite of technical development yet we still use the rules of harmony and proportions introduced by ancient Greeks and Egyptians. These rules enable us to manage complicated graphic arrangements of publications. The usage of the rule of thirds, absolute and relative measures, Fibonacci or Renard numbers, or Karl Gerstner's grid of 58 equal units provides legible transfer of information.

Thanks to that the structure, which reflects reality, is created. That ensures the balance of the composition. At the same time it is possible to preserve the element of creation as a consequence of diversified details. The utilisation of established rules does not guarantee that a project would be accepted positively.

There are many ways to create a good layout and the most important thing is to use generally accepted principles in an individual manner that lead us to a formation of an innovative project.

Ryszard Bienert
3group

Layout and Concept Design of a Book

From the view of designers, design is inseparable with life, music, food and friends. Earlier before designing a book, conception is the soul of the overall design. At this time, designers need more inspiration to fresh the book and thus catch the readers' eyes.

Book design is "propositional", so the inspiration of designers always comes from the content of a book. Designers usually combine what they had acquired in books and living experience with the proposition of the book on hand, and eventually turn it into the designing process. While thinking about the overall design of a book, designers should take the diversity of book design into account, which according to different propositions and types of books deffers the conception. What's more, the form of book must be based on the nature, content, readers and other factors of the book.

Cover design is top priority of book design. Cover design can be conceived as a kind of visual communication artwork, which means that it could arouse a visual and psychological resonance of readers in terms of vision and conception. The conception of cover is a concentrated expression of the designers' own artistic culture and cultural deposits. The cover should be full of sense of times and vividness. It is through different forms of choice and comparison that the conception and the design could really arouse the readers' feelings. "Light to see" means that the cover is just to give a beam of sunlight onto the invisible content of the book, and thus make the book full of vitality.

According to the book content, designers in the process of conceiving and sketching always try to combine the view of point, line, surface, body, space, texture, colour and living experience into design ideas.

The Expression of the Book's Content and Form

Only after the designers have understood the content of a book do they start to choose the form of art to express the book content. The integrated visual language of the cover, title page, text layout and top margin could give a perfect presentation of the book's content. A classic design could really present the original creativity and fascinating spirit of the designer.

The expression of the book's content is always realised by the form design. Form design does not simply refer to a kind of form or design, but to focus on the content, which determines the form and grasps the book overall from the view of microworld to macroworld. Designers who could apply the form design flexibly to present the book's content will be able to integrate the content with form completely. In addition, the creation of the layout design's aesthetics is an important part in the visual communication design of a book. That is to say, form design should not only be consistent with the message that the book expresses from the view of logic, but also need giving strong visual aesthetic impact. In the book design, any subtle changes of the fonts, lines, colours and other elements could provide a different experience for readers. The book design always consists of words, images, colours and other elements, including the capture of any disposable visual image and management to convey the content and core of the text. A rational expression of the imagery thinking can go beyond the expression of the words, so as to generate added value for the book.

Book is not an instant static solid, so in the conveying of the book's content we should pay more attention to the visual process, which is a kind of movement in the visual space. It refers to the process that the sight with various visual elements in a certain space goes along a certain trajectory. It aims to guide the eyes following with the design elements to convey the messages of the design. A good book design should include two aspects of time and space, which is a thread that runs through the book and could be invisible. Designers need to turn this invisible thread into graphic or figurative language to show the readers. Therefore, designers need to use the interrelated and interactive relationship between various components to create a rational and emotional visual design environment. They should control the content of design and various elements associated with the form subjectively and re-combine them, so as to make the whole text clear and integrated.

The expression of the book's content refers to the integration and unification of the form and the content, for the content needs to be presented by the form. Any work that separates from the content to pursue form would turn to be a failure. In another perspective, the content determines the form, and the form serves for the content. Needless to say, they complement each other, "never betray". Designers need to be aware of the structure of time and space on the book content, and understand the hierarchical space and time as well as the temporal flow in sight, so as to catch the readers' eyes.

Component Design of a Book

A book that gives a unique aesthetics from the overall to the details is not just an ordinary book; it could be a kind of artwork. Stunning appearance is not everything; only the perfect details of design can bring readers to get the double resonance in mind and feeling.

1. Cover

If a book is seen as a product, then there is no doubt that cover is the packaging of the product. In traditional industry, packaging design is a vital category, which means that the failure of packaging design would cause a series of negative reaction for sales and others. Cover is an expression of a book. Whether it could touch the readers' mind or not became a key to the success of a book.

Cover is not only to reflect the content, nature, but also to provide readers with the aesthetics, and well protect the book. Cover design includes the design of title, names of the author and publishers as well as the decorative images and colours. How to make the cover reflect the content of the book and how to make it affect the readers' mind are the most important parts in the cover design.

The colour of cover is always determined by the content of book as well as the readers' age, educational level and other characteristics. Bright colours are always applied in children's books; soft and pleasing colours always can be seen in the elderly reading; while colours between bright and grey should be used in young people's books. In addition, the content of the book also has specific requirements for colours; for instance a book that focuses on the revolutionary theme is suitable to red tones; a theme that emphasises on exposing the dark social evils is appropriate for white or black colour; while the fresh and energetic book prefers bright colours, etc. Readers with different cultural awareness, nationality and occupation could have different colour preferences for books.

An innovative cover requires the designer to master a wide range of knowledge. The knowledge of architecture, music, drama, film literature and so on can provide rich and fresh inspiration for designers. Designers in designing the cover must have a good solid foundation and a certain space of imagination in order to have the ability to fully express the book's shape, colour and texture to touch the readers' feeling.

2.Spine

Design of the book spine is an important visual language second to that of cover in a book. Hans Pitt Virbo mentioned in his book *Developing of the Books Art* that "It is spine that presents ninety percent of a book." Generally, most of books sold in bookstores are always inserted in the shelf and cannot be completely displayed. At this time, book spine turns to be the first visual language to express the style of a book. Therefore, design of the spine is very important.

The space of spine is usually narrow and small, which needs the designers to provide a refined layout design to make this special place play its supreme role. Usually, spine is often appropriate to use unique composition and brilliant colours to form a strong visual impact and thus stands out from the crowd. However, the design of spine should go harmoniously with the style and content of the whole book.

3. Fly Page

The fly page is a bridge between cover and inside of a book. A classic book that lacks of the fly page is just like a flaw on the white jade, greatly reducing the value of it. The fly page includes expansion page, blank page, like page, frontispiece inserts or title page (the amount of books), copyright page, inscription, thank offering, etc. With the improvement of the aesthetics, the quality of the fly page is also getting better and better, some of which use high quality specialty paper, and some fly pages even emit fragrance; while some with a number of decorative patterns or illustrations relate with the content of the book. Undoubtedly, this improvement will be a joy for book lovers and thereby increases the value of book, attracting more buyers.

The design of fly page is required to reflect the theme of the book content just as the cover design. In order to construct a good bridge between the cover and content of a book, illustrations, photography, calligraphy and other art forms or printing processes should be employed. As an integral part of the overall design, the fly page should go harmoniously with the cover and other design. Designers should inherit the design tradition and also be innovative. The emergence of the new materials and new craft not only plays a breakthrough role in the traditional design concept, but also calls the designers to take advantage of these new technologies to design more innovative and unique books.

4. Contents

From the award-winning design of the contents of books, we can see that the layout design of contents has got rid of the coloured thread and changeable font as much as possible. Some designers are interested in the application of colour, with some beautiful colour preferences listed in the directory layout design; the "bulge" or "depression" results could cause the readers' visual fatigue while turning over the book. A good designer will not abuse the colour; he will just let the book's tone be close to nature. If he chooses multi-colour to achieve aesthetically pleasing results, he would pay attention to the order of composition of neon. In many masterpieces, there are some blanks just like that in the Chinese painting that could give readers a sense of relaxing and pleasing. The more important the title is, the more blanks are needed. Blank in the dense layout of the contents is just like a beam of sunlight in the darkness, giving a sense of pleasure.

5. Layout

Layout design refers to format design of the full text in a book. Generally, besides the cover, the lining papers and the title page, the forewords are also included. The layout design should be original, beautiful, simple and popular and go harmoniously with the book's contents. Visual sense is the main sense organ of the human's appreciation of the beauty. Therefore, the layout design comes before the book content to impress the readers; an excellent layout design will attract readers to read the book content further. In contrast, a book without a sense of design whose layout design even gives a sense of suffocation will be hard to attract the readers. This means that the layout design has an "advertising effect". Colour, line and other elements of each particular object in the layout design are able to arouse the reader's feelings.

In the layout design, symmetry as a design form has been used widely. This design gives a sense of stability, unification and elegance. In practice, absolute symmetry of the layout design is rare, and too much emphasis on symmetry is also easy to make the layout look stiff. Designers will usually cleverly use the form of balance on typography to make up for the shortcoming of symmetry. Subtle changes in the layout that are a little "breaks" of the absolutely symmetrical layout could give a sense of novelty. This sense is generated by applying the form of balance to coordinate the contradiction between absolute symmetry and unbalance. In the design process, designers should avoid imbalance caused by too much changes.

Generally, in a book with texts and images, unique images will give the readers a strong visual impact. Sometimes, quality of the picture will directly affect the layout design. Images can be enlarged according to the needs of composition or even dealt with cross-page order and bleeding. This will make layout more lively and bring a sense of relaxing. What's more, the arrangement of text should correspond with the human engineering. Overlong lines will cause reading fatigue and reduce the reading speed.

Most of the layout is two-dimensional graphic design. Adjustment of the layout elements in accordance with the distance could create a three-dimensional visual effect. The changes of the font size and colour could contribute to a sense of layer. Compared with dark colours, light colours seem closer to the readers. In addition, the improvement of the arrangement of layout elements which refers to the scale, directions, colours and other details could help forming a mature perfect visual sense of space gradually. This is so called a three-dimensional illusion of space based on a two-dimensional plane. It aims to make the entire layout full of rhythm, appear flexible and far-reaching, but also to convey information clearly. It will attract the reader's attention and enhance their comprehension.

6. Copyright Page

Copyright page includes book title, the name of author, editor, criticiser, publisher and the name and location of printer and license number of book publishing business permits as well as format, printed sheet, number of words. In addition, there are also date of publication, order in the edition and printed, printing number as well as ISBN and pricing.

The title types in the copyright page are larger than other types in this page, and the rest of the text is arranged according to the classification. Some designers also use columns and decorative lines to fresh the page.

Design Methods

Design methods now are various. For a new case, the designer uses the existing design methods in mind and re-creates them to greatly improve the design and make the book design always being fresh.

1. Gridding

Gridding is not simply to put the words and pictures together, but a form of rule that is developed from the interrelated composition. It emphasises the sense of proportion, order, continuity, clarity, times, accuracy and rigour. It perfectly coordinates the relationship between the design elements. In essence, grid is the skeleton of layout design which can bring a sense of order and structure for design.

2. The Selection of Fonts

Font plays an important role in the book design, which should have distinct characteristics and styles. The ideal design is to select different fonts to guide the readers. Text itself is an art form; whether Chinese or English, it can be with handsome, vigorous, lively, soft and other styles. It is convenient for readers to read if the font goes harmoniously with the content and style.

The brightness of pages varies with the difference of the font, size, thickness, row spacing and kerning distances which determine the layout of the composition in the colour of black and white and grey. The changes of font size and the choice of font could reflect the content of the text elements, giving readers a taste of publications from the spirit and the content. The type of the title should not be too illegible or unrecognisable. Brief and small type should not employ the strong and thick black font. Font which is made up with simple lines and arcs gives a sense of softness and calmness; the beautiful and elegant "decorated letters" always give a sense of nobleness; round and thick font always could be used in cartoons. These general knowledge and disciplines are the base of designing a good book. In the designer's opinion, the choice of font is a combination of understanding and intuition, while the intuition comes from the accumulation of experience.

3. The Combination of Colours

Generally, colours are usually given to the feelings. In a sense, colours reflect human's character. In a similar way, the colour sometimes can show the spirit of a book. Actually, the colour content has not definitive meaning, while it always causes physical and mental activity on us. For example, the monotonous and simple colours of black, white, and yellow always bring a sense of solemnity. The symbolism of colour is formed with experience accumulation and habits while people cognising and using colours.

4. The Arrangement of Images

In recent years, blank layout is gradually developed into an effective means to fresh the layout. Bold and rational use of blank could perfectly present the good aesthetic taste of designers and break the old and dull layout, so as to give the whole page a sense of transparence, openness and brightness as well as cleanness.

BIS / BNO. Real Dutch Design Biennial

Design Agency:

...,staat creative agency

Production Date:

2006

Client:

BIS / BNO

Description:

The Dutch Design books are published every two years, showing an uncensored cross-section of the current state of affairs in Dutch design, representing over 300 agencies. ...,staat created the concept and design for the 06/07 edition. This nearly 1000-page book is based around the question: "What exactly is real Dutch design?" The creative agency asked various key players in different design areas this question – from Stefan Sagmeister and Wim Crouwel to Anton Corbijn and Marc Newson. You will find their answers and thoughts in Real Dutch Design 0607, together with the most recent work of more than 300 Dutch design agencies. The set consists of two books and is all about contrast in material and in design – fluorescent plastic combined with basic cardboard binds the pages together. Between these contradictory extremes, everything is possible. Real Dutch Design can be read from either side, and is published in Dutch, German and English.

REAL DUTCH DESIGN 0607
REAL DUTCH DESIGN 0607

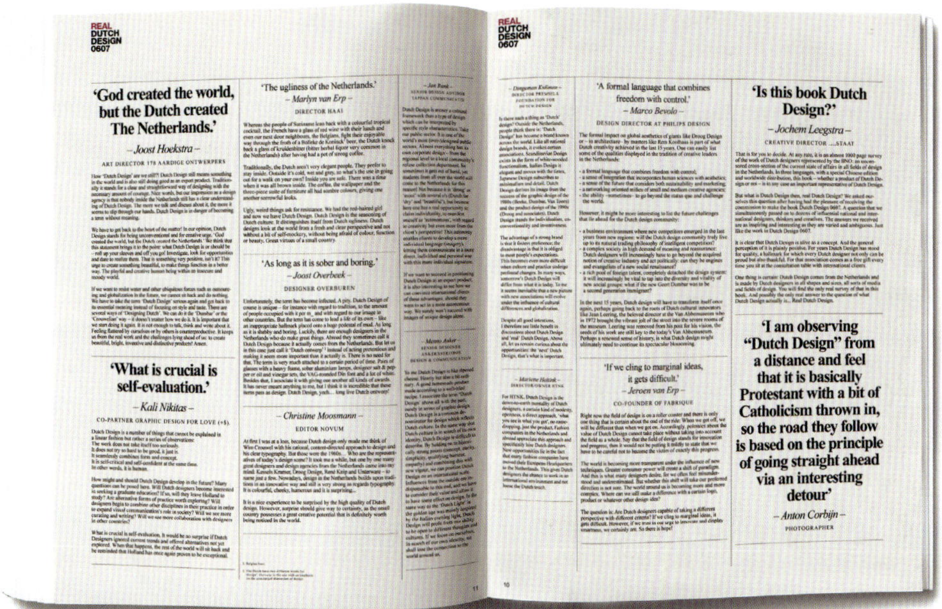
REAL DUTCH DESIGN 0607
'God created the world, but the Dutch created The Netherlands.'
'What is crucial is self-evaluation.'
REAL DUTCH DESIGN 0607
'Is this book Dutch Design?'
'I am observing "Dutch Design" from a distance and feel that it is basically Protestant with a bit of Catholicism thrown in, so the road they follow is based on the principle of going straight ahead via an interesting detour'

REAL DUTCH DESIGN 0607
'The true story of Dutch Design.'
'What Alberto Alessi thinks of Dutch Design'
REAL DUTCH DESIGN 0607
'I prefer to stop designing before it is finished.'
'Dutch Design is in a very good starting position for the future.'

016—017

The World According to Concrete

Design Agency:

...,staat creative agency

Production Date:

2007

Client:

Concrete

Description:

The designer, ...,staat saw this book as a "space". In collaboration with Thonik, ...,staat created square space within a book, or a book within a book; a shape within a shape. The book (content) is a square; the book (material) is a rectangle. It shows Concrete's vision of the world and contains work from various artists, such as Erwin Olaf, Fritz Kok, Damien Hirst, Vincent van Gogh, Blommers & Schumm, KesselsKramer, Banksy, Marcus Harvey and Maurice Scheltens.

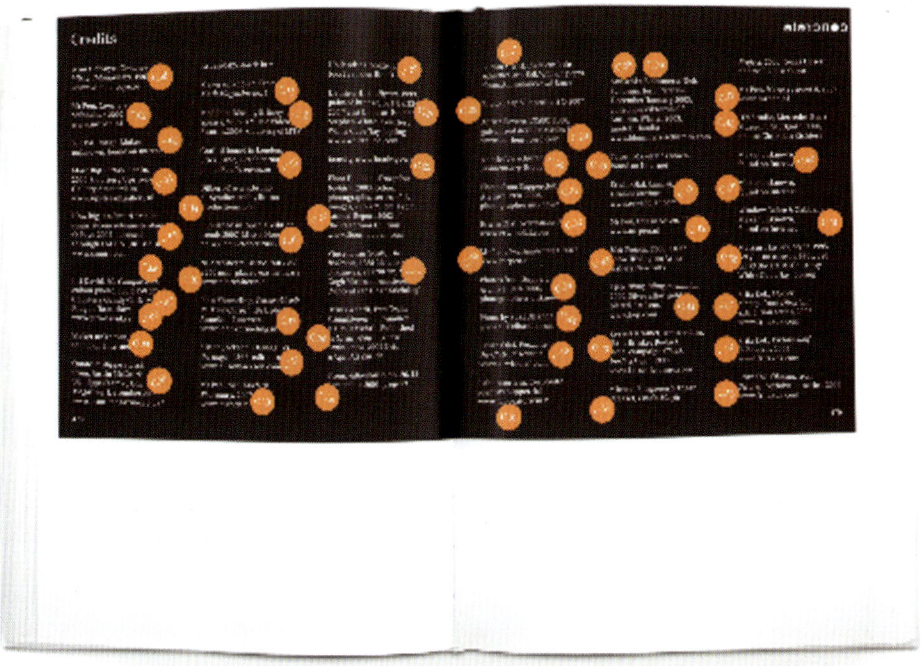
Credits

03 CREATING SHOPS,
BUILDING BRANDS

A Miracle of Modern Colour Photography

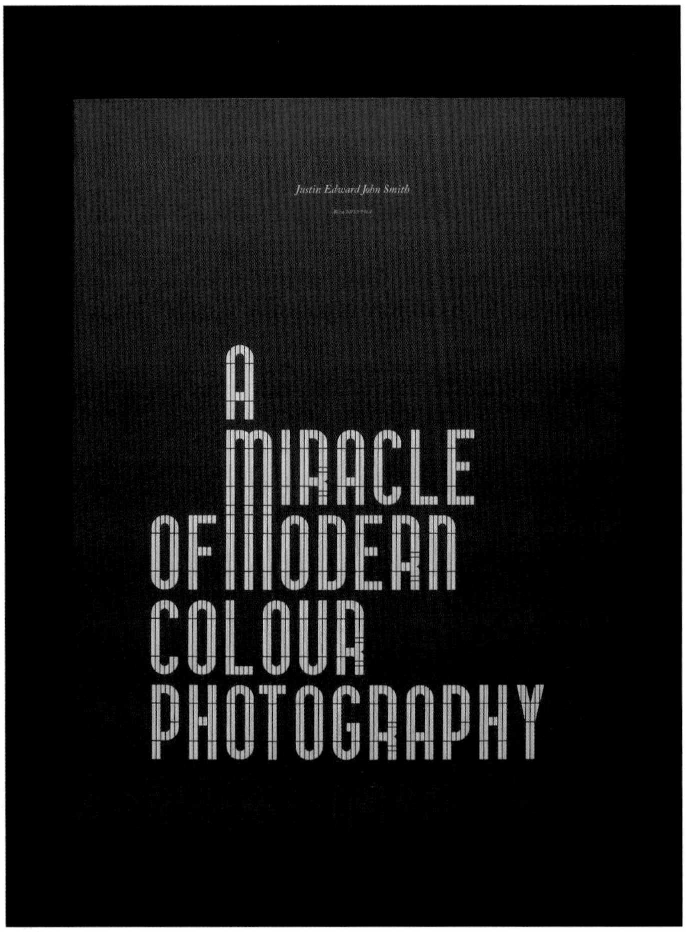

Design Agency:
3 Deep Design
Production Date:
2007
Client:
Justin Edward John Smith
Description:
A Miracle of Modern Colour Photography was a publication designed by 3 Deep Design to accompany an exhibition of the same name at the Goddard de Fiddes Gallery, in Perth, Western Australia. The artist, Justin Edward John Smith, is an English-born artist, who now lives in Perth and who has a lineage in Fashion photography and the performing arts. Julian Goddard, principal of Goddard de Fiddes Gallery comments here on the exhibition and Justin's work.

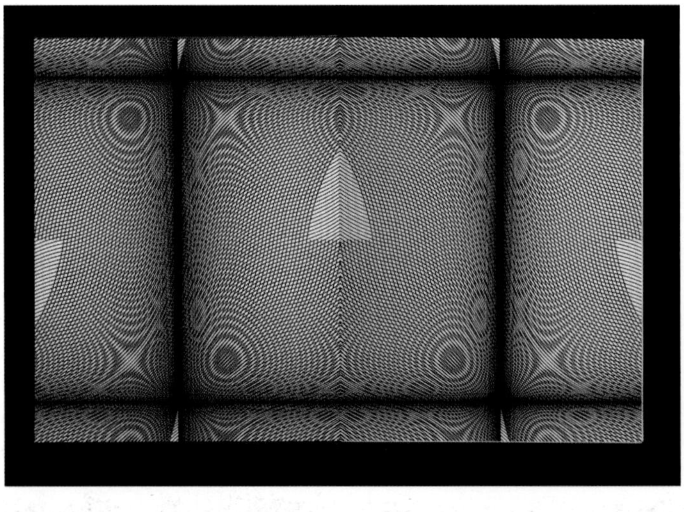

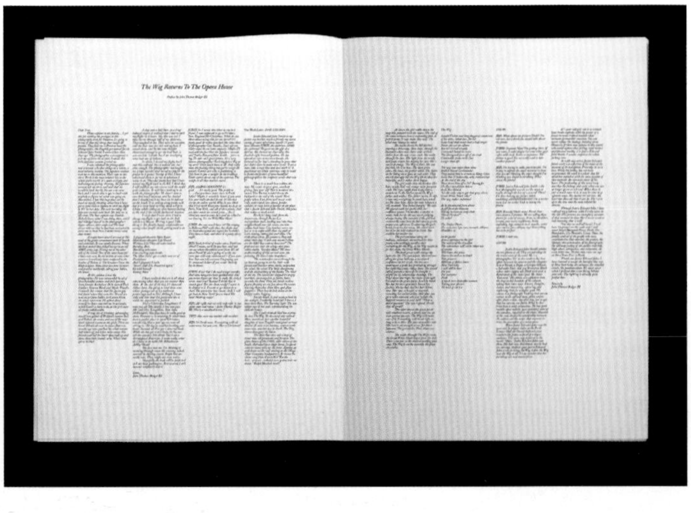

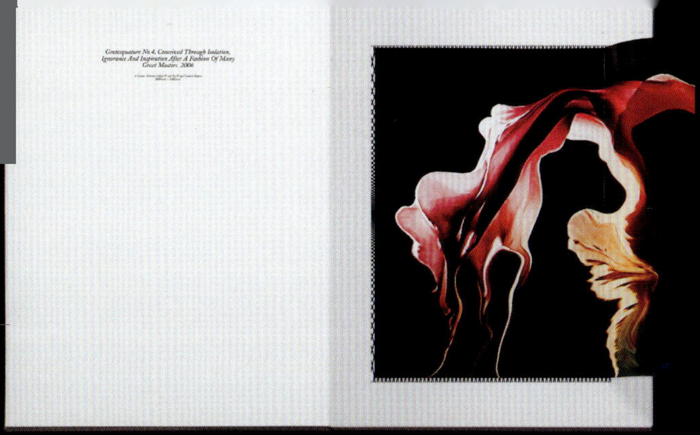
Grotesquature No.4, Conceived Through Isolation,
Ignorance And Inspiration After A Fashion Of Many
Great Masters. 2006

Grotesquature No 7, Conceived Through Isolation,
Ignorance And Inspiration After A Fashion Of Many
Great Masters. 2006

Justin Edward John Smith
A
MIRACLE
OF MODERN
COLOUR
PHOTOGRAPHY

Grotesquature No.7, Conceived Through Isolation,
Ignorance And Inspiration After A Fashion Of Many
Great Masters. 2006
6 Colour Solvent Inkjet Print On Vinyl Coated Nylon
2400mm x 1698mm

Goalkeeper Forever

Design Agency:
3group
Designer:
Ryszard Bienert
Production Date:
2009
Client:
Galeria Piekary
Description:
Book "Goalkeeper Forever" was designed for the photography exhibition of Zbigniew Sosnowski in Piekary Gallery in Poznan, Poland. Its character design relates to 1970s' photography style. There are five different kinds of paper used inside the book: coated matt, offset white, cream, handmade paper and different grammature of "newspaper-like" stock. Shots are printed by use of duotone Black and Pantone Grey. Cover has two differently-sized sleeves: the bigger one is a poster printed on uncoated paper, and the smaller one is gloss laminated. The inserts of different sizes in the book are printed on the thin stock, gloss laminated throughout.

Chel
sea
LeNny pidgeleY
Kiedy goalkeeper CHELSEA, LENNY PIDGELEY przyczynił się do porażki 4 – 0 swojego klubu z HERTFORDSHIRE w rozgrywkach PUCHARU ANGLII.

GROSIC
GYUL GROSIC

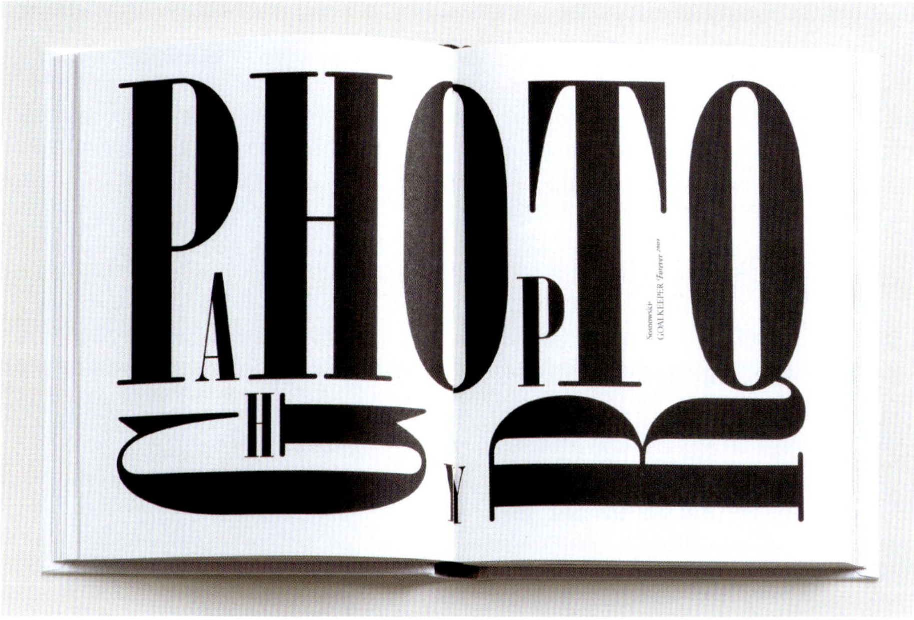
PHOTO

THIS WAS A COMPLETELY NEW KIND OF LIFE.
KEEPER
GOALKEEPER forever,
SOSNOWSKI

Kingdom

kingdom

an unwanted kingdom

an unwanted kingdom
ON SATIN PILLOWS AND ENCLOSED CABINETS

Born in 1973 in Gdańsk. Graduated from the State High School of Art in Gdynia - Orłowo and from the Sculpture Department of The Academy of Fine Arts in Gdańsk (prof F. Duszeńko's sculpture studio and multimedia studio of prof G. Klaman) in 1999. 1998 - 2002 cooperation with Wyspa Gallery and Wyspa Progress Foundation.

an unwanted kingdom
kingdom
kingdom

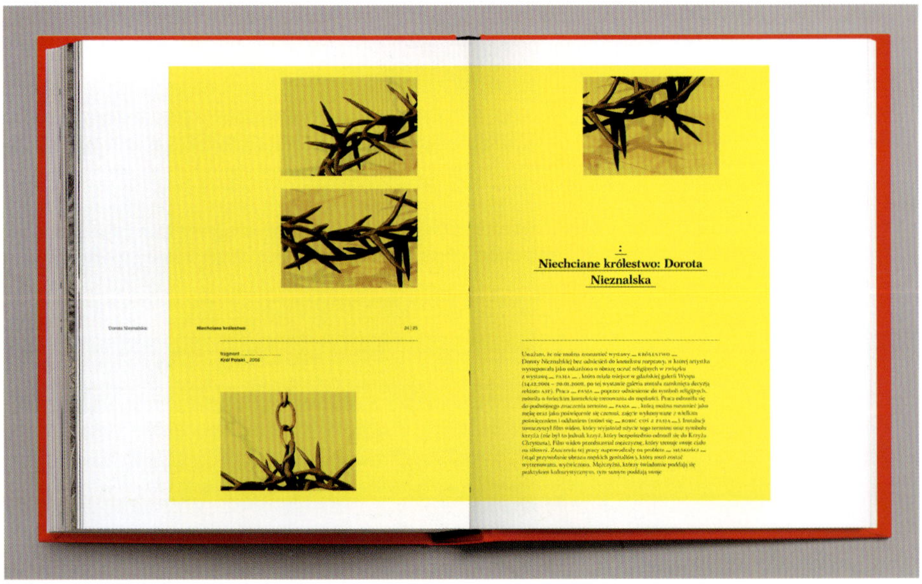
Niechciane królestwo: Dorota Nieznalska

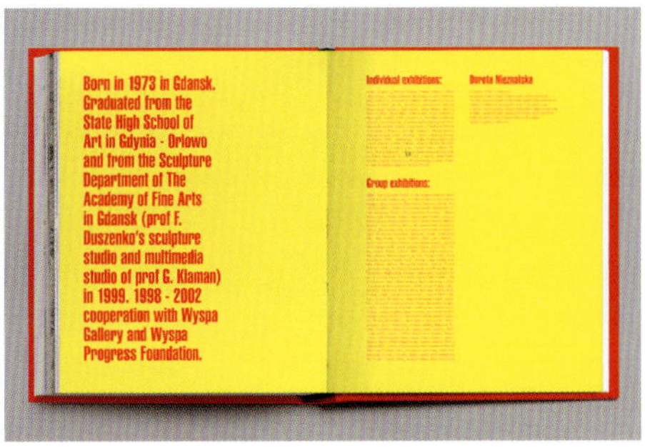

Design Agency:

3group

Designer:

Ryszard Bienert

Production Date:

2010

Client:

Galeria Piekary

Description:

Book "Kingdom" was designed for the exhibition of Dorota Nieznalska in Piekary Gallery in Poznan, Poland. Its character design relates to 1970s' style. There are two different kinds of paper used inside the book: coated matt, offset white. Book is printed by use of full colour and Pantone Red 032. Cover is matt laminated. Catalogue is full of strong typography.

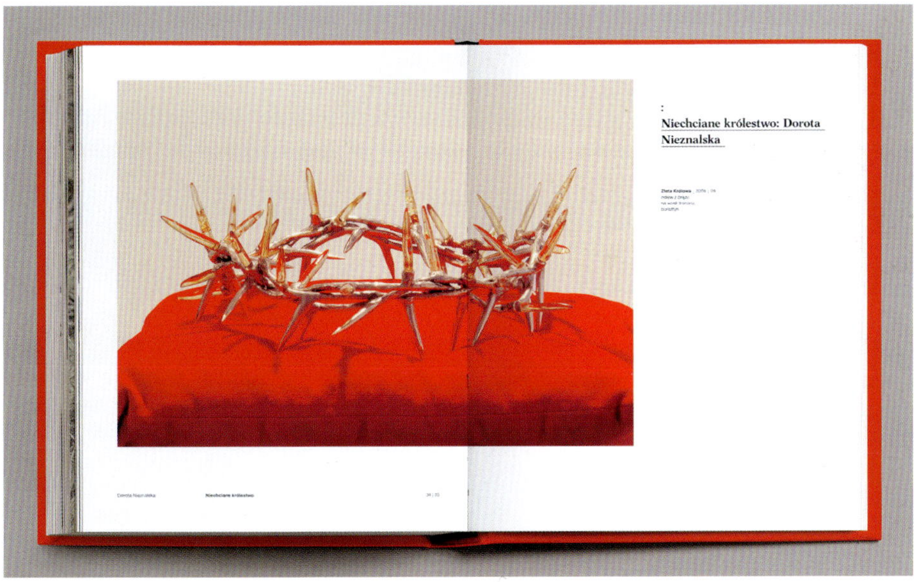

Ska

Design Agency:
3group
Designer:
Ryszard Bienert
Production Date:
2009
Client:
Galeria Wozownia
Description:
Ska catalogue was designed for Wozownia Gallery in Torun, Poland. It consists of over 100 pages printed in 6 colours. Printed on Munken Print Cream 15-150 gsm. Cover is made with 350 gsm cardboard printed with two pantone colours, matt laminated and covered with brocade/sparkling foil.

HWD
PRACY

0+0+0
3XU

WAG
IN
A

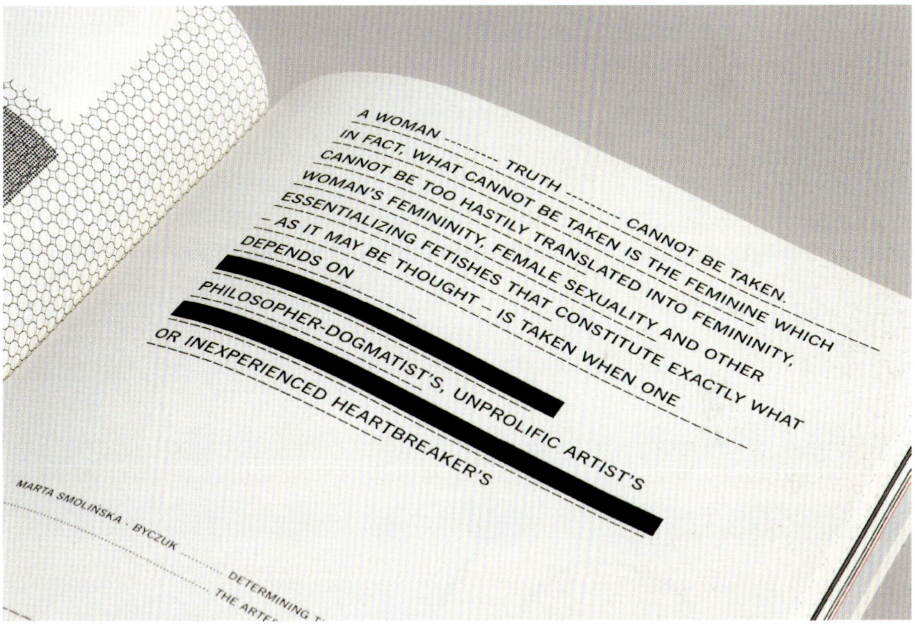
A WOMAN ------- TRUTH ------- CANNOT BE TAKEN.
IN FACT, WHAT CANNOT BE TAKEN IS THE FEMININE WHICH
CANNOT BE TOO HASTILY TRANSLATED INTO FEMININITY,
WOMAN'S FEMININITY, FEMALE SEXUALITY AND OTHER
ESSENTIALIZING FETISHES THAT CONSTITUTE EXACTLY WHAT
– AS IT MAY BE THOUGHT – IS TAKEN WHEN ONE
DEPENDS ON
PHILOSOPHER-DOGMATIST'S, UNPROLIFIC ARTIST'S
OR INEXPERIENCED HEARTBREAKER'S
MARTA SMOLIŃSKA - BYCZUK

Spinka

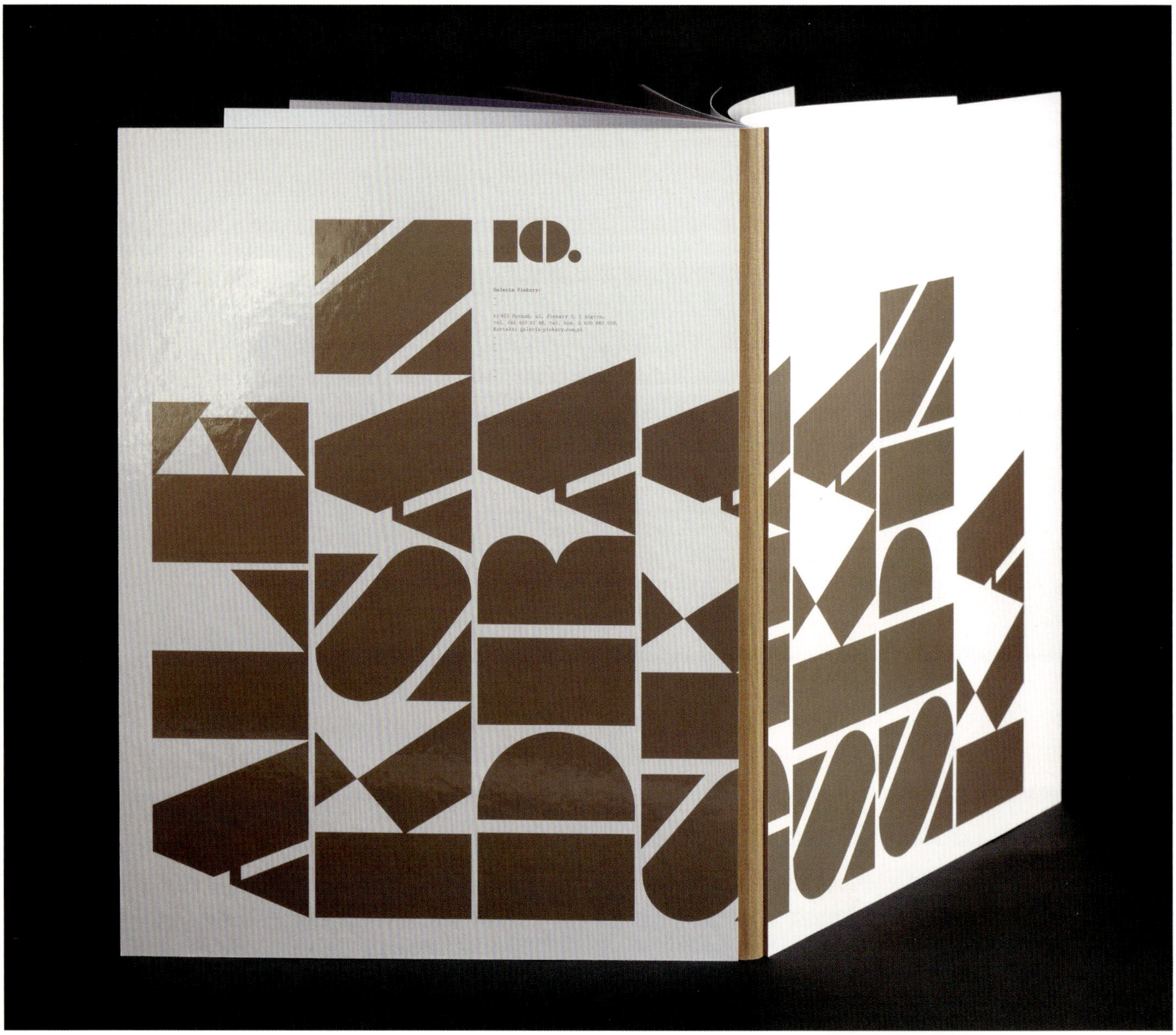

Design Agency:
3group
Designer:
Ryszard Bienert
Production Date:
2006
Client:
Galeria Piekary
Description:
Limited edition of two hundred copies of the catalogue for the young artist Aleksandra Ska. There are two different cover designs to accentuate the special edition, each printed in quantity of 100. The large format of the catalogue - 34 cm (width) x 45 cm (height) when folded - lets the viewer appreciate the artist's work in much detail, and see the materials they are created from. Three spreads in the catalogue show fragments of works in scale 1:1. For this reason, an unusual solutions to the construction of the cover and spine was created. Cover used 3 mm cardboard, DH Board, and was glued with coated stock, in addition with silk screen printed with metallic pantone, UV spot varnish, steel stapled, and was finished with canvas spine. The canvas colour was selected with care to match yellow metallic ink.

SKA
PIRA
CE

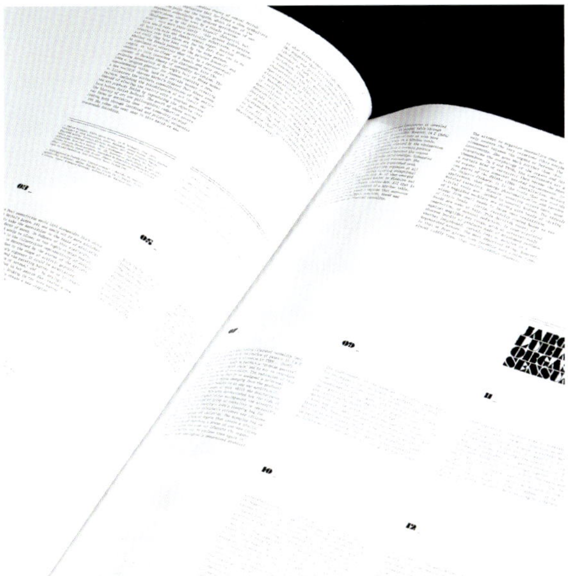

10.

The Truth of Painting

Design Agency:

3group

Designer:

Ryszard Bienert

Production Date:

2010

Client:

Galeria Piekary

Description:

The catalogue "The Truth of Painting" was designed for an artist, Kamil Kuskowski and presents his works from the last few years. Different kinds of papers were used throughout the book (seven different stocks, coated and coloured) to accentuate several techniques used by the artist. Stock colours were matched with particular distinctive colours in the artist's works. There are four chapters in the catalogue, each one having its colour and different kind of stock. The aim of the catalogue was to resemble techniques used by the artist but at the same time keep it simple, similarly to the style of works.

GOYA
Hughes
STR.
THE RIGHT TO PAINTING

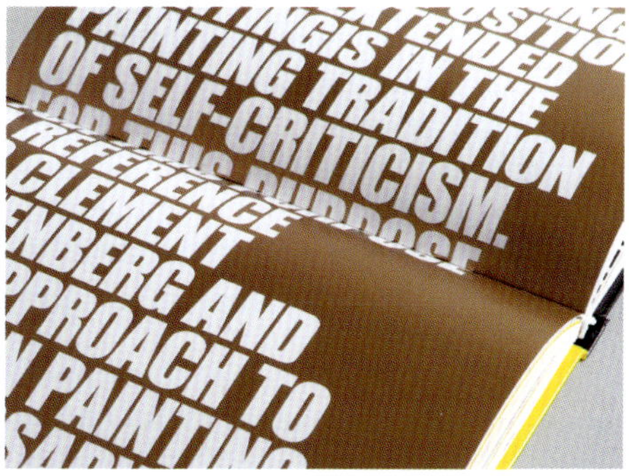
PAINTING TRADITION
OF SELF-CRITICISM.
CLEMENT
ENBERG AND
PROACH TO
PAINTING

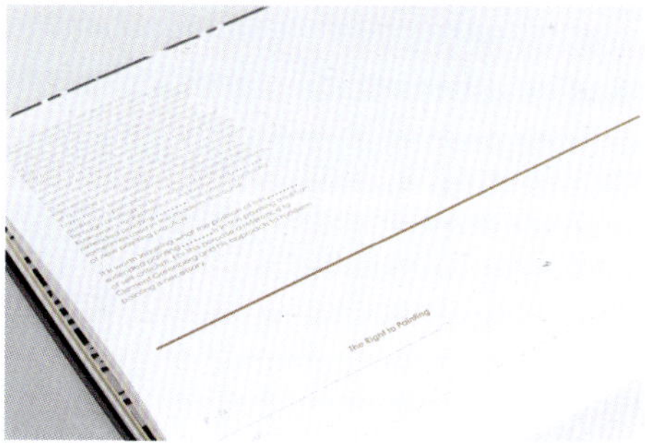

Kuskowski's new project is a peculiar exhibition-installation, realized in Galeria Piekary in Poznań in April 2009, entitled The Truth of Painting. The exhibition's structure is narrative. Kuskowski places three plinths in the middle of the gallery. Each of them holds an art exhibition catalogue from the successive Art Basel Miami Beach exhibitions of 2006 and 2007, and the 38th Art Basel of 2007. Since each catalogue is presented in a transparent wrapper-cabinet, made of Plexiglass, its purpose the ability to be read is suspended, and exchanged for a contemplative and exhibitory value. In other words, the catalogues from the art exhibitions are shown as the objects of art here, as works of art.

THE
RIGHT
TO
PAINT
ING

DE
FIL
DA
Uczta malarska __ 2007
THE RIGHT TO PAINTING
STR
93

Waiting for the Barbarians

Design Agency:
3group
Designer:
Ryszard Bienert
Production Date:
2007/8
Client:
Galeria Piekary
Description:
"Waiting for the Barbarians" - limited publication of 200 copies for two artists who held exhibition at the Piekary 5 Gallery. Both of them have different reative approaches to art so 3group decided to use two different typographic approaches (serif and sans-serif) throughout the parts relating to them. Delicate and massive fonts were used to enhance the contrast/difference in styles. Inside covers, different for each artist, designed in black and white, and in a different typographic style respectively. Binding these two covers together is a wrap around cover, matt laminated on uncoated stock. Covers were made of 3 mm-cardboard, glued together with uncoated stock and UV printed. Inside is printed on uncoated stock with special hexachrome black ink to intensify the contrast between white and black colour.

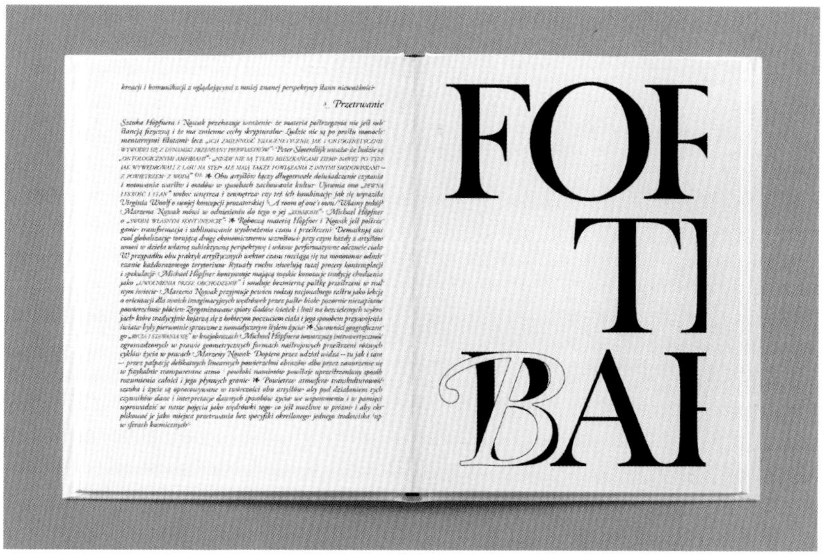
Przetrwanie

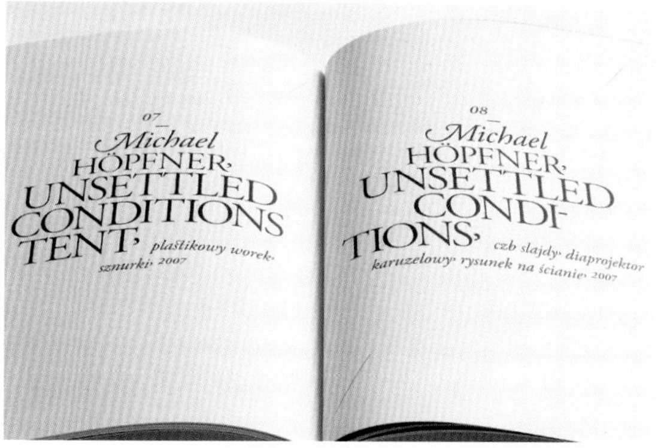
07_
Michael HÖPFNER,
UNSETTLED CONDITIONS TENT, plaštikowy worek, sznurki, 2007
08_
Michael HÖPFNER,
UNSETTLED CONDI-TIONS, czb slajdy, diaprojektor karuzelowy, rysunek na ścianie, 2007

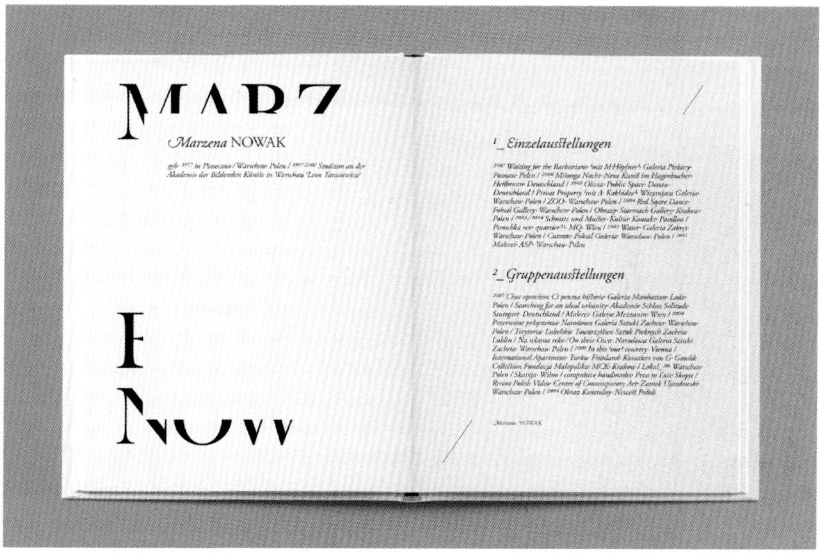
Marzena NOWAK
1_ Einzelausstellungen
2_ Gruppenausstellungen

Goschka Gawlik, WIEDEN, Kwiecień 2007
ABOUT
CEN
TRE,
TTLED

Satellites Mistaken for Stars

Design Agency:

Alexander Egger

Designer:

Alexander Egger

Production Date:

2010

Client:

Rupa Publishing

Description:

Everybody gets a little bit lost sometimes. It is a monograph, with 180 pages, softcover and dustjacket.

Dokument – Designforum Wien

Creative Director:

Alexander Egger

Designer:

Alexander Egger, Isolde Fitzel

Photography:

Lisa Fleck

Client:

Designforum Vienna

Production Date:

2010

Nationality:

Italy/Germany

Description:

The third edition of a loose series of publications edited by Designforum Vienna documents its activities in the first four years of its existance. Designforum Vienna is located since 2006 in the Museumsquartier in Vienna and presents itself as a centre of competence, of interest intermediation and service whose function consists of propagating and increasing the interest in design and its underlying conditions to the public awareness and to deepen the dialogue about design, its fuctions and its importance for economy and society, which is achieved through exhibitions, lectures, symposiums, podium discussions, events and competitions. With its manifold programmes Designforum Vienna sucessfully presented in the period of the last four years substantial design topics to a growing audience and left also a lasting impression in the Austian media landscape. DOKUMENT-Designforum Wien 2006–2010 describes the framework of the activities originated by the institution and the motivation of its initiators, supporters and sponsors.

The book breathes a raw and strong power with tendencies to an open discourse. An approach which is reflected also in the design: a thick bound portfolio of work encased by two heavy cardboard covers, embossment, open spine, conceptual playful typography, experiments of codes and space in the opening spreads of the different chapters, strong and clear colours which determine the single. The book comes infolded in a double-sided poster which gives variation in appearance, underlines the processual and temporary character of the book and generates a flexibility of viewpoints through seemingly two different covers.

NIMBUS XXI

Designer:
Andreas Preis
Client:
Georg Simon Ohm University of Applied Sciences
Production Date:
2009
Description:
Increasingly fewer people call themselves religious. Only 15 percent of registrated Christians in Germany attend church on Sundays. At the same time, masses surge to football games, concerts and other major events. People worship brands, idols and lifestyles and behave just as devoutly as the most obedient believer. On 164 pages this illustrated book describes how nowadays the church and belief are replaced by modern surrogate religions and new created gods.

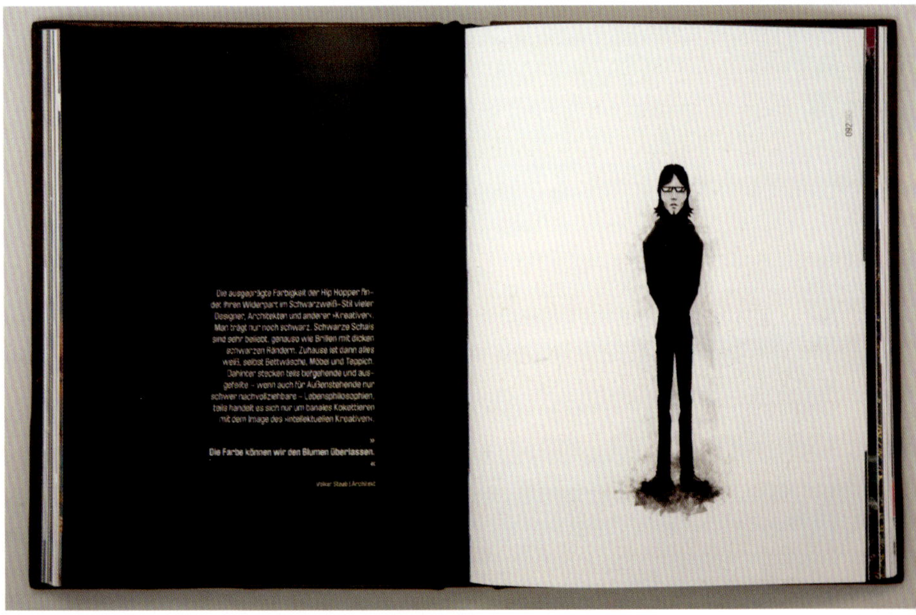

COME JOIN US
Die in Berlin ansässige studiVZ Ltd. besteht inzwischen aus drei sogenannten *Social Networks*, dem namensgebenden *studiVZ* für Studenten, *meinVZ* für Berufstätige und *schuelerVZ* logischerweise für Schüler. Insgesamt sind momentan über 12 Millionen Mitglieder registriert, die bislang gut 600 Millionen Fotos online gestellt haben. Jeden Tag kommen mehr als eine Million neuer Bilder dazu. Über 5,9 Milliarden Seitenaufrufe pro Monat machen das schuelerVZ aktuell zur meistgeklickten Seite im deutschsprachigen Raum, direkt gefolgt vom studiVZ mit monatlich gut 4,2 Milliarden Aufrufen.
Facebook hat weltweit über 150 Millionen aktive User, die wiederum circa 19 Millionen aktive Gruppen gegründet haben. Dabei hat der durchschnittliche Nutzer im Schnitt 100 Freunde. Jeden Monat werden über 700 Millionen Fotos und mehr als 4 Millionen Videos hochgeladen. Jeden Tag verbringt die Welt circa 2,6 Milliarden Minuten auf Facebook.
Das ursprünglich vor allem als Plattform für Musiker gedachte Netzwerk *MySpace* besitzt über 180 Millionen registrierte Mitglieder. MySpace ist mit monatlich 50 Milliarden Seitenaufrufen die wichtigste Web-Community der Welt. Anfänglich tauchte MySpace vor allem in Musikzeitschriften und Plattenkritiken auf. Circa 2 Millionen registrierte Musiker und Bands stellen sich hier dar. Interpreten wie die Arctic Monkeys und Lily Allen verdanken ihre ersten Erfolge praktisch ausschließlich ihrer Präsenz auf MySpace. Zum Präsidentschaftswahlkampf in den USA 2008 gaben alle Kandidaten Pressekonferenzen via MySpace und legten sich eigene Profile als Wahlwerbung zu.
Mehr als 6,5 Millionen Mitglieder zählt heute das selbst ernannte Business-Netzwerk *XING*. Konzipiert ist es im Grunde einzig und allein für Geschäftsleute und Berufstätige. XING arbeitet in 16 Sprachen und versteht sich als Möglichkeit zur Vernetzung und Kontaktpflege für Geschäft, Beruf und Karriere.

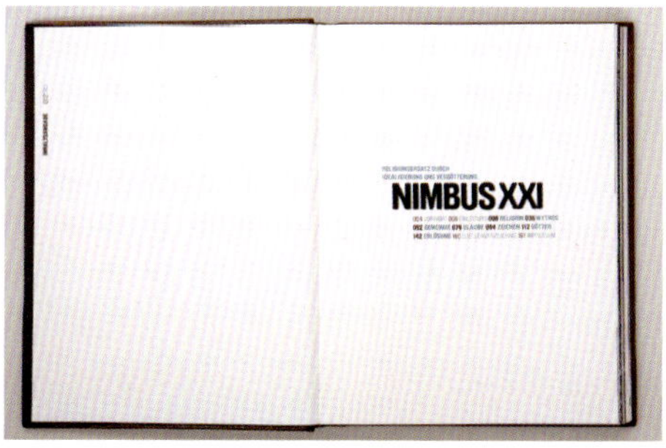
NIMBUS XXI

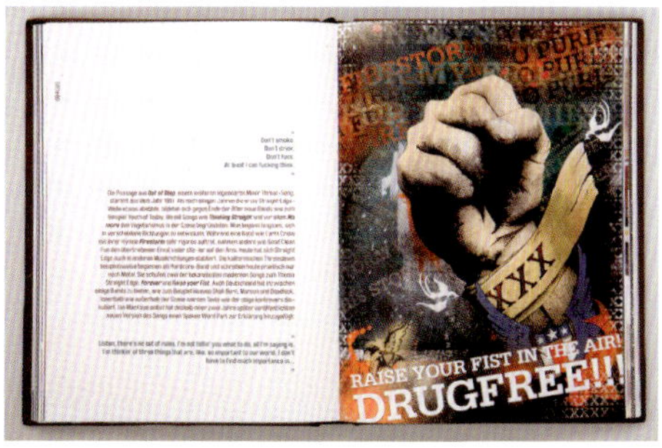
RAISE YOUR FIST IN THE AIR!
DRUGFREE!!!

THE PRODUCT IS
THE EXPERIENCE

BRANDS ARE
THE NEW
RELIGION
John Elkins | Gründer und ehemaliger CEO von Futurebrand
»
Die Brandingapostel sind oft ideologisch derart verbohrt, dass ihnen nicht einmal auffällt, wie komisch sie sind (…) Um es deutlich zu sagen: Die Predigten, die die *Marken-Evangelisten* in Richtung der Belegschaft halten, erinnern halb an Gehirnwäschetechniken, wie man sie aus dem Sektenwesen kennt, halb an kuriose Parolen, wie sie im Sozialismus alltäglich waren.
«
Robert Misik | Schriftsteller

Rolling Stone

Designer:
Anthonys Timola
Client:
Student work
Production Date:
2010
Description:
The project was to rebrand a company that falls into a defined set of criteria: dead, dying, or defunct. The designer was to bring the brand back to life through relevant and well thought out branding techniques.

The designer defined Rolling Stone as a brand that was dying in comparison to its prior prowess as the go-to-magazine for all things counter culture. The designer chose to call on the DIY movement in order to bring back the brand's connection with the counter culture and provided a brand extension of high pigment spray paint and markers. In addition there are gallery spaces that are also locations for community centers; creating a venue for expression.

Comments:
This project is the culmination of the past two years; the MFA programme at the Academy of Art is highly competitive, and pushes you to be the best. The designer is very proud of this project, as it came together in a strong way.

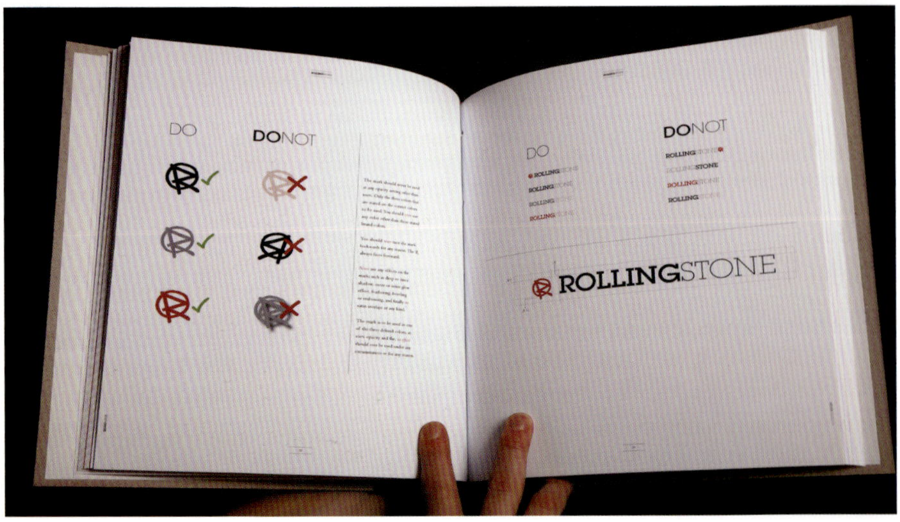

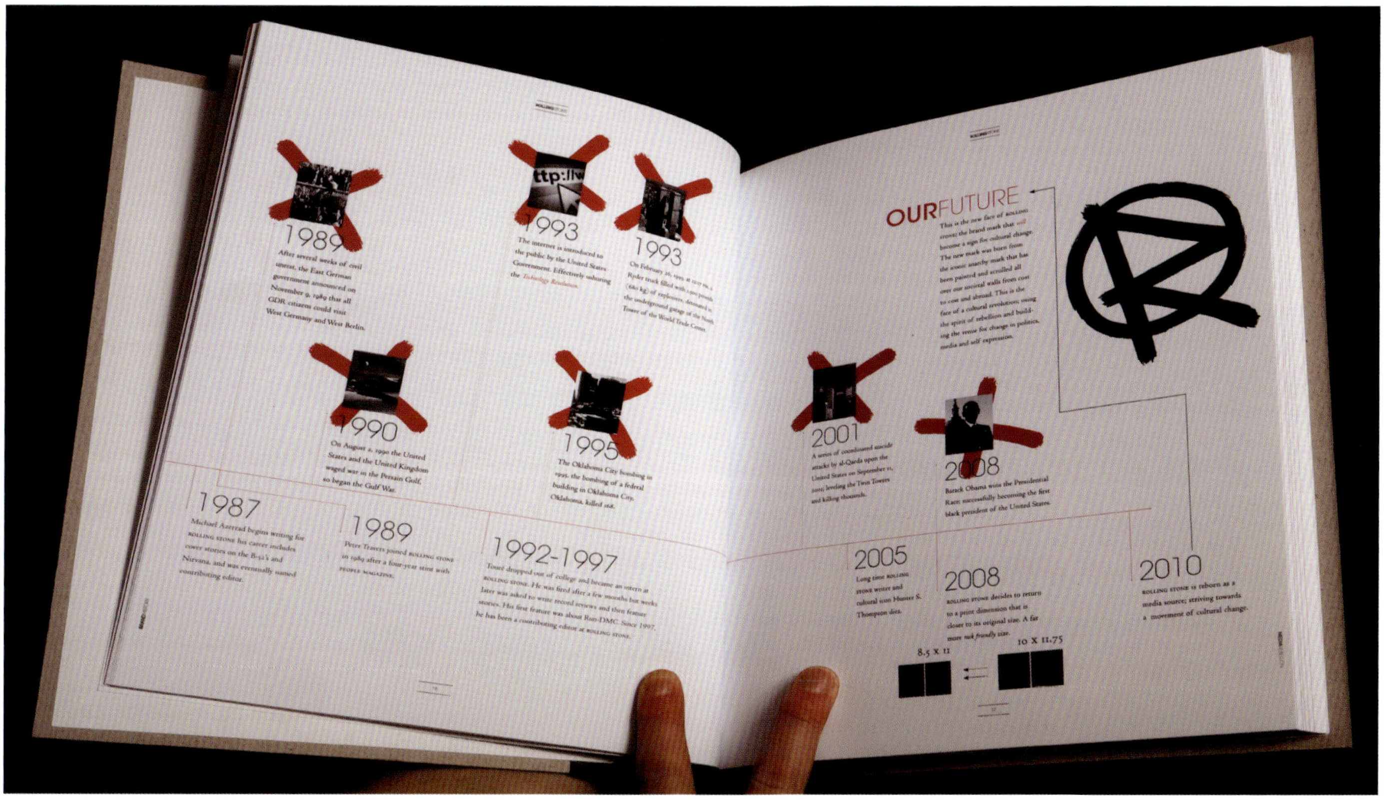
1989
After several weeks of civil unrest, the East German government announced on November 9, 1989 that all GDR citizens could visit West Germany and West Berlin.
1993
The internet is introduced to the public by the United States Government. Effectively ushering the Technology Revolution.
1993
1990
On August 2, 1990 the United States and the United Kingdom waged war in the Persain Gulf, so began the Gulf War.
1995
The Oklahoma City bombing in 1995, the bombing of a federal building in Oklahoma City, Oklahoma, killed 168.
1987
Michael Azerrad begins writing for ROLLING STONE his career includes cover stories on the B-52's and Nirvana, and was eventually named contributing editor.
1989
Peter Travers joined ROLLING STONE in 1989 after a four-year stint with PEOPLE MAGAZINE.
1992-1997
Touré dropped out of college and became an intern at ROLLING STONE. He was fired after a few months but works later was asked to write record reviews and then feature stories. His first feature was about Run-DMC. Since 1997, he has been a contributing editor at ROLLING STONE.
OURFUTURE
2001
A series of coordinated suicide attacks by al-Qaeda upon the United States on September 11, 2001; leveling the Twin Towers and killing thousands.
2008
Barack Obama wins the Presidential Race; successfully becoming the first black president of the United States.
2005
Long time ROLLING STONE writer and cultural icon Hunter S. Thompson dies.
2008
2010
ROLLING STONE is reborn as a media source; striving towards a movement of cultural change.
8.5 x 11
10 x 11.75

SPRAYPAINT

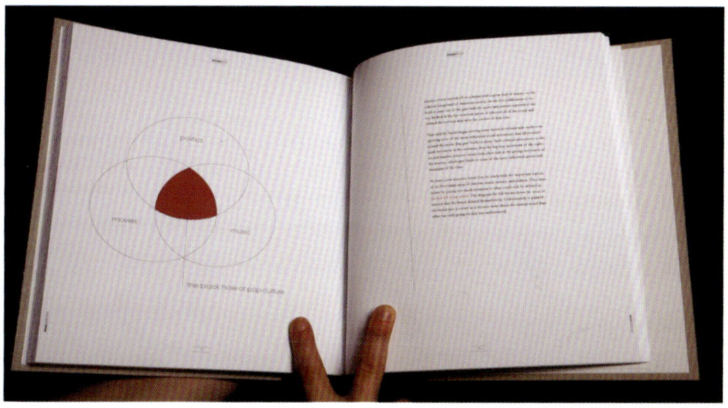

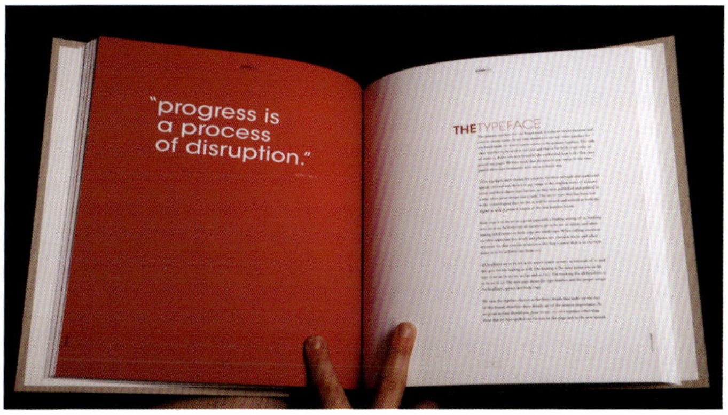
"progress is a process of disruption."
THETYPEFACE

Friendly Fire

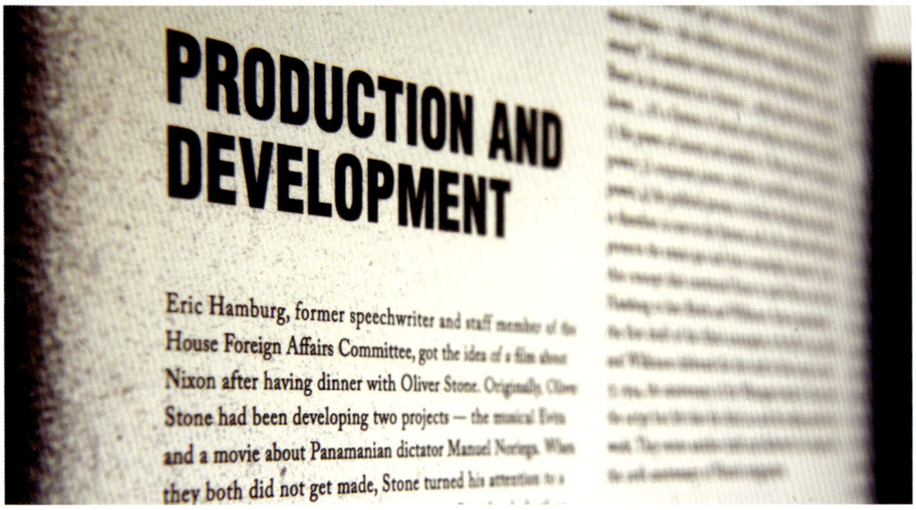

Designer:

Anthonys Timola

Photography:

Dominic Stimola

Client:

Student work

Production Date:

2010

Description:

This book was created as an informational and archival guide for the Friendly Fire Film Festival. Friendly Fire is a fictitious film festival that celebrates the filmmaker Oliver Stone, and an era of social turbulence in America and South East Asia. The three locations of the film festival, New York City, Washington DC, and Ho Chi Min City were chosen to comemorate the many momentous occasions of the era.

Comments:

The designer put in a lot of personal heart and soul into the piece as the era is an important one in his family. His father is a Vietnam veteran and it was very important to him to aim this towards his fellow veterans. He found it difficult to put persoanl feelings aside; if he was to do it again, he would have steered clear of such personal subjects.

"I WILL COME OUT WITH MY **INTERPRETATION**. IF I AM WRONG, FINE. IT WILL BECOME PART OF THE DEBRIS OF HISTORY, IT'S PART OF THE GIVE AND TAKE."

OLIVER STONE

PLATOON
BORN ON THE FOURTH OF JULY
HEAVEN AND EARTH
JFK
NIXON

FILMS

The films chosen for this film festival all fall into a common thread that ties the group together. The irreversible devastation of the Vietnam War on both society and politics in the nineteen sixties is visually laid out across the five chosen films. These films show the impact of war that took place from September twenty sixth of nineteen fifty nine to April thirtieth of nineteen seventy-five. Oliver Stone chose to display the reach of war on man as an individual and a group in both Platoon and Born on the Fourth of July, while exploring the unheard stories of the villagers who were thrown into the middle of the conflict in Heaven and Earth. JFK and Nixon both explored the interior struggles of political figures of the time as they made the important decisions that affected some many people's lives. The corruption of the soul and mind are another running theme through out all five films.

PRODUCTION AND DEVELOPMENT

Eric Hamburg, former speechwriter and staff member of the House Foreign Affairs Committee, got the idea of a film about Nixon after having dinner with Oliver Stone. Originally, Oliver Stone had been developing two projects — the musical Evita and a movie about Panamanian dictator Manuel Noriega. When they both did not get made, Stone turned his attention to a biopic about Richard Nixon. The former President's death on April 22, 1994, was also a key factor in Stone's decision to make a Nixon film. He pitched the film to Warner Bros. ,according to the director, they saw it, "as a bunch of unattractive older white men sitting around in suits, with a lot of dialogue and not enough action".

In 1993, Hamburg mentioned the idea of a Nixon film to writer Stephen J. Rivele with the concept being that they would incorporate all of the politician's misdeeds, both known and speculative. Rivele liked the idea and had previously thought about writing a play exploring the same themes. Hamburg encouraged Rivele to write a film instead and with his screenwriting partner, Christopher Wilkinson, they wrote a treatment on November 1993. They conceived of a concept referred to as "the Beast", which Wilkinson describes as "a headless monster that lurches through postwar history," a metaphor for a system of dark forces that resulted in the assassinations of John F. Kennedy, Robert Kennedy, and Martin Luther King, Jr., the Vietnam War, and helped Nixon's rise to power and his fall from it as well. Stone said in an interview that Nixon realizes that "the Beast" "is more powerful than he is. We can't get into it that much, but we hint at it so many times — the military-industrial complex, the forces of money". In another interview, the director elaborates, "I see the Beast in its essence as a System ... which grinds the individual down ... it's a System of checks and balances that drives itself off: 1) the power of money and markets; 2) State power, Government power; 3) corporate power, which is probably greater than state power; 4) the political process, or election through money, which is therefore in tow to the System; and 5) the media, which mostly protects the status quo and their ownership's interests". It was this concept that convinced Stone to make Nixon and he told Hamburg to hire Rivele and Wilkinson. Stone commissioned the first draft of the film's screenplay in the fall of 1993. Rivele and Wilkinson delivered the first draft of their script on June 17, 1994, the anniversary of the Watergate break-in. Stone loved the script but felt that the third act and the ending needed more work. They wrote another draft and delivered it on August 9th, the 20th anniversary of Nixon's resignation.

Stone immersed himself in research with the help of Hamburg. With Hamburg and actors Hopkins and James Woods, Stone flew to Washington, D.C. and interviewed the surviving members of Nixon's inner circle: lawyer Leonard Garment and Attorney General Elliot Richardson. He also interviewed Robert McNamara, a former Secretary of Defense under the Kennedy and Johnson administrations. The director also hired Alexander Butterfield, a key figure in the Watergate scandal who handled the flow of paper to the President, as a consultant to make sure that the Oval Office was realistically depicted, former deputy White House counsel John Sears, and John Dean, who made sure that every aspect of the script was accurate and wrote a few uncredited scenes for the film. Butterfield also appears in a several scenes as a White House staffer. To research their roles, Powers Boothe, David Hyde Pierce and Paul Sorvino talked to their real-life counterparts, but J.T. Walsh decided not to contact John Ehrlichman because he had threatened to sue after reading an early version of the script and was not happy with how he was portrayed. Hopkins watched a lot of documentary footage on Nixon. At night, he would go to sleep while the Nixon footage playing, letting it seep into his subconscious. Hopkins said, "It's taking in all this information and if you're relaxed enough, it begins to take you over."

Stone originally had a three-picture deal with New Regency Films which included JFK, Heaven and Earth, and Natural Born Killers. After the success of Killers, Arnon Milchan, head of New Regency, signed Stone for three more motion pictures. Stone could make any film up to a budget of $42.5 million. When he told Milchan that he wanted to make Nixon, Milchan, who was not keen on the idea, told the director that he would only give him $35 million, thinking that this would cause Stone to abandon the project. Stone took the project to Hungarian financier Andrew Vajna who had co-financing deal with Disney. Vajna's company, Cinergi Films, were willing to finance the $38 million film. This angered Milchan who claimed that Nixon was his film because of his three-picture deal with Stone and he threatened to sue. He withdrew after Stone paid him an undisclosed amount. Stone was finalizing the film's budget a week before shooting was to begin. He made a deal with Cinergi and Disney's Hollywood Pictures in order to supply the $43 million budget. To cut costs, Stone leased the White House sets from Rob Reiner's film, The American President.

ORIGINAL RELEASE DATE:	December 22, 1995	FEATURING:	Anthony Hopkins
RUNNING TIME:	212 minutes		Joan Allen
MUSIC BY:	John Williams		Paul Sorvino
WRITTEN BY:	Stephen J. Rivele		Bob Hoskins
	Christopher Wilkinson		Powers Boothe
	Oliver Stone		James Woods
DIRECTED BY:	Oliver Stone		Ed Harris
DISTRIBUTED BY:	Hollywood Pictures		E.G. Marshall

MANHATTAN, NY

LOCATION: The Film School At NYU
Washington Square Park

DATES: September 15th thru 19th of 2014

The Friendly Fire Film Festival will be extending it's celebration of Oliver Stone's films to include the celebration of his seventieth birthday. The board chose to bring the celebration to the door step of where Oliver Stone began his journey as a film maker. The film festival will take place in Washington Square Park in the midst of NYU where Stone was a film student.

The Many Faces of San Franciso's Architecture

Designer:
Anthony Stimola

Production Date:
2010

Description:
This book is the product of two individuals who have a great love and also distain for the very different social structure of San Francisco. The designer wanted to produce a piece that would display the beauty of San Francisco without using the clichés of colour and bright content. The idea is to show the city through a lens that has not yet been utilised.

Comments:
The designer would have liked to see this book build out further, however short turnaround time and tight deadlines kept the book short. The structure of the book is there and it could be reformated to reflect any city.

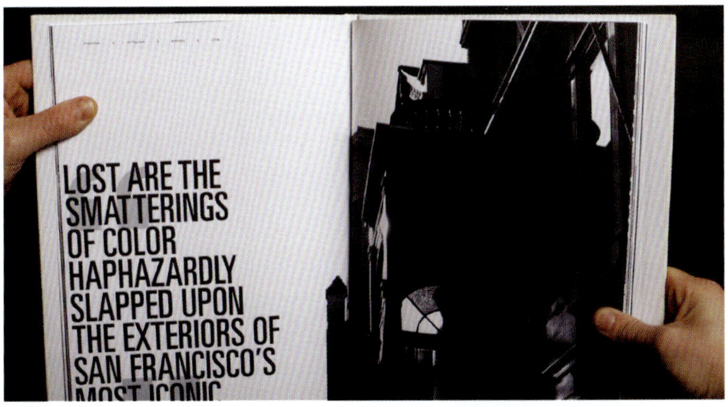
LOST ARE THE
SMATTERINGS
OF COLOR
HAPHAZARDLY
SLAPPED UPON
THE EXTERIORS OF
SAN FRANCISCO'S

THE MANY
FACES OF
SAN FRANCISCO'S
ARCHITECTURE
FOREWORD

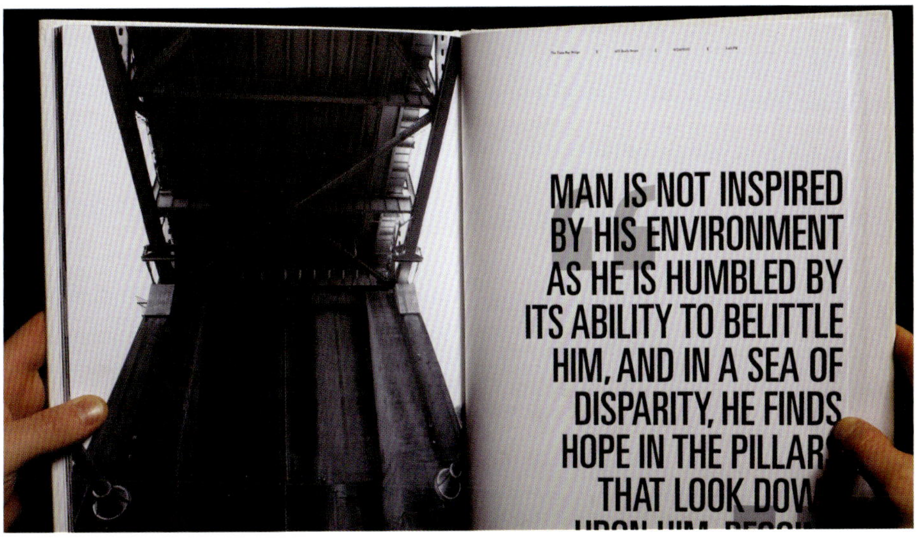
MAN IS NOT INSPIRED
BY HIS ENVIRONMENT
AS HE IS HUMBLED BY
ITS ABILITY TO BELITTLE
HIM, AND IN A SEA OF
DISPARITY, HE FINDS
HOPE IN THE PILLAR
THAT LOOK DOW

Lezioni di Paesaggio

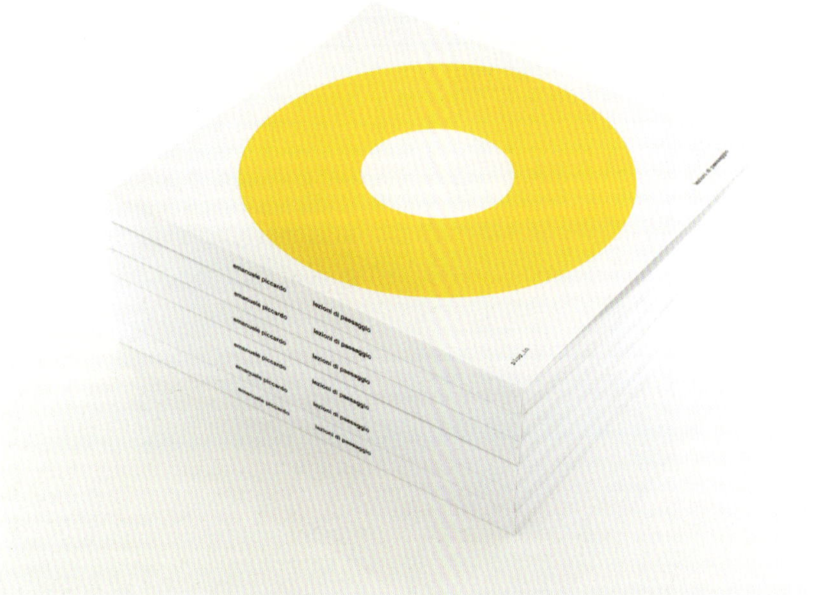

Design Agency:
Artiva Design

Designer:
Daniele De Batté, Davide Sossi

Client:
Plug_in Edition

Production Date:
2008

Description:
The book is a collection of writings and photos on the landscape not only in terms of architectural and artistic heritage.

Comment:
The cover represents the duality between open and closed space.

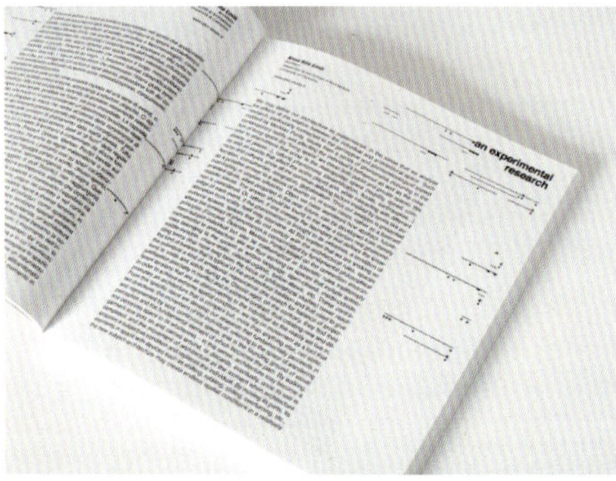

;
Artisti / Artists

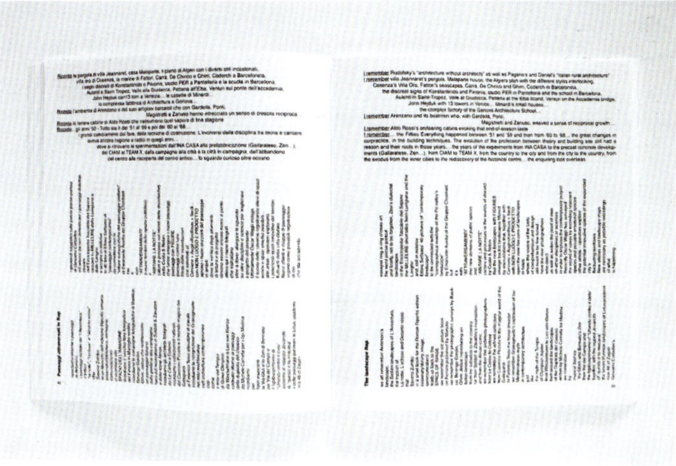

ringraziamenti
acknowledgments

Guido Guidi
128 -/(1995)
Marcello Galvani

Utopia & Comunità

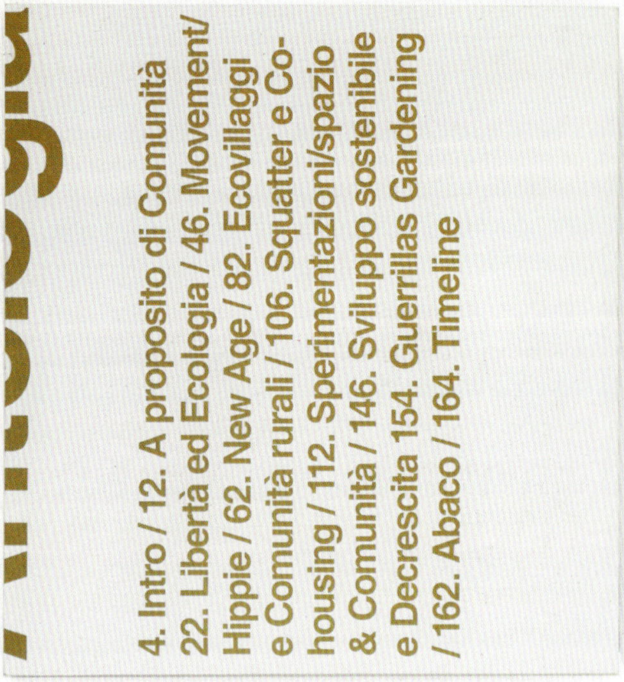

Design Agency:
Artiva Design
Designer:
Daniele De Batté, Davide Sossi
Client:
Plug_in Edition
Production Date:
2009
Description:
The book deals with communities and cohousing, reading and consultation are facilitated by the division in cards and the integration of photographic materials.
Comment:
The use of black and white is a reference to the underground magazines of the 1960s. Designers also used on some pages typefaces olivetti's typewriter to have a more different and original typography.

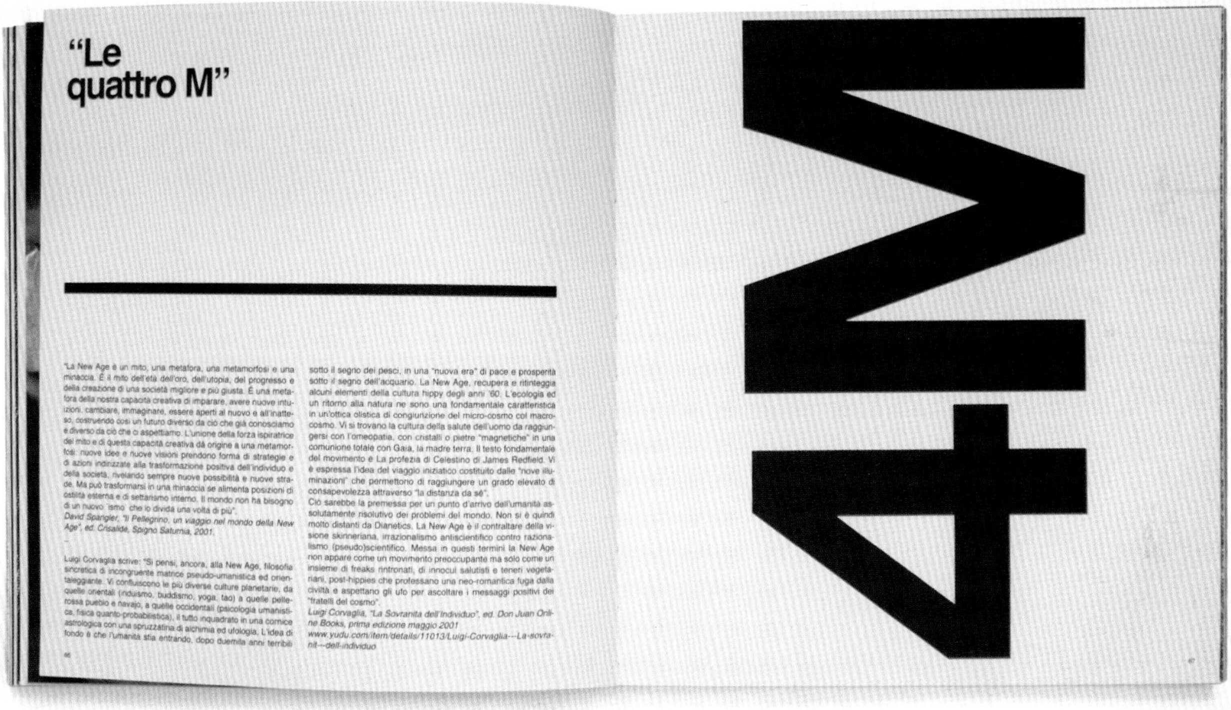

"Le quattro M"

"La New Age è un mito, una metafora, una metamorfosi e una minaccia. È il mito dell'età dell'oro, dell'utopia, del progresso e della creazione di una società migliore e più giusta. È una metafora della nostra capacità creativa di imparare, avere nuove intuizioni, cambiare, immaginare, essere aperti al nuovo e all'inatteso, costruendo così un futuro diverso da ciò che già conosciamo e diverso da ciò che ci aspettiamo. L'unione della forza ispiratrice del mito e di questa capacità creativa dà origine a una metamorfosi: nuove idee e nuove visioni prendono forma di strategie e di azioni indirizzate alla trasformazione positiva dell'individuo e della società, rivelando sempre nuove possibilità e nuove strade. Ma può trasformarsi in una minaccia se alimenta posizioni di ostilità esterna e di settarismo interno. Il mondo non ha bisogno di un nuovo 'ismo' che lo divida una volta di più".
David Spangler, "Il Pellegrino, un viaggio nel mondo della New Age", ed. Crisalide, Spigno Saturnia, 2001.

–

Luigi Corvaglia scrive: "Si pensi, ancora, alla New Age, filosofia sincretica di incongruente matrice pseudo-umanistica ed orienteggiante. Vi confluiscono le più diverse culture planetarie, da quelle orientali (induismo, buddismo, yoga, tao) a quelle pellerossa pueblo e navajo, a quelle occidentali (psicologia umanistica, fisica quanto-probabilistica), il tutto inquadrato in una cornice astrologica con una spruzzatina di alchimia ed ufologia. L'idea di fondo è che l'umanità stia entrando, dopo duemila anni terribili sotto il segno dei pesci, in una "nuova era" di pace e prosperità sotto il segno dell'acquario. La New Age, recupera e ritinteggia alcuni elementi della cultura hippy degli anni '60. L'ecologia ed un ritorno alla natura ne sono una fondamentale caratteristica in un'ottica olistica di congiunzione del micro-cosmo col macro-cosmo. Vi si trovano la cultura della salute dell'uomo da raggiungersi con l'omeopatia, con cristalli o pietre "magnetiche" in una comunione totale con Gaia, la madre terra. Il testo fondamentale del movimento è La profezia di Celestino di James Redfield. Vi è espressa l'idea del viaggio iniziatico costituito dalle "nove illuminazioni" che permettono di raggiungere un grado elevato di consapevolezza attraverso "la distanza da sé".
Ciò sarebbe la premessa per un punto d'arrivo dell'umanità assolutamente risolutivo dei problemi del mondo. Non si è quindi molto distanti da Dianetics. La New Age è il contraltare della visione skinneriana, irrazionalismo antiscientifico contro razionalismo (pseudo)scientifico. Messa in questi termini la New Age non appare come un movimento preoccupante ma solo come un insieme di freaks rintronati, di innocui salutisti e teneri vegetariani, post-hippies che professano una neo-romantica fuga dalla civiltà e aspettano gli ufo per ascoltare i messaggi positivi dei "fratelli del cosmo".
Luigi Corvaglia, "La Sovranità dell'Individuo", ed. Don Juan Online Books, prima edizione maggio 2001
www.yudu.com/item/details/11013/Luigi-Corvaglia---La-sovranit---dell-individuo

46

4M

47

Poetry Books and Covers

Design Agency:

Massachusetts College of Art and Design

Award:

Bookbuilders of Boston Scholarship, 2008

Production Date:

2008

Description:

Books are hardcovered with a dust jacket, uncoated paper.

Comment:

The book covers and interior design from this series are a modern visual interpretation of the writings of Federico Garcia Lorca. Metaphorical representation, bold use of colour and of shapes hint at the important influence of Spanish folklore on Lorca's work. Its initial illustrated capital letters invite the reader to embark on a journey of sensuality, music, longing, and love.

CANCION

SONG

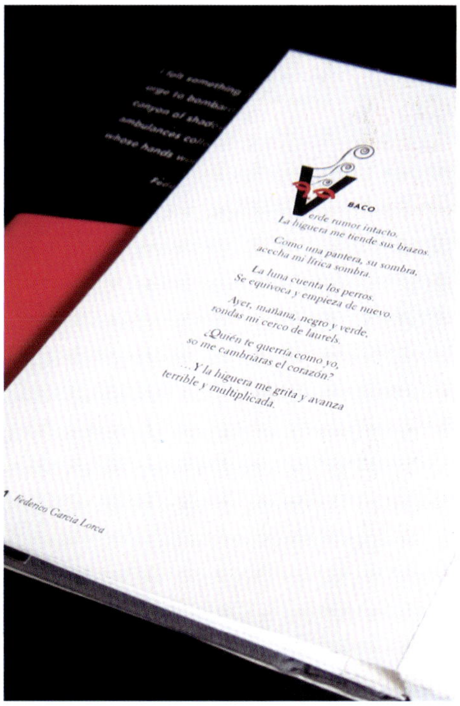
BACO
Verde rumor intacto.
La higuera me tiende sus brazos.
Como una pantera, su sombra,
acecha mi lírica sombra.
La luna cuenta los perros.
Se equivoca y empieza de nuevo.
Ayer, mañana, negro y verde,
rondas mi cerco de laurels.
¿Quién te querría como yo,
si me cambiaras el corazón?
...Y la higuera me grita y avanza
terrible y multiplicada.
Federico García Lorca

LIGHT MADRIGAL

John Cage: Music of Changes

Design Agency:
Massachusetts College of Art and Design
Client:
Massachusetts College of Art and Design
Award:
Bookbuilders of Boston Scholarship 2008
Production Date:
2008
Description:
Hardcover, uncoated and special paper.
Comment:
This book celebrates the creative work and philosophy of American avant-garde composer John Cage. The visual language of this publication reflects the textures and dynamism found in Cage's music, while the structure of the book retains a sense of unpredictability. The book's design is based on a lecture on composition given by Cage in Darmstadt which was in sync with the length of "Music of Changes", the musical piece.

Humans

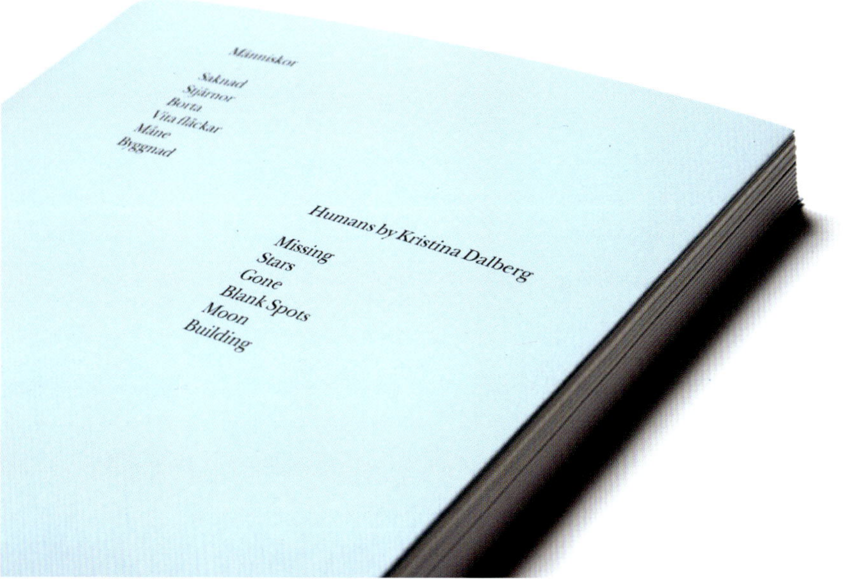

Design Agency:
Ateljé Altmann HB
Designer:
Christian Altmann, Oskar Holmquist
Client:
Kristina Dalberg
Production date:
2009
Description:
'This performance was inspired by a dream. It combines films (Boat, Bridge, Building, Moon, Stars, and Wall) with short stories, personal reflections and facts in order to tell a bigger story about people, cities and the human condition. Kristina is transfering her films and lecture 'Humans' into book form. The designers decided to release it with four different coloured dust jackets made of the finest muted coloured Kolorit paper available from the swedish paper distributor Map. Kristina loved the idea to clad the stories in this slightly dusted coat in fine colour nuances. Very personal views deserve warm regards for it. Together with Oskar Holmquist we delivered something we will be proud for many years to come.

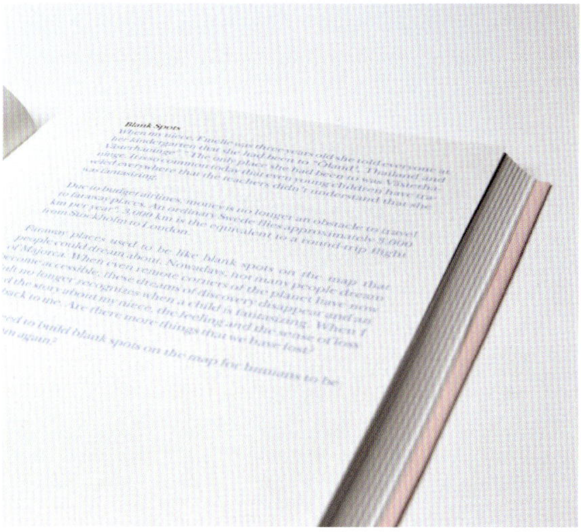

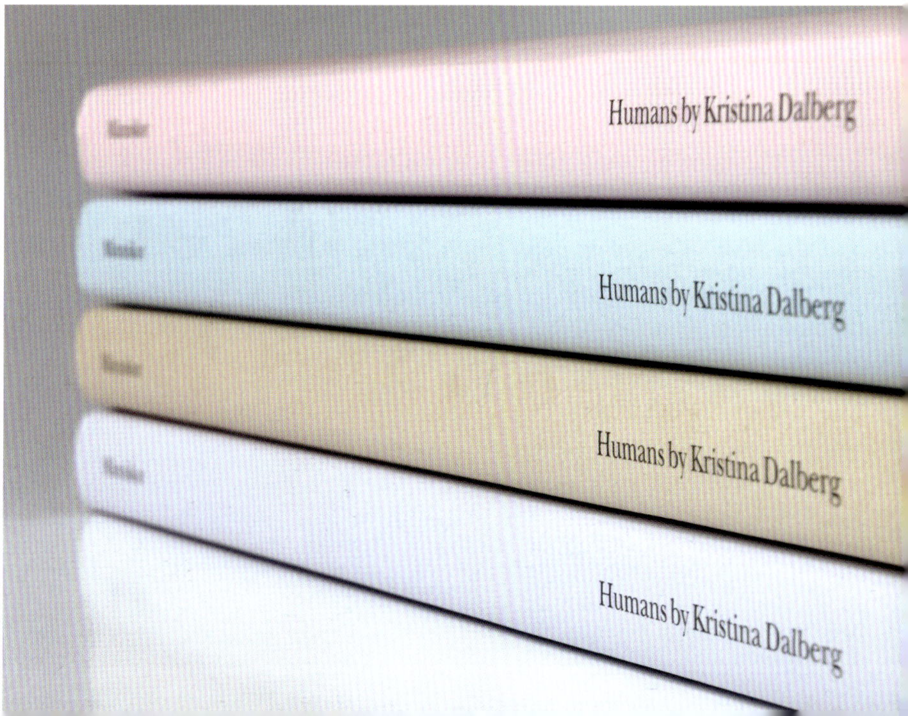

KI Arkitektur Och Kunskapsmiljö

Design Agency:

Ateljé Altmann HB

Designer:

Christian Altmann

Client:

Akademiska Hus

Production Date:

2010

Description:

The book presents historical content about KI's campus development from the 1940s through to today and is complimented with spacial analysis models from the School of Architecture/KTH.

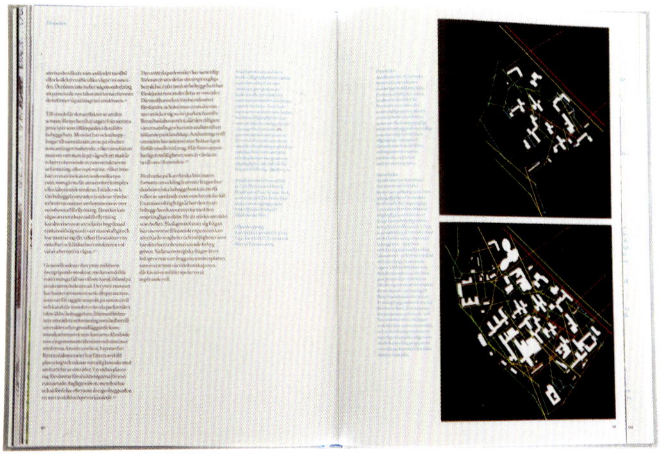

Occupying Time

Design Agency:

Ateljé Altmann HB

Designer:

Christian Altmann

Client:

Ramia Mazé

Production date:

2007

Description:

Ramia came to the designers with the aim to get the best possible appearance of her texts and dress them into a bold but timeless book design. They designed cover and layout with the intention to inform in a straight forward but elegant way. Keep the cover simple black and white with a hint to typographic abstraction. They wanted it to pop out on the bookshelves.

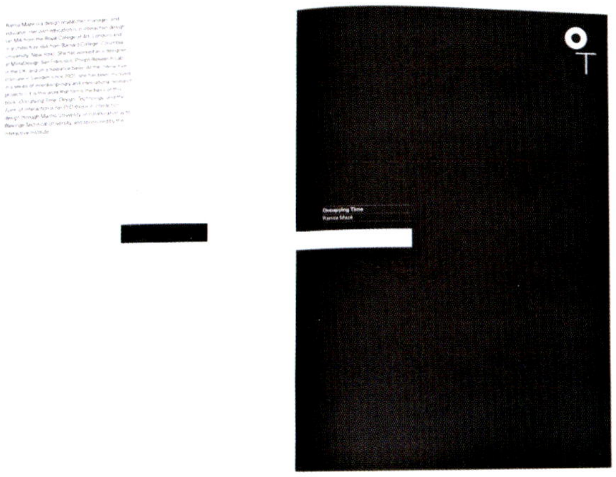

Static! Designing for Energy Awareness

Design Agency:

Ateljé Altmann HB

Designer:

Christian Altmann, Oskar Holmquist

Client:

The Interactive Institute

Production Date:

2010

Description:

This book presents the Static! design examples and perspectives on issues in (sustainable) design today. Grounded in passion and humour, as well as rigour and research, the book asks designers and consumers – that is, all of people – to rethink the form, and future, of electricity in the world.

International Space Syntax Symposium

Design Agency:

Ateljé Altmann HB

Designer:

Christian Altmann

Client:

Architecture School/KTH

Production Date:

2009

Description:

Christian Altmann designed a logo that consists of two vertical bars, set apart to allow for space... That mark became the visual metaphor for the 7th Space Syntax Symposium 2009. The commission included an organisational website, an on-screen event animation (in collaboration with Kristofer Vahlström at Propeller), poster series for different architectural events, a conference pack containing the book of proceedings, programmes, noteblock and other materials.

Die 15-Minuten-Welt

Design Agency:

BEIHOFER+ADOLF

Designer:

Rainer Beihofer, Ronald Adolf

Client:

HfG Schwäbisch Gmünd

Production Date:

2008

Description:

Die 15-Minuten-Welt is a book about the development of the Tagesschau, Germany's most important newscast. Besides a background report with a lot of information about newscasts the book offers a newly-created visual system that translates real parameters like responsibility, time, command structure, technics, etc. into graphic parameters which allows the reader to analyse the steps very fast and easily. Every chapter is introduced by an decoration font which was especially created for this book. While the most pages use uncoated paper with soft haptics and very low opacity the single steps of the newscast's genesis, which are place in the middle of the book, were printed on double coated paper.

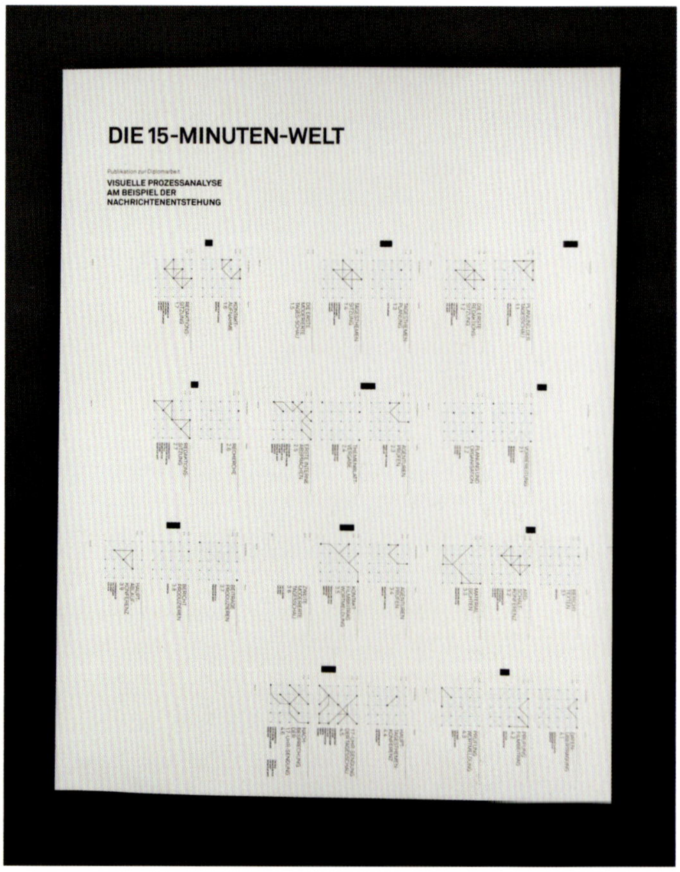

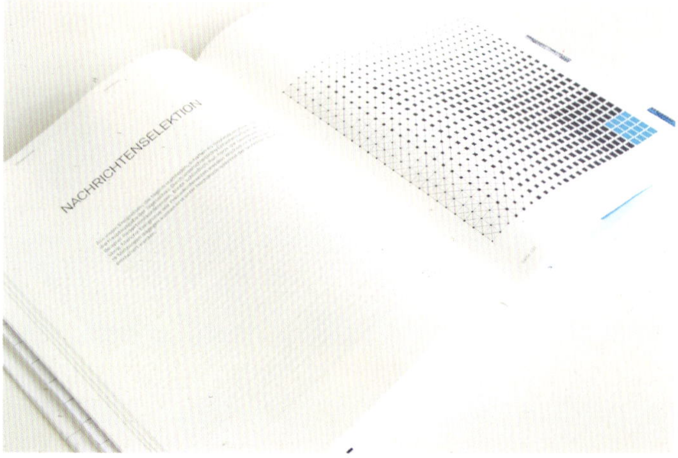

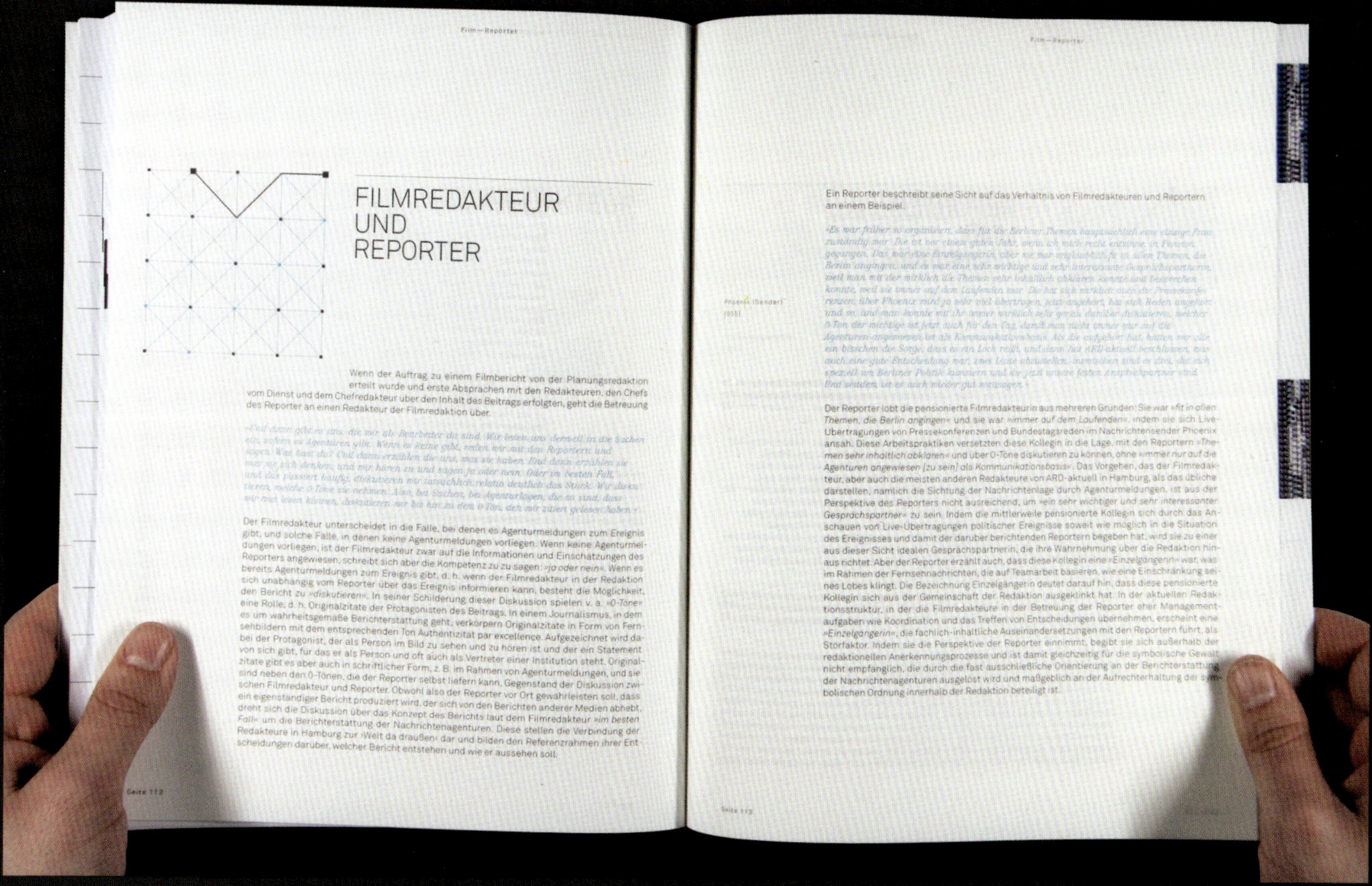
FILMREDAKTEUR
UND
REPORTER

WORTMELDUNGEN -
DAS SIEBENZEILIGE
EXTRAKT

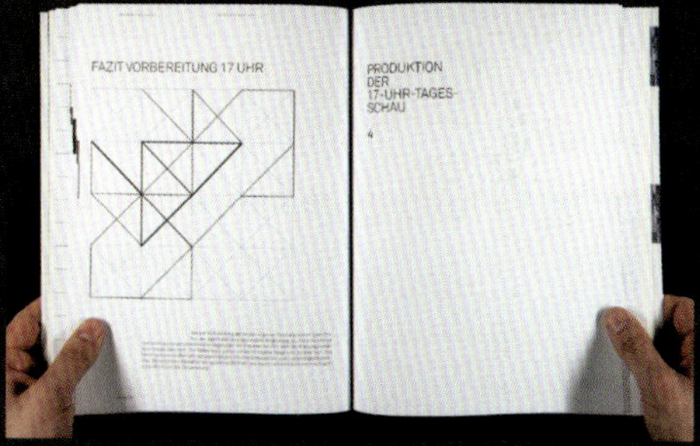
FAZIT VORBEREITUNG 17 UHR
PRODUKTION
DER
17-UHR-TAGES-
SCHAU
4

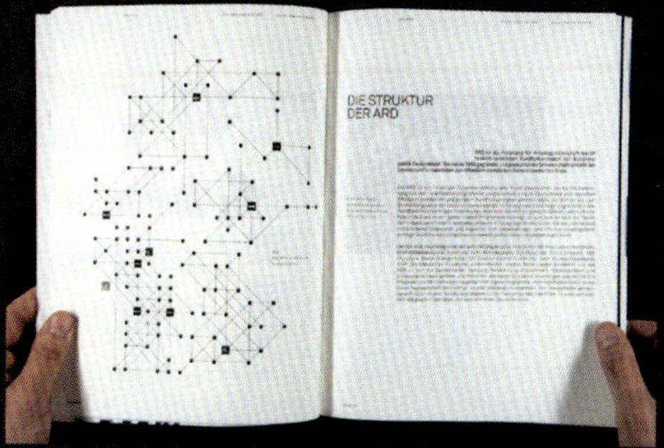
DIE STRUKTUR
DER ARD

LYSE
DIE 15-MINUTEN-WELT
VISUELLE PROZESSANALYSE
AM BEISPIEL DER
NACHRICHTENENTSTEHUNG

Abschlusskatalog 10

Designer:

Britta Siegmund, Christina Eike

Client:

University of Applied Sciences and Arts Hannover

Production Date:

2010

Description:

This publication shows all final projects from the University of Applied Sciences and Arts Hanover. The last projects from the old diploma programme were shown along with the first projects from the new bachelor's and master's projects.

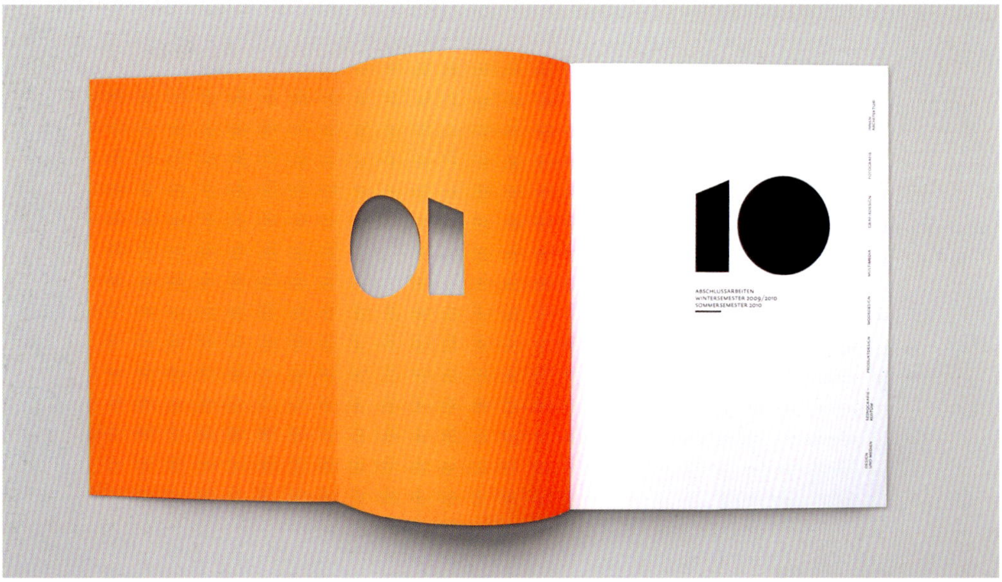

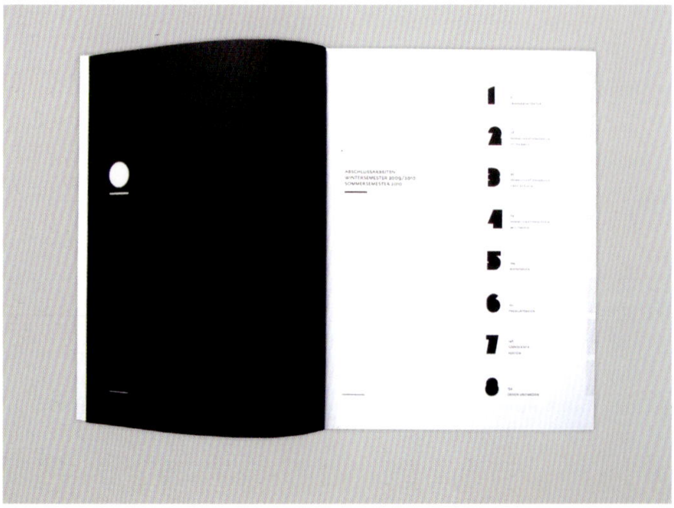

KÜNSTLERISCHE AUFNAHMEPRÜFUNG
— ARTISTIC ENTRANCE EXAMINATION
11. – 12. MAI 2010

EiGEN/ARTIG

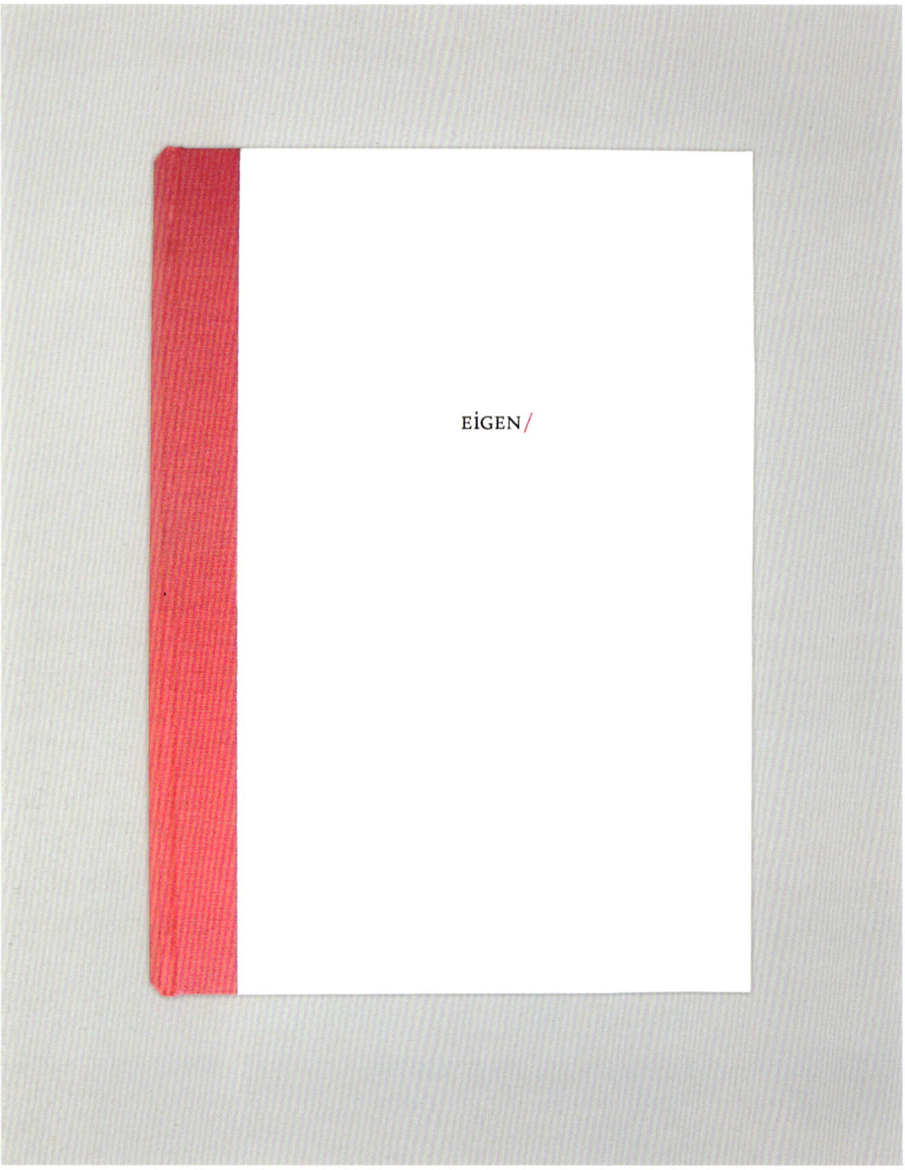
EiGEN/

WENN ICH
ALLEINE BIN,
REDE ICH IN
EINER ART
FANATASIE-
SPRACHE.

MMER
TEN
ERST AN.
ICH ZIEH
DEN RECHT
SCHUH ZU

DEN WIDERSTÄNDEN
ZUM TROTZ –
DAS ENDE IST DER
ANFANG
DESPITE
ALL RESISTANCE –
THE END IS
THE BEGINNING

BEIM ZUCKERN
DES KAFFEES
MUSS ICH MIT
DEM ZEIGE- UND
MITTELFINGER
DER LINKEN
HAND ZWEIMAL
AUF DEN TISCH
TIPPEN.

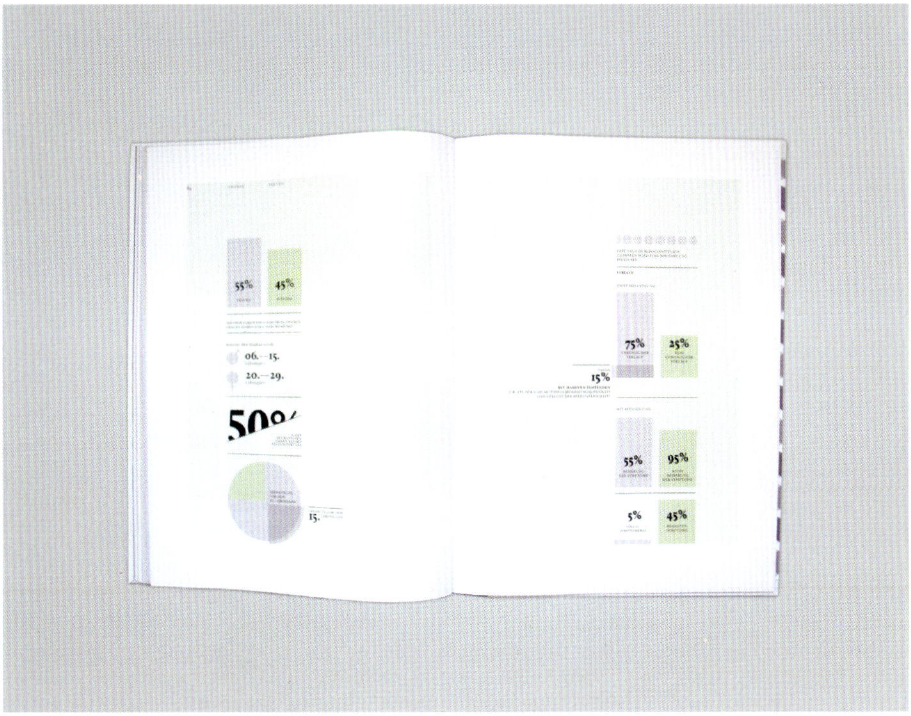

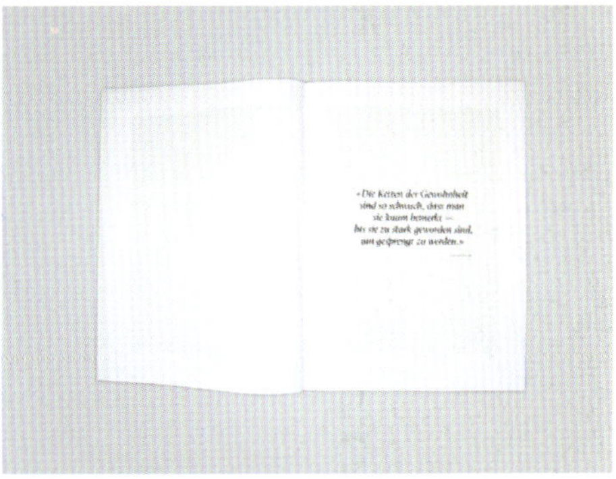

Designer:

Britta Siegmund

Production Date:

2010

Description:

Everyone has his or her little idiosyncrasies. One person always puts his right shoe on first; another counts steps as she goes up or down. This is all merely human. But when these little habits become compulsions a little habit turns into a complicated system of rituals. Over time, a compulsion can become a great burden.

I Am You

Designer:

Ellen Tongzhou Zhao

Location:

Paris, France

Production Date:

2007

Description:

This project "I Am You" is a book which talks about itself, its conception, its construction and its reading. It can be read in two directions and it has two beginnings. It highlights the moment of reading, this both solitary and shared meeting between the object of the book and the person who reads it. It is also in this moment that the two identities (of the book and the author, or of the book and the reader, or of the reader and the author) confront each other. This book invites the reader to think about the meaning of the book, the author, the reader, and the act of reading.

WHEN
WE
ET
IN?
I AM
A BOOK
WITHIN A
BOOK
I AM WORDS
ABOUT
A BOOK
I AM
PHOTOS OF
A BOOK

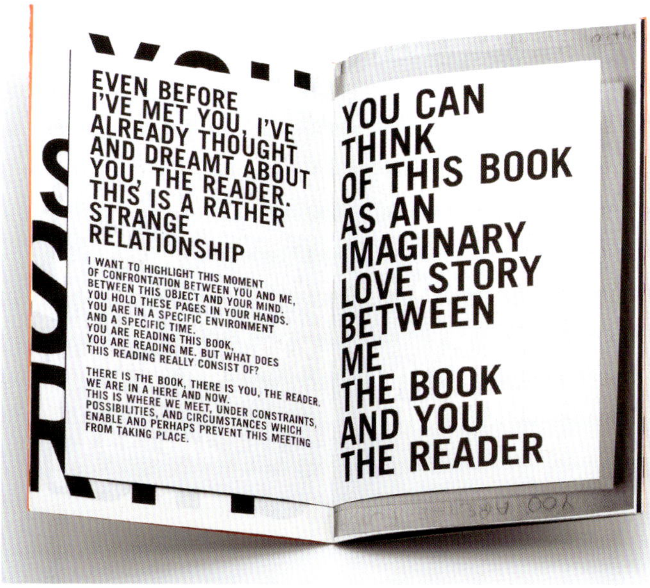
EVEN BEFORE
I'VE MET YOU, I'VE
ALREADY THOUGHT
AND DREAMT ABOUT
YOU, THE READER.
THIS IS A RATHER
STRANGE
RELATIONSHIP
I WANT TO HIGHLIGHT THIS MOMENT
OF CONFRONTATION BETWEEN YOU AND ME,
BETWEEN THIS OBJECT AND YOUR MIND.
YOU HOLD THESE PAGES IN YOUR HANDS.
YOU ARE IN A SPECIFIC ENVIRONMENT
AND A SPECIFIC TIME.
YOU ARE READING THIS BOOK,
YOU ARE READING ME. BUT WHAT DOES
THIS READING REALLY CONSIST OF?
THERE IS THE BOOK, THERE IS YOU, THE READER.
WE ARE IN A HERE AND NOW.
THIS IS WHERE WE MEET, UNDER CONSTRAINTS,
POSSIBILITIES, AND CIRCUMSTANCES WHICH
ENABLE AND PERHAPS PREVENT THIS MEETING
FROM TAKING PLACE.
YOU CAN
THINK
OF THIS BOOK
AS AN
IMAGINARY
LOVE STORY
BETWEEN
ME
THE BOOK
AND YOU
THE READER

WHAT
IS
THIS
MOM
WE
SHAR
YOU ARE
THE
FUTURE

WHO ARE
YOU?
WHERE
ARE YOU?
WHAT
ARE
YOU DOING?
HOW ARE
YOU
FEELING?
I WAS READING
GEORGES PEREC'S
SPECIES OF SPACE
IN THE FIRST CHAPTER, HE TALKS ABOUT
THE PAGE, AND EVENTUALLY THE SPACE
EXPANDS TO INCLUDE THE ROOM,
THE NEIGHBORHOOD, THE CITY AND THE PLANET.
PEREC'S WORDS MAKE ME THINK ABOUT THIS
CONFRONTATION OF THE PAGE WITH THE
READER. I WONDER WHAT YOU ARE DOING AT
THIS MOMENT WHEN YOU ARE READING
THIS BOOK, I ASK YOU:
WHAT TIME IS IT? WHAT MONTH IS IT?
WHAT DAY IS IT? WHERE ARE WE?
WHAT YEAR IS IT?
WHAT ARE YOU FEELING?
ARE YOU SITTING OR STANDING?
WHAT DO YOU SMELL AROUND YOU?
WHAT DO YOU HEAR AROUND YOU?
HOW DOES THIS PAPER FEEL?
WHAT DO YOU TASTE?
HOW FAST ARE YOU MOVING?
WHAT IS AROUND YOU? IN 10 METERS?
100 METERS? 1000 METERS?
WHAT IS THE WEATHER LIKE?
WHAT IS THE TEMPERATURE?
WHAT ARE YOU THINKING ABOUT?
WHERE ARE YOU FROM?
WHERE WILL YOU GO FROM HERE?

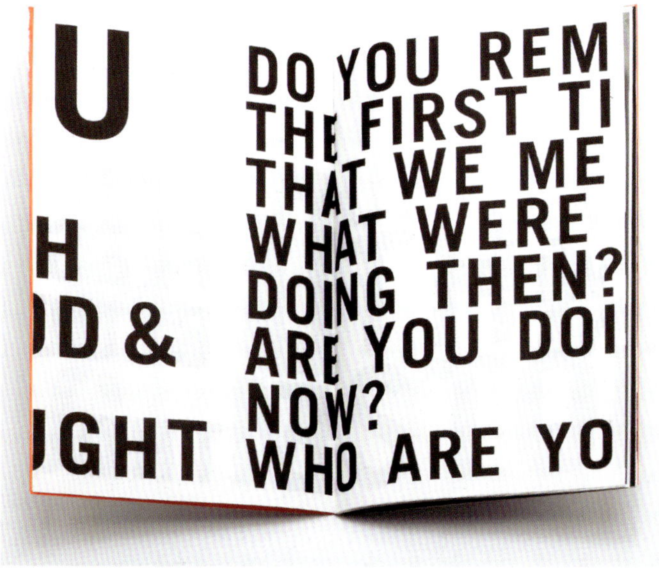
U
H
D &
GHT
YOU REM
FIRST TI
T WE ME
AT WERE
NG THEN?
YOU DOI
NOW?
WHO ARE YO

Cool Readings Book Collection

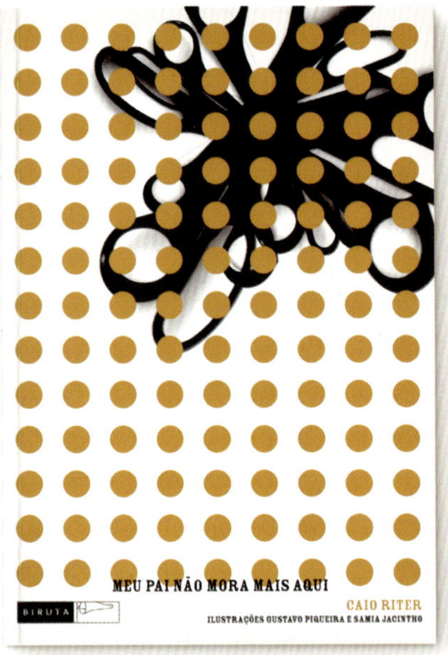

Design Agency:
CASA REX
Creative Director:
Gustavo Piqueira
Designer:
Gustavo Piqueira, Samia Jacintho
Illustration:
Gustavo Piqueira, Samia Jacintho
Client:
Editora Biruta
Production Date:
2009
Description:
The project developed for the early teen's books Cool Readings Collection published by Editora Biruta propose a new paradigm of teen literature and creates a complementary narrative, more adjusted to the visual repertory of current youth. The illustrations were produced from pictures shot by not so orthodox techniques, since were taken from cellphone cameras, eliminating the barrier of a illustration that works only as a text support. More than just a visual treatment or a series of regular illustrations, each book brings a parallel visual narrative (exploring colours and different images for each publication), almost in a cinematographic way, subverting what we know as an early teen's publication.

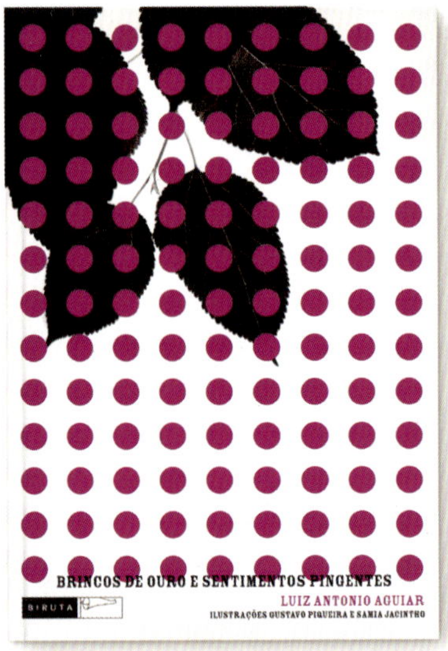

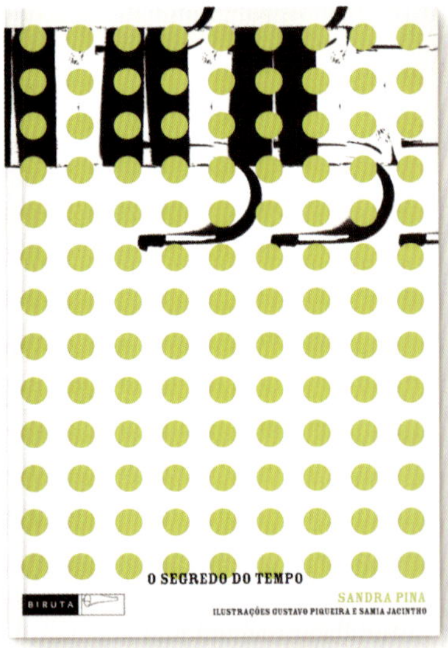

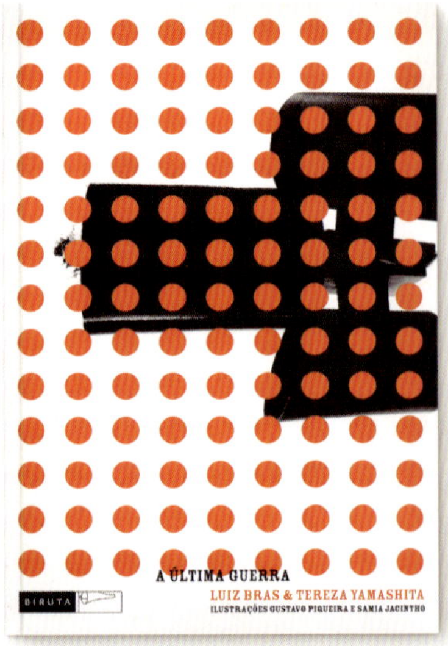

DO DIÁRIO DE LETÍCIA

18

Diário, ontem uma notícia caiu feito uma bomba na cabeça da gente. O Tadeu não apareceu na aula, aí, a diretora entrou e disse que tinha ocorrido um acidente com o pai dele. Coisa grave. Que ele estava mal no hospital. Mas, na verdade, era pior ainda. Parece que um caminhão bateu de frente no carro do pai do Tadeu. Ele tava vindo de uma de suas tantas viagens.

O pai do Tadeu morreu, Diário.

Nossa, foi um silêncio na aula. Ninguém sabia direito o que fazer. A diretora disse que as aulas seriam suspensas para que quem quisesse pudesse ir ao velório e ao enterro. Eu nunca fui a um enterro, Diário. Nunca. Será no final do dia.

Eu e as gurias, mais o Pedro Henrique e o Cícero, demos uma passada no velório. Coisa terrível. O caixão, no meio da capela; o corpo, entre as flores; aquele cheiro de velas queimando. Tudo só tristeza. E o Tadeu agarrado na mãe dele. O rosto inchado de tanto chorar. Coitado. Me deu uma pena. Nós o abraçamos, uns disseram algumas coisas, eu não. Não sabia o que falar, não tinha o que falar. O mundo do Tadeu desabando bem ali na nossa frente. Um horror.

Aí, dei o sinal, o Cícero tocou uns acordes na guitarra e o som explodiu. Eu comecei a cantar meu (nosso) discurso. Falava de vencer dificuldades. Falava de não desistir jamais dos sonhos. Falava de descobertas e do quanto vale ter amigos e amores. Falava também da saudade que, com certeza, a gente ia sentir daqueles tempos de escola.

Eu cantava.

Lá embaixo, toda linda, Letícia acompanhava a letra. Só ela conhecia a surpresa que eu tinha inventado. Sabia que era eu quem tinha escrito. Tava feliz. E eu também. Não sei até quando esta felicidade toda vai durar. Mas isto não importa.

Ou será que importa?

Vai saber.

Our Movie

Design Agency:

CASA REX

Creative Director:

Gustavo Piqueira

Designer:

Gustavo Piqueira, Samia Jacintho

Illustration:

Gustavo Piqueira, Samia Jacintho

Client:

Jogo de Amarelinha

Production Date:

2010

Description:

Our Movie is a book that tells a story about two young lovers. Instead of creating illustrations that portray the book's narrative, the designer used visuals in the form of soft shapes that weave through the pages in parallel to the narrative, almost like a sound track. These emotive fluid graphics follow the relationship and story of the couple from their first date through to the romance, the sex, and finally, their split.

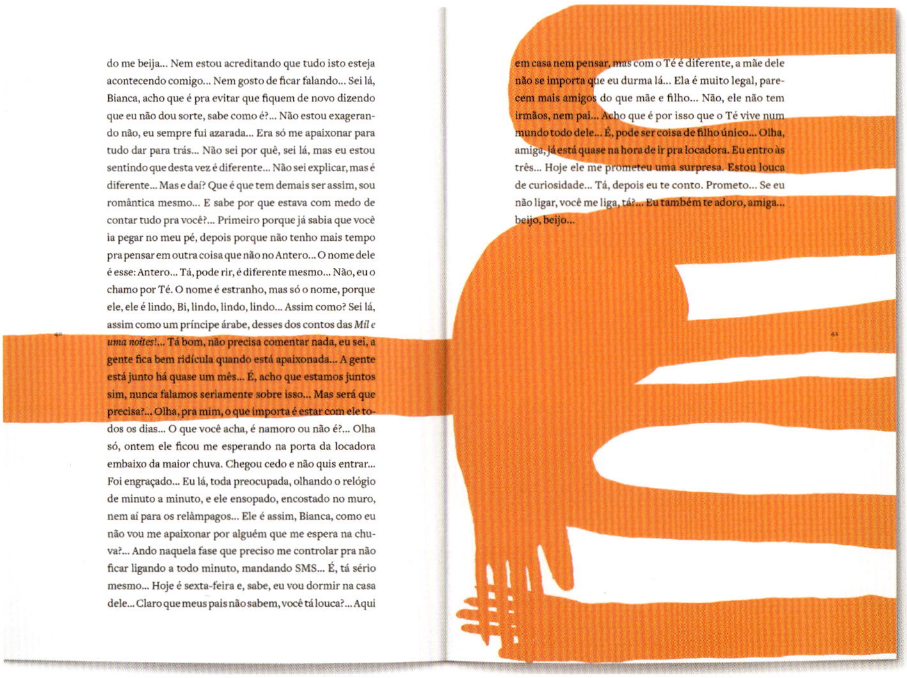

My Amerindian Friend

Design Agency:
CASA REX
Creative Director:
Gustavo Piqueira
Designer:
Gustavo Piqueira, Samia Jacintho
Client:
Editora Biruta
Production Date:
2009
Description:
The adolescent book "My Amerindian Friend" traces the story of friendship and conflicts that arise when Amerindian children start to study at a school with other kids who come from different backgrounds and traditions. While it broaches the subject of inclusion at school, the book also inevitably deals with the other side of the story - the exclusion and the prejudice. In developing the book graphics, this theme of portraying different sides of a story have been taken into consideration. The result is a unique project that has made unusual use of illustrations positioned at different angles creating a metaphoric sense of perspective.

Writings About Jade - Classic Chinese Poetry

Design Agency:

CASA REX

Creative Director:

Gustavo Piqueira

Designer:

Gustavo Piqueira, Samia Jacintho

Client:

Ateliê Editorial

Production Date:

2010

Description:

"Writings About Jade" is a classic Chinese poetry book translated by one of Brazil's best known "concrete" poets (modern poetry that uses visual composition as part of its structure). To portray this unusual relationship, the designer created a book cover that integrated ancient Chinese books and their main design characteristics with a modern approach. The open bookbinding beautifully showcases the intricate and colourful Chinese drawing on the front page. Visual appeal is further enhanced by the contrasting black and white treatment used on the inside pages.

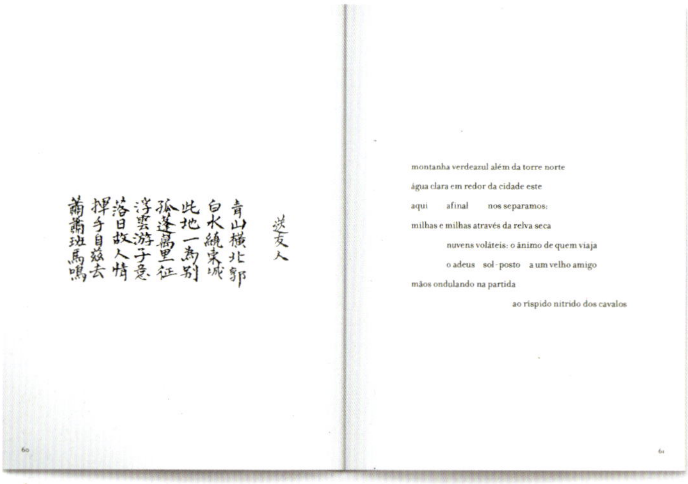

Science, History and Art

Design Agency:
CASA REX
Designer:
Gustavo Piqueira, Samia Jacintho
Assistant Designer:
Camile Leão
Creative Director:
Gustavo Piqueira
Client:
Editora EDUSP
Production Date:
2010
Description:
This book is a compilation of a series of rare and special works of science, history and art from the Bioscience Institute, which is part of one of the most renowned Universities in São Paulo. The antique elements and images have been retained and are showcased in a contemporary setting augmented by beautiful hand-drawn line illustrations, all designed to accentuate the exclusiveness of the publication.

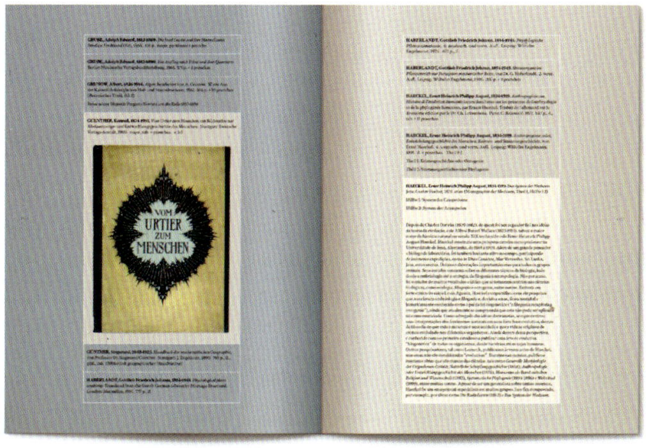

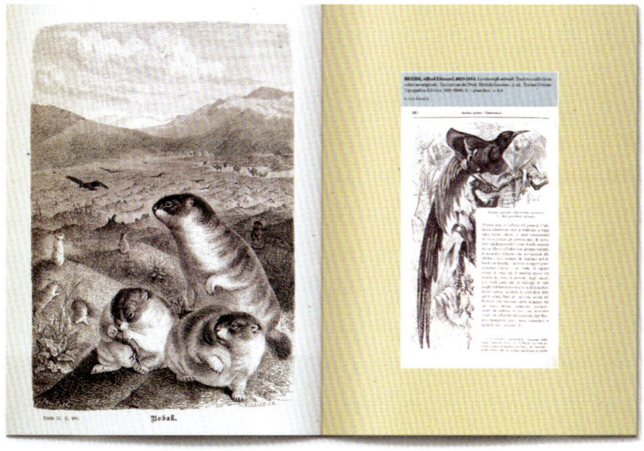

Information - In Formation

Designer:

Christian Grutsch

Client:

Information - In Formation

Production Date:

2010

Description:

Diploma thesis on abstraction. The book is divided into two sections. On the one hand there is a short overview on abstract theory, on the other hand a personal interpretation. For personal interpretation the designer collected printed matter and made a selection. Out of this selection the designer created abstract compostitions, leaving only colour and basic geometric shapes. Some compositions, even when abstracted, are still readable, and others remain a miracle.

Pizzeria Ristorante
Da CORRADO
Tel 894 31 66
Fax 990 68 46
www.dacorrado.at
Penzinger Strasse 22, 1140 Wien
Samstag 17 - 23 Uhr
DA CORRADO
1989
TÄGLICH
Für Parties und Feste
70 Plätze
zur Verfügung !!!
GRATISZUSTELLUNG
Ab €8,50 Bestellwert
13., 14. und 15. Bezirk
ANGEBOT Sa. 17-23 Uhr
Nur bei Zustellung oder Abholung jede Pizza nur € 5,90
Ab einem Bestellwert von € 25, 2L cola GRATIS
Im Lokal und bei Selbstabholung
JEDE Pizza
außer mittlerer und Familienpizza
5,50

SONNTAG MIT FREUNDEN
WIEN MUSEUM KARLSPLATZ
WIEN MUSEUM

EX LIBRIS

The LAB Book

Design Agency:
Creative Inc
Creative Director:
Mel O'Rourke
Designer:
Ciara Cantwell
Client:
Dublin City Council
Production Date:
2009
Description:
The objective of the book was to showcase the work of 40 Artists that have exhibited in The LAB Gallery on Dublin's Foley Street. This book was part of The LAB's overall visual identity.Using interesting combinations of stock and alternating between four colour process and spot printing, the designer's aim was to produce a compelling and unique backdrop which showcased the work without distracting from it.

Clouds
The Fold
Issue Two
Cora Cummins and Alison Pilkington

36
Seamus Nolan Demesne
In the work of Seamus Nolan, the object is often secondary to the ideas and questions his art inspires. Hotel Ballymun was one such project, a temporary 'boutique hotel' in one of the condemned tower blocks of Ballymun. There, the art lay less in the rooms of the hotel, than in the series of transactions (the relational aesthetics) and discussions around it. With Demesne, the 'object', in this case, a holiday caravan, constructed entirely from discarded cardboard (wheels, tow hitch and all), presents a striking presence, and yet it too demands considered thought, and raises a complex series of implications.
Complicating things is the exhibition's title, 'Demesne', bringing issues of property rights and ownership, landlords and tenancies into play. The material from which Nolan's caravan is constructed, and which is also the medium for a series of wall pieces, adds to this – adding ideas of waste, refuse, recycling and consumption to the mix. There is also the dichotomy between the caravans towed to seaside spots of holidays, and the ones inhabited by those with no ownership of land at all. Does siting a caravan give one temporary title to the land on which it stands? How are boundaries and territories negotiated, when the dwelling is as impermanent and transitional as this?
Multi-layered as ever, Demesne transformed The LAB into a challenging space of ideas, and yet one that also had a strong and satisfying aesthetic presence.
Demesne originated in the Wexford Arts Centre, as part of the inaugural 2006 Emerging Visual Artist Award.

The Fold
Issue II : Clouds

Joseph R. Wolin

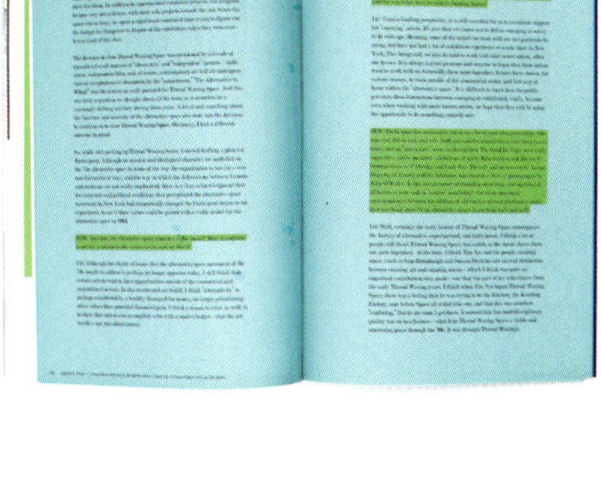

Barnardos Wizard of Words

Design Agency:
Creative Inc
Creative Director:
Mel O'Rourke
Designer:
Tony Matthews
Client:
Barnardos
Production Date:
2009
Description:
Barnardos Wizard of Words is a school reading programme, undertaken by volunteers from an older age bracket, designed to improve childrens' reading abilities and also to improve their social and personal skills through their interaction with their mentor. The design uses strong, vibrant colour and impactful type to engage the participant and is visibility compliant according to EU regulations.

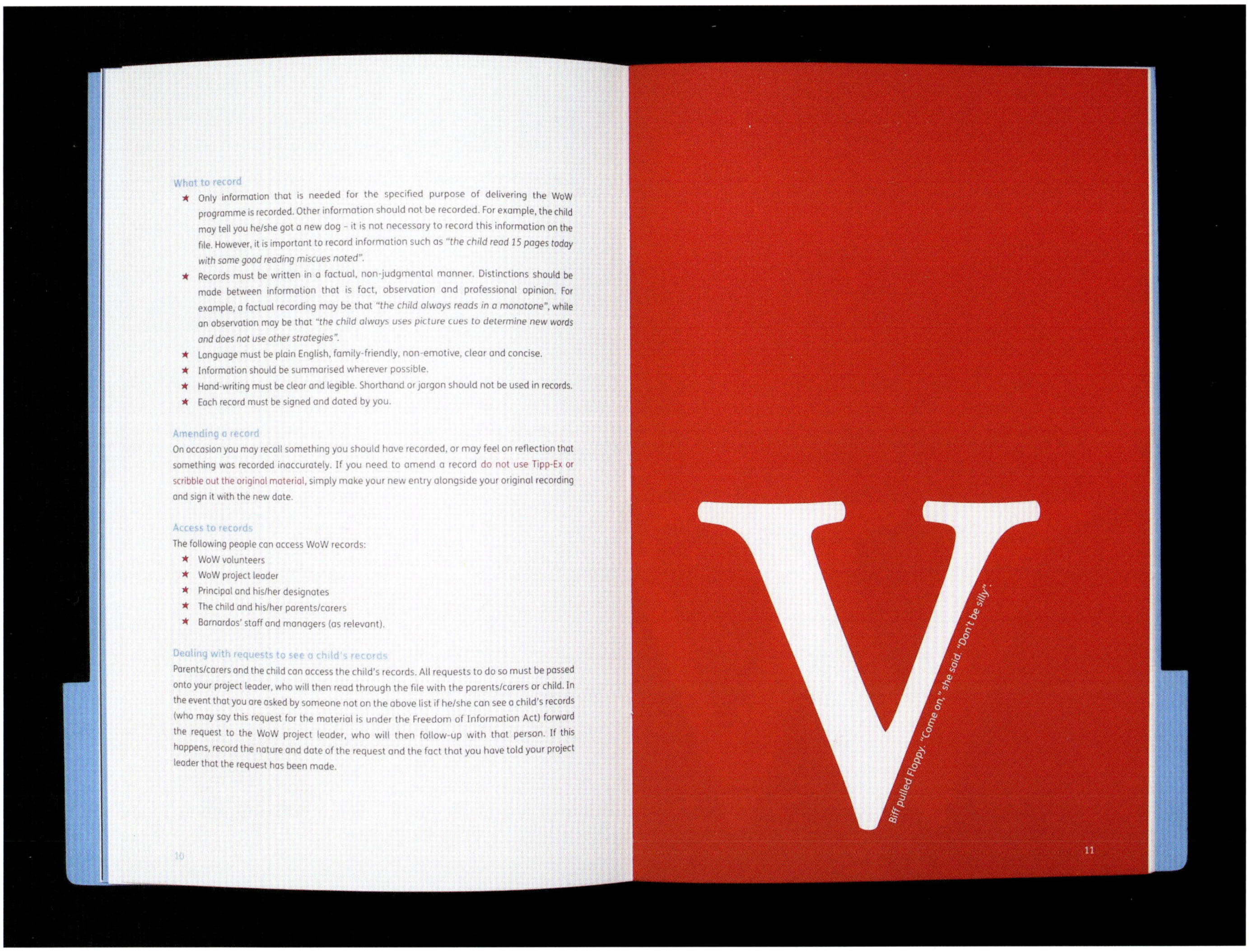
What to record
★ Only information that is needed for the specified purpose of delivering the WoW programme is recorded. Other information should not be recorded. For example, the child may tell you he/she got a new dog – it is not necessary to record this information on the file. However, it is important to record information such as "the child read 15 pages today with some good reading miscues noted".
★ Records must be written in a factual, non-judgmental manner. Distinctions should be made between information that is fact, observation and professional opinion. For example, a factual recording may be that "the child always reads in a monotone", while an observation may be that "the child always uses picture cues to determine new words and does not use other strategies".
★ Language must be plain English, family-friendly, non-emotive, clear and concise.
★ Information should be summarised wherever possible.
★ Hand-writing must be clear and legible. Shorthand or jargon should not be used in records.
★ Each record must be signed and dated by you.
Amending a record
On occasion you may recall something you should have recorded, or may feel on reflection that something was recorded inaccurately. If you need to amend a record do not use Tipp-Ex or scribble out the original material, simply make your new entry alongside your original recording and sign it with the new date.
Access to records
The following people can access WoW records:
★ WoW volunteers
★ WoW project leader
★ Principal and his/her designates
★ The child and his/her parents/carers
★ Barnardos' staff and managers (as relevant).
Dealing with requests to see a child's records
Parents/carers and the child can access the child's records. All requests to do so must be passed onto your project leader, who will then read through the file with the parents/carers or child. In the event that you are asked by someone not on the above list if he/she can see a child's records (who may say this request for the material is under the Freedom of Information Act) forward the request to the WoW project leader, who will then follow-up with that person. If this happens, record the nature and date of the request and the fact that you have told your project leader that the request has been made.
10
V
Biff pulled Floppy. "Come on," she said. "Don't be silly".
11

1
Gran had a hut, by the sea.
2
It was fun in the Jolly Jean. "I can see a seal,"
3
4
"The door is open," said Biff. The magic was working. It took the children inside. It took Floppy too.
Acknowledgements
Suzanne Connolly

Everything is Going to be Alright

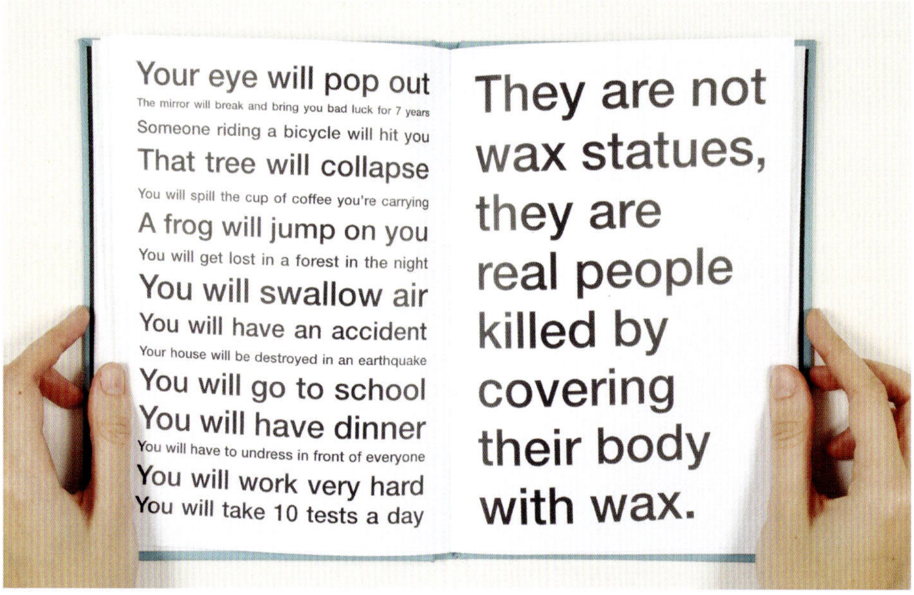

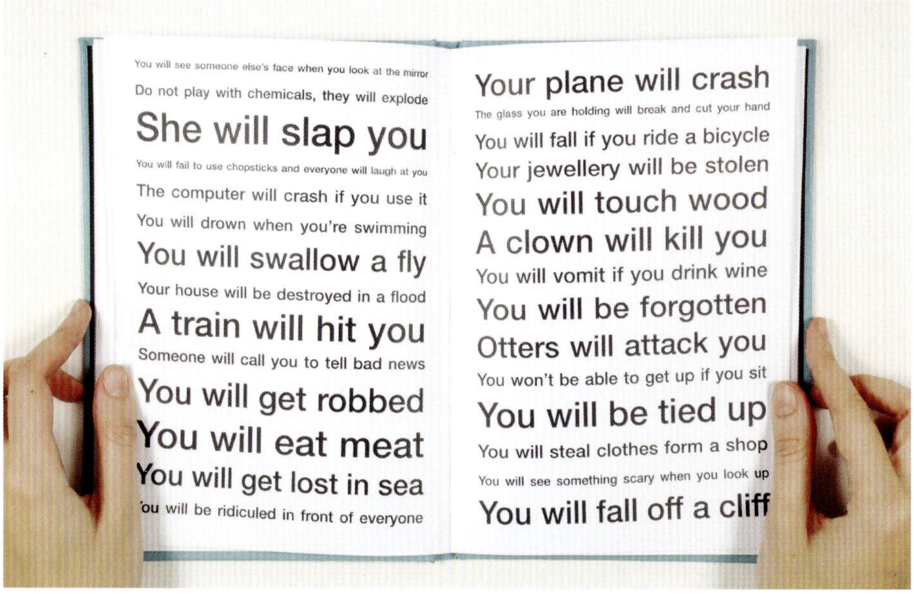

Designer:

Deniz Tekkul

Production Date:

2008

Description:

As his final project on his MA, Deniz Tekkul produced two books as a critique of the culture of fear that is promoted by the media.For the first book, Deniz took pictures of his everyday life surroundings, in his flat and outside, then numbered in these pictures the phobias from the phobia list he found. The numbers were explained in the index on the back of the book.

MA Research Book

Designer:

Deniz Tekkul

Production Date:

2008

Description:

Deniz Tekkul designed this book to document all his research and design process during the MA Graphic design communication at Chelsea College of Art and Design, London.

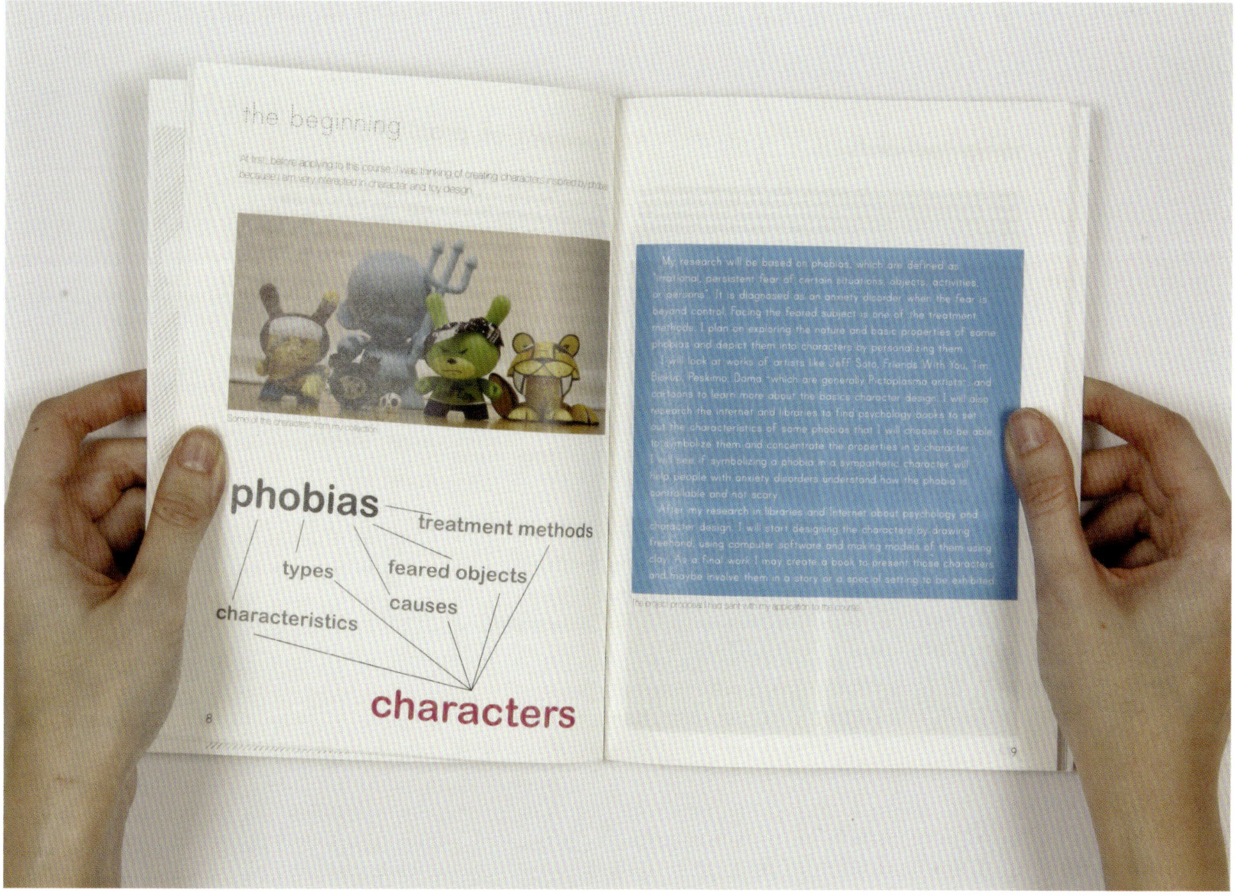
the beginning
phobias
treatment methods
types
feared objects
causes
characteristics
characters
8
9

experiments
YOU WILL SPILL
THE COFFEE YOU
your house will be destroyed and all your relatives will die in an earthquake
28
29

Tons Líricos

Designer:

Diogo Montes

Photography:

Paula Abreu, Diego Correia and Stock.XCHNG

Client:

Editora Eldorado and Ronei Recker

Production Date:

2009

Description:

Tons Líricos (Lyric Tones) is a prose poetry book written by Ronei Recker.

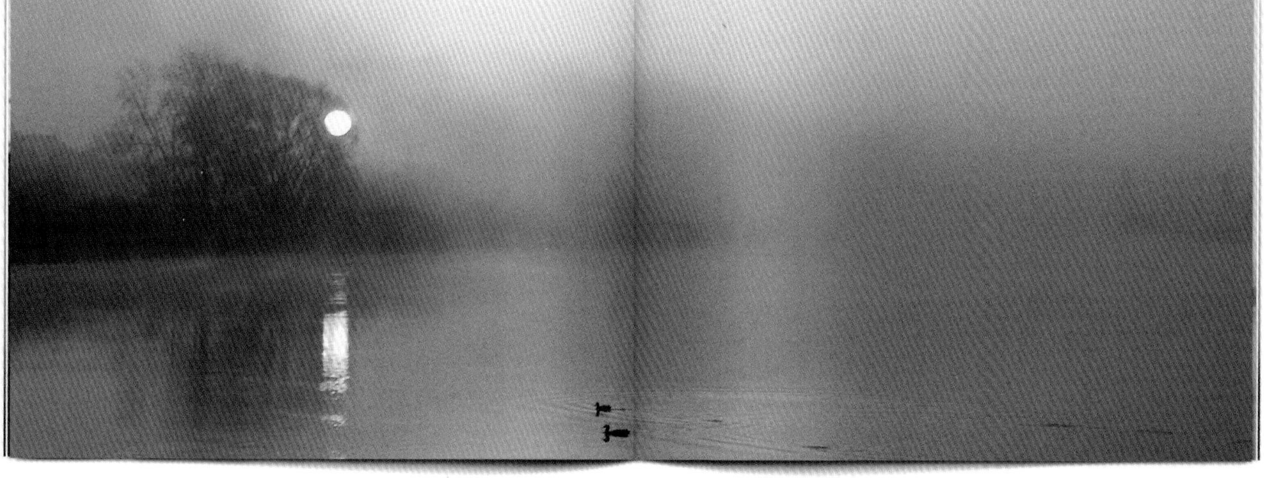

Alimente-a a cada dia, com mais e mais informações, e cultive em seu corpo o dicionário do saber. E não queira você saber de barreiras ou mágoas. Transponha seus problemas como se fosse o mais simples dos atos.

Às vezes penso:
"E se eu fosse a própria flor em que pouso pesado, fazendo-a curvar-se de dor?"

Não sente dor a rosa mais linda, pois se sentisse a mim, com seus espinhos me alvejaria; mas as rosas não falam, elas apenas se calam para a elas enfeitar.

Quando paro, sinto a sensação de tudo ser igual; olho para as flores e as vejo de frente. Na minha altura, vejo de perto o pólen laranja caindo no chão. Por que será que tudo que olho cai no chão? Será assim o fim de tudo? O chão?

Existe algo de belo que em toda manhã escuto bem alto, com seus tons quase líricos percutindo para todos. Às 6:00, no cume da torre da igreja do vale, via a mascote de bronze rangendo notas que todos conhecem. Os garotos franzinos protegem seus ouvidos do celeste barulho. As pessoas correm nas ruas e nós, circulando por tudo, olhamos para o dia que mal despertou.

É assim a vida no vale; os sons viram uma rotina gostosa que, se um de nós faltar para este concerto, o som fica baixo. Cantamos para tudo acordar, e, no banco da praça, até os pombos, bem gordos, comendo o farelo do chão, nos olham também.

Hering Berlin

Design Agency:
Edenspiekermann
Client:
Hering Berlin
Production Date:
2009
Description:
The complex shapes and decorations of Hering porcelain come to life in the image brochure; blind embossing, die cuts, metallic paints and spot varnishes make the porcelain look as lifelike as objects can possibly get in print. There's also the 700-page general catalogue with the highest standard of clarity and design. No wonder then that the company's appearance has caused such a stir in the industry. The product catalogue and the brochure won Silver European Design Award in May 2009.

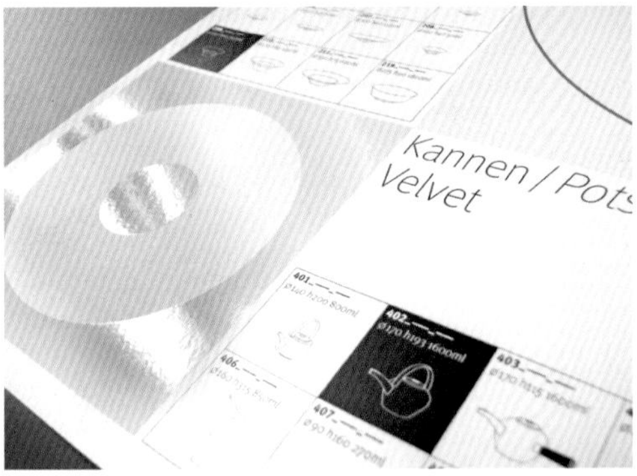

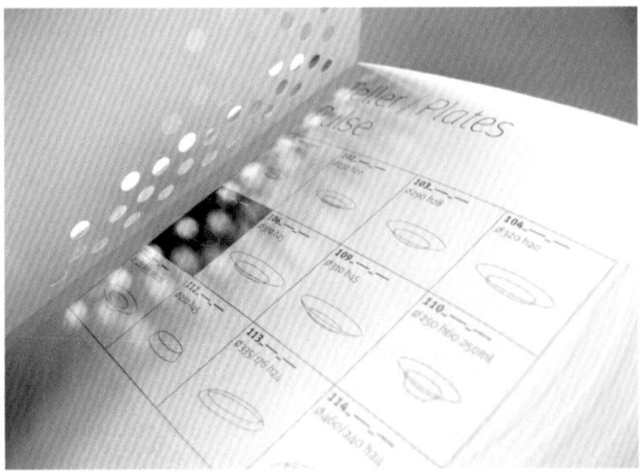

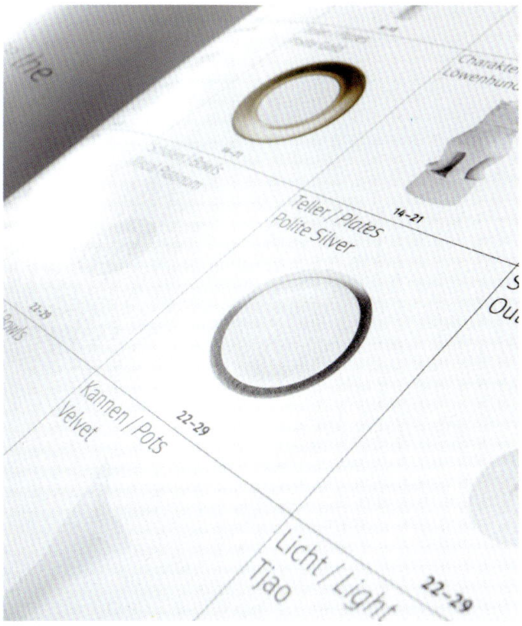
Teller / Plates
Polite Silver
14–21
22–29
Kannen / Pots
Velvet
Licht / Light
Tjao
22–29

201
ø75 h60 70ml
202
ø110 h75 200ml
206
ø220 h45 60ml
207
211
ø330 h75 600ml
212
ø100 h54 160ml
216
ø350 h125 6000ml
217
ø175 h140 1500ml
221
ø105 h37

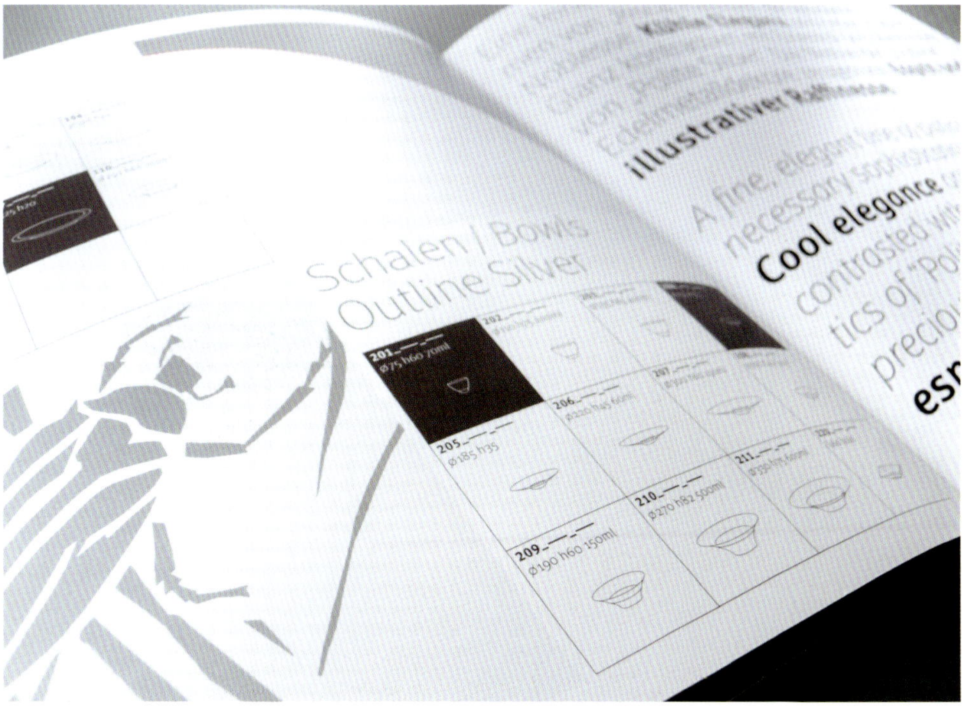
illustrativer Raffinesse.
Cool elegance
Schalen / Bowls
Outline Silver
201
ø75 h60 70ml
205
ø185 h35
206
209
ø190 h60 150ml
210
ø270 h82 500ml
211

Futu Design Guide

Design Agency:

Publishing and Design Guide

Creative Director:

Edgar Bąk

Client:

Publishing and Design Guide

Production Date:

2009

Description:

It is a guide about design, fashion, architecture and music, published bimonthly.

FUTU Design Guide
Living
ST 904, TR 9 LAMPS, TOM ROSSAU
Kariera Duńczyka Toma Rossau rozpoczęła się od składania klocków Lego w piwnicy rodzinnego domu. Gdy dorósł, przerzucił się na drewno i projektowanie. Z dobrym skutkiem. Brzozowe lampy jego autorstwa otrzymały na Furniture Fair w Kopenhadze specjalną nagrodę publiczności.
www.tomrossau.dk
SQUARE
Efektowny, ciemnobrązowy stolik kawowy z dębowego forniru Planika Fires to nie tylko ozdoba nowoczesnego salonu, ale - przede wszystkim - niepowtarzalny klimat. Wbudowany stalowy talerz otoczony szklanym cylindrem pozwala cieszyć się domowym ogniskiem przy jednoczesnym zachowaniu bezpieczeństwa i całkowitym wyeliminowaniu nieprzyjemnego zapachu charakterystycznego dla zwykłych kominków. Nowa kolekcja powstała przy współpracy z designerem Christophe Pilletem.
www.planikafires.com
DEESAWAT STICK UP, CUBIC, GREEN WALL COLLECTION
Deesawat to tajska firma specjalizująca się w produkcji drewnianych mebli. Założona w 1972 roku szybko stała się hitem eksportowym odnosząc sukces zarówno w Europie jak i Stanach Zjednoczonych. Trzystu wykwalifikowanych pracowników ręcznie wykańcza każdy produkowany w niej przedmiot.
www.deesawat.com

SYGNAŁY
LUKSUSU

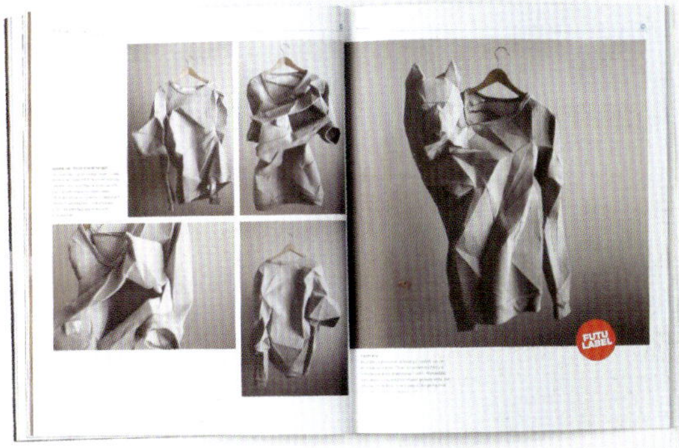
FUTU
LABEL

THE ALLURE
OF BEAUTY
WOMEN IN HOLLYWOOD
ASSOULINE
water
THE LIGHT OF
TOKYO
THE
INGMAR
BERGMAN
ARCHIVES
the eco-travel
handbook
HEARTBREAK
LIES
RAPHAEL
SAADIQ
FUTU
LABEL
DARK
WAS
THE
NIGHT
AMY
WINEHOUSE
FRANK &
BACK TO
BLACK

Patinir

Design Agency:

Erretres

Client:

Museo del Prado

Production Date:

2007

Description:

With over 400 pages, Erretres designed the catalogue for Museo del Prado as part of the exhibition of the famous Flemish painter, Joaquim Patinir.

Horacio Coppola Fotografía

Design Agency:
Erretres
Designer:
Erretres
Client:
Fundacion Telefonica, Madrid, Spain
Production Date:
2008
Description:
Fundación Telefónica organised an exhibition about the works of Argentinean photographer, Horacio Coppola. This catalogue highlights his works as one of Latin America's prominent photographers during the 20th century. In addition, Erretres designed the exhibition's logo, its entire environmental graphics and website. The design team received the 2008 Visual Award for Best Book Design.

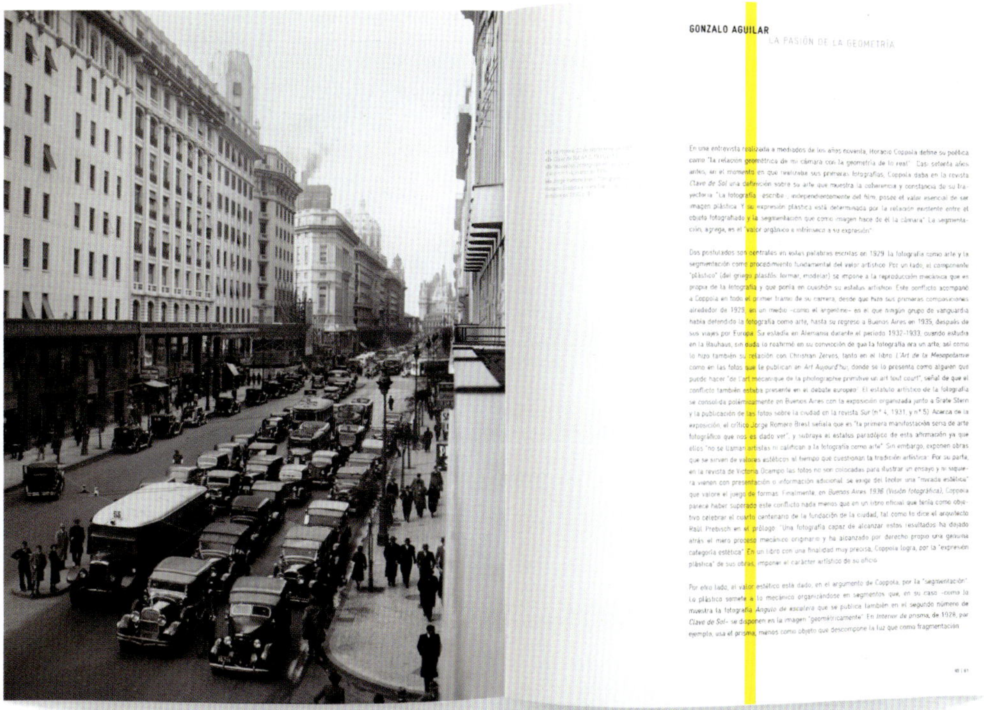
GONZALO AGUILAR
LA PASIÓN DE LA GEOMETRÍA

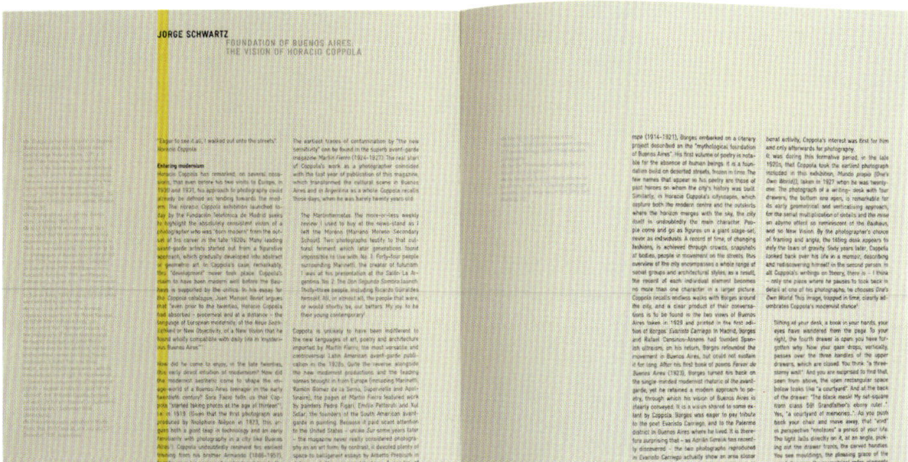
JORGE SCHWARTZ
FOUNDATION OF BUENOS AIRES:
THE VISION OF HORACIO COPPOLA
Entering modernism

Marín

Design Agency:

Erretres

Client:

Fundación Telefónica, Madrid, Spain

Production Date:

2007

Description:

Erretres designed the logo and exhibition graphics, as well as the catalogue and website for the exhibition Marín, showcasing a selection of the works of the unknown photographer, Luis Ramón Marín, now considered one of the precursors of photojournalism in Spain. The design team received the 2008 PHotoEspaña Award for Best Photography Book.

Obras Maestras

Design Agency:

Erretres

Client:

La Fábrica, Madrid, Spain

Production Date:

Since 2009

Description:

Obras Maestras are books designed in big format that offer a deep analysis of the life and works of the most important contemporary photographers of Spain. Two books are published each year and amongst the material edited, personal albums and chronologies of the authors are included. The most recent books include the works of Chema Madoz, Català-Roca and Isabel Muñoz.

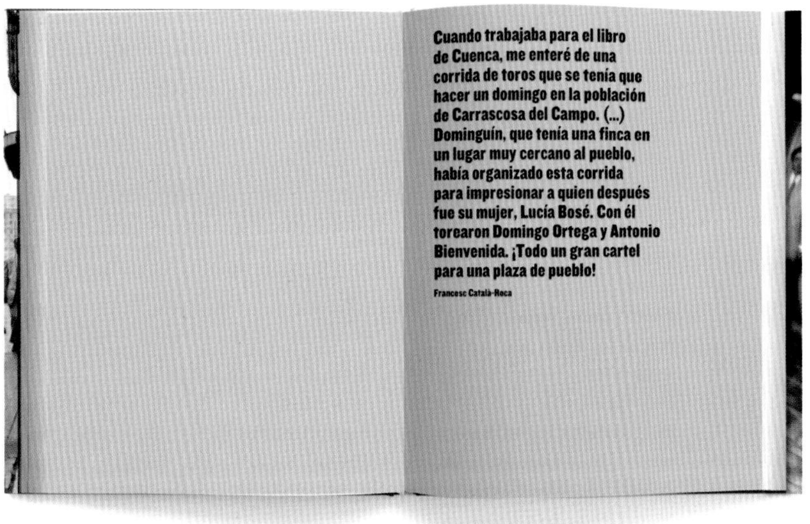
Cuando trabajaba para el libro de Cuenca, me enteré de una corrida de toros que se tenía que hacer un domingo en la población de Carrascosa del Campo. (...) Dominguín, que tenía una finca en un lugar muy cercano al pueblo, había organizado esta corrida para impresionar a quien después fue su mujer, Lucía Bosé. Con él torearon Domingo Ortega y Antonio Bienvenida. ¡Todo un gran cartel para una plaza de pueblo!
Francesc Català-Roca

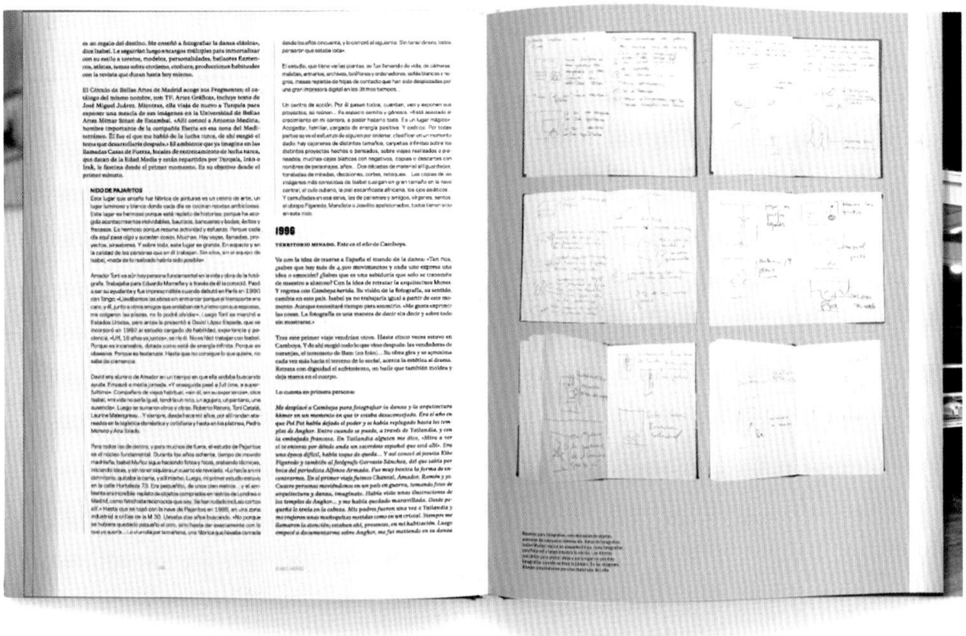
1996

PHotoEspaña Books

Design Agency:

Erretres

Client:

PHotoEspaña, Madrid, Spain

Production Date:

Since 2010

Description:

PHotoEspaña is the leading photography festival in Europe. To date, twelve editions have taken place since its beginning and 723 works have been presented in main museums, exhibition halls, galleries and art centres in Madrid. PHE is characterised by being a very influential festival that provides the opportunity to showcase photographic projects, videos and artistic installations, and the works of national and international photographers. Erretres developed their new book collection called PHE Books. Erretres designed the logo and oversaw the entire editorial project. The use of typography was rigorous and the materials selected for printing were of the upmost quality, resulting in an effective and recognisable collection, intimately tied to the PHE brand.

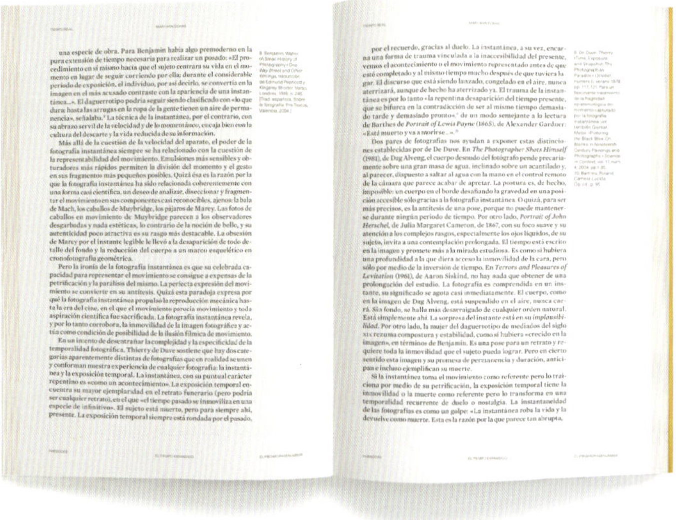

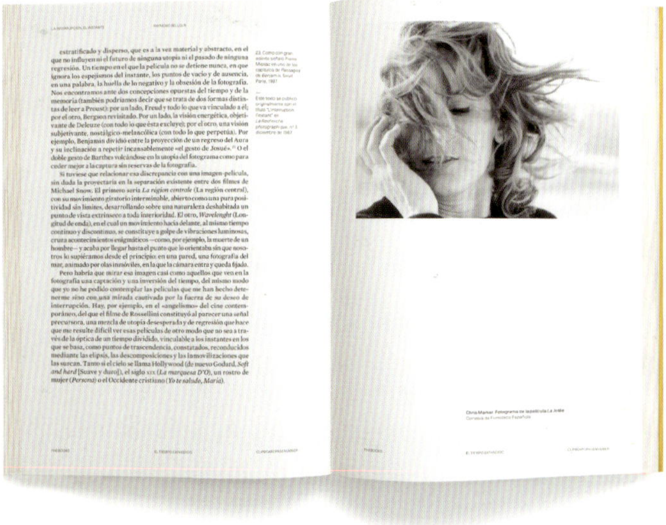

de Robledo se trata de lograr el efecto opuesto: se borra cualquier indicio referencial de la realidad para poner la imagen al servicio de la luz y dejar que ella se nos presente en su máxima esencia. Las obras se realizan en espacios desolados en donde el tiempo discurre a una velocidad diferente. La paciencia, que es discípula del tiempo, será la herramienta necesaria para captar instantáneas desprovistas de una temática preestablecida. La realidad que generalmente disfraza la fotografía se verá mitigada para potenciar la aparición de su esencia, es decir, la luz.

Desde sus trabajos iniciales a mediados de los setenta, la fotografía única fue insuficiente para mostrar el paso del tiempo y se hizo necesaria la «serialidad». Lo estático quedó desplazado y la instalación y el vídeo entraron en escena. En las imágenes de Robledo, la luz y la sombra son mecanismos para visualizar la prolongación del paso del tiempo; así veremos figuras geométricas y líneas de luz y sombra que se mueven en el espacio, como metáforas de un reloj solar.

El exceso de imágenes impuesto por la cultura mediática actual nos enfrenta a una agresiva velocidad en la asimilación de la fotografía. Robledo pretende huir de esta medida acelerada del tiempo para instar a una reflexión y así abstrae el referente para darle un espacio prioritario al paso del tiempo. En su obra *Diarios de luz* (2004) se ve el tránsito de un rayo de sol por un espacio. La luz es protagonista, pero no en su capacidad de viajar a velocidades insuperables, sino más bien en su poder de dilatarse en el espacio y el tiempo. Al dar prioridad a la luz como objeto a fotografiar más allá del instante, Robledo logra captar un ambiente, unos fenómenos efímeros que se presentan en los momentos aparentemente inocuos que existen entre una y otra imagen. Sus series son el antes y el después, no existe un momento central, la narración se desmaterializa y vemos un signo sin código, una imagen incierta.

En la obra *Fotos de otros* (2001-2002), de Julio Grinblatt, surge un interés similar por huir del instante y jugar con el tiempo. Sus series registran transiciones y observamos momentos que estarían entre un instante fotográfico y otro. Como resalta el artista, lo interesante es ver esa fracción de tiempo en la que algo deja de ser una cosa para transformarse en otra diferente. Una fotografía generalmente está cargada de información. Grinblatt supera la función de espejo de la realidad adjudicada a esta disciplina para crear una experiencia reflexiva en donde se resaltan los experimentos con la luz por encima del objeto, buscando que el observador se descubra en el acto de mirar. En la serie mencionada, el artista juega con dos temporalidades: una lenta, que se manifiesta con una luminosidad tenue que poco a poco marca el negativo detrás del obturador abierto permanentemente, generando figuras amorfas y fantasmagóricas y, por otro lado, la del flash de otro fotógrafo que de manera improvisada congela esa temporalidad instantánea que detiene el flujo extendido habilitado por el artista.

Grinblatt quiere explorar una fotografía que, más allá de una representación de la realidad, puede tener varias manifestaciones en torno a lo cotidiano. El artista menciona, retomando a Philippe Dubois, que el acto fotográfico, en su poder de estupefacción, arroja en cada toma un velo transparente y paralizante que él quiere abandonar. Trabaja con el

Óscar Muñoz, *Narcisos (vídeo)*, 2001-2002
© Óscar Muñoz

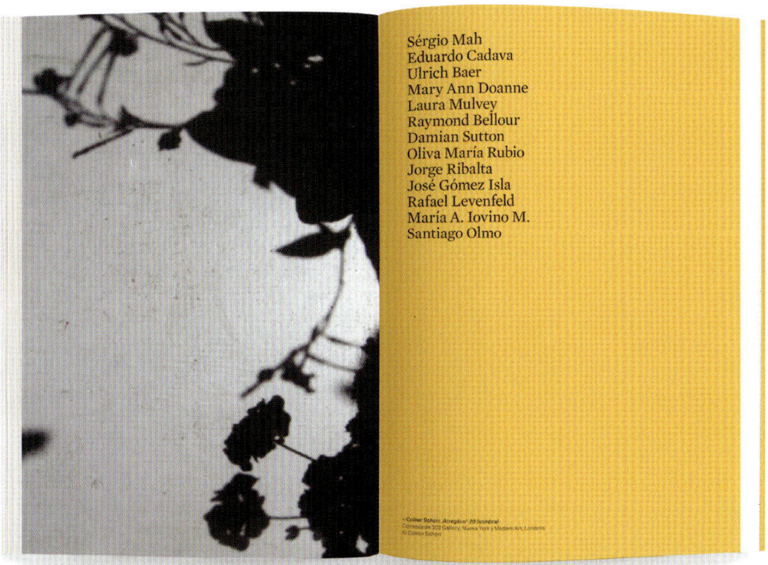

Sérgio Mah
Eduardo Cadava
Ulrich Baer
Mary Ann Doanne
Laura Mulvey
Raymond Bellour
Damian Sutton
Oliva María Rubio
Jorge Ribalta
José Gómez Isla
Rafael Levenfeld
María A. Iovino M.
Santiago Olmo

El tiempo expandido
Sérgio Mah
1

Dossier Trasatlántica
Christopher Fraga Wiley
María Wills
Rita Ferrer
Irving Domínguez
Inés Yujnovsky

Batecs A Mig Cami

Design Agency:

Esteve Bou

Client:

Joaquima Nolla

Production Date:

Since 2009

Description:

Design and illustration of "Batecs A Mig Cami", a poetry book that speaks about the essence of the human condition: emotions, pain, joy, love and hope... important moments of the designer's aunt Joaquima Nolla, collected after half a lifetime and a long road travelled and lived.

20
Com una onada en maregassa
Com una onada en maregassa
el meu navili
va sense veles, cercant rumb
sense timó.
Ona que ve empeny amb força un cec deliri,
Ona que va allunya el port on retornar.
Vent de llevant torna la calma,
mentre lluita
vent de ponent obrint-se pas
fugint del mar
i un ventijol desconegut, tot d'una, enfonsa
la gran carcassa que em serveix per navegar.
21
I feta a trossos va surant la meva vida
tota preguntes que no em saben contestar,
la incongruència de la incògnita profunda
del vell misteri que no ensenyen a esbrinar.
Com una onada en maregassa
el meu navili
va sense veles cercant rumb
sense timó.
I un ventijol desconegut, tot d'una enfonsa,
la gran carcassa que em serveix de salvació.

"Batecs a mig camí"
és un conjunt de 62 poemes,
més dos "Cançonetes d'amor
al son de la mare", que parlen
de l'essència de l'ésser humà
i del seu caminar pel món;
dels seus moments de llum i
de foscor, de vida i de mort.
A través dels poemes passem
pels batecs de dol, d'amor,
del jo que es desgrana, de la
seva continuïtat i de la seva
constància d'ésser pensant
que s'adona que els moments
són irrepetibles i efímers.
Un petit món de sensacions,
emocions i desitjos fets
paraula empresonada en uns
poemes, però volàtils com la
pròpia existència.

Índex

Batecs
del jo

Cami "Road"

Design Agency:

Esteve Bou

Client:

Pilar Gonzalez & Esteve Bou

Production Date:

Since 2009

Description:

Creation and design of a road that runs through the city in two routes that intersect throughout the day at different urban crossroads.

In these meeting points, special moments: a bouquet of flowers, a good movie, quiet dinner... and at the end of the routes, the most special moment of all: a hand requested in marriage, a declaration of commitment. Conceptually the ring represents the union between two people. Simple lines and robust sculpturality emphasise that union.

17:50

21:45

19:10

25-4-2009
Barcelona

Spaghetti Grafica 2: Contemporary Italian Graphic Design

Design Agency:
Ginette Caron
Designer:
Ginette Caron
Photography:
Marirosa Toscani Ballo
Client:
Ministero della Grafica
Production Date:
Since 2009
Description:
Spaghetti Grafica 2: Contemporary Italian Graphic Design is the title of an exhibition. The logo plays with spaghettis and the number "2" to emphasise the second edition of the exhibition. The book was divided into chapters where the studios were classified regarding to their areas of occupancy. The dividers in fact represent in a photographic way the quantity of square metres from 1 to 500.

0_30 mq studios

31_60 mq studios

61_90 mq studios

91_120 mq studios

121_160 mq studios

161_500 mq studios

Individual Portfolio

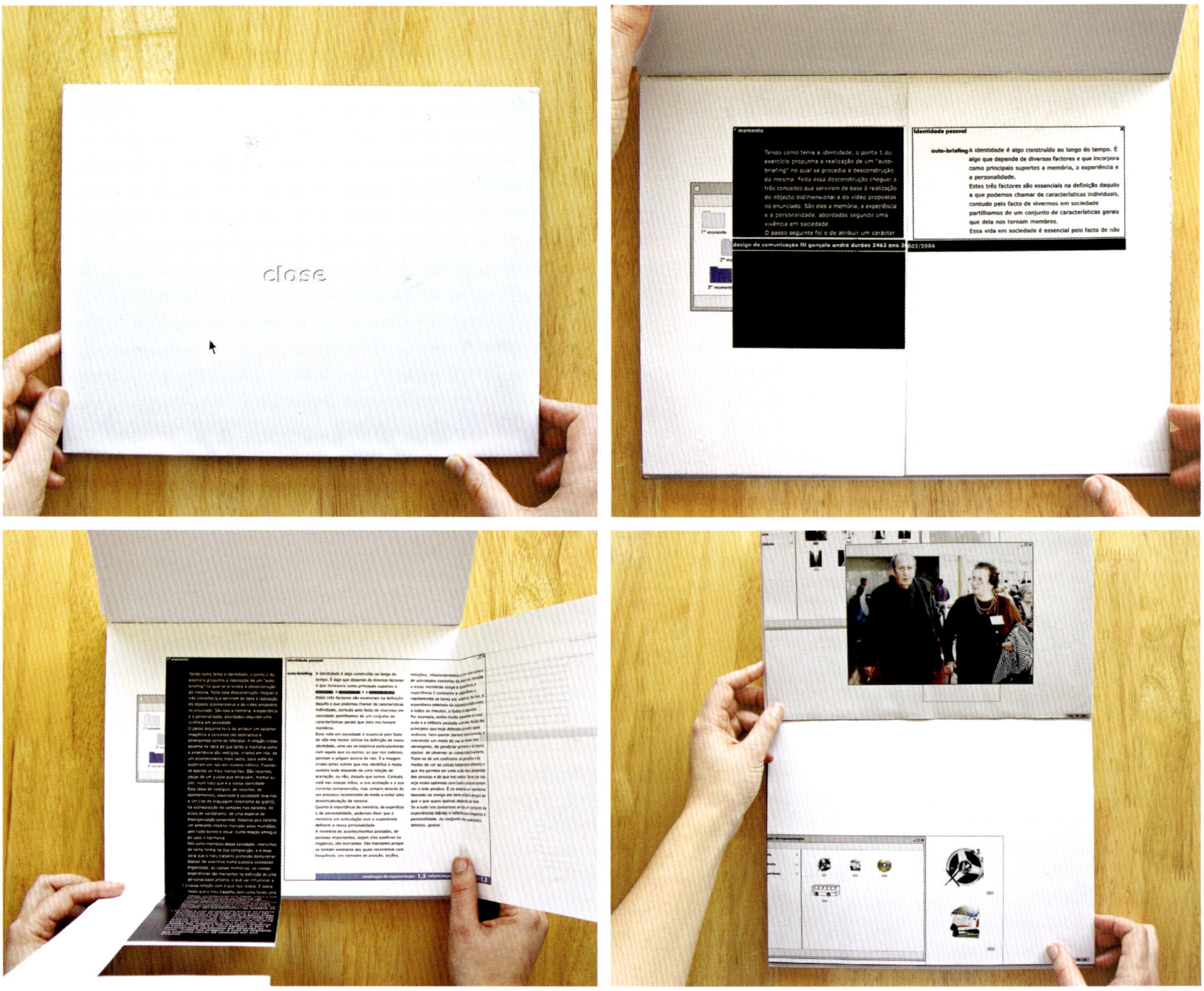

Designer:

Goncalo Dures

Client:

Individual Portfolio

Production Date:

2004

Description:

Final course project where the designer had to create an object to present their works from the past year. The designer chose to make an interactive book, a book that replies a multimedia presentation.

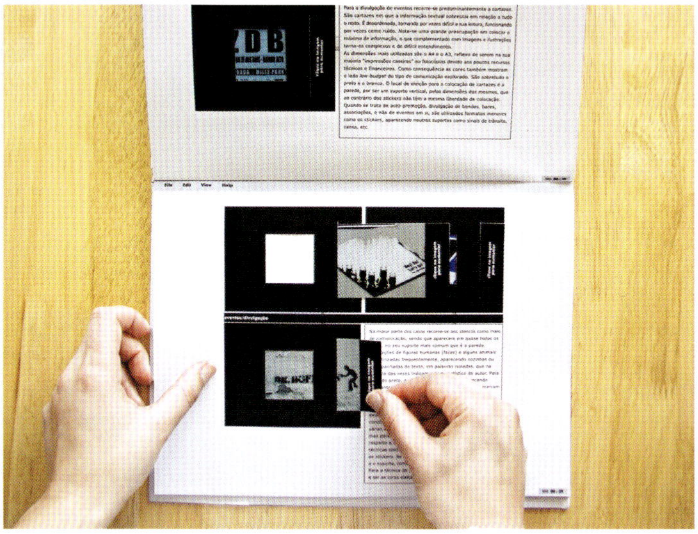

M.P.
M.S.

Uma História Chamada Tipografia

Designer:

Gonalo Dures, Pedro Motta, Rita Alves

Client:

Proposal

Production Date:

2003

Description:

Academic project of a book was developed to present a theoretic research about typography. Designers created a short story, a tale, with characters made of letters who go explaining the rules of typography.

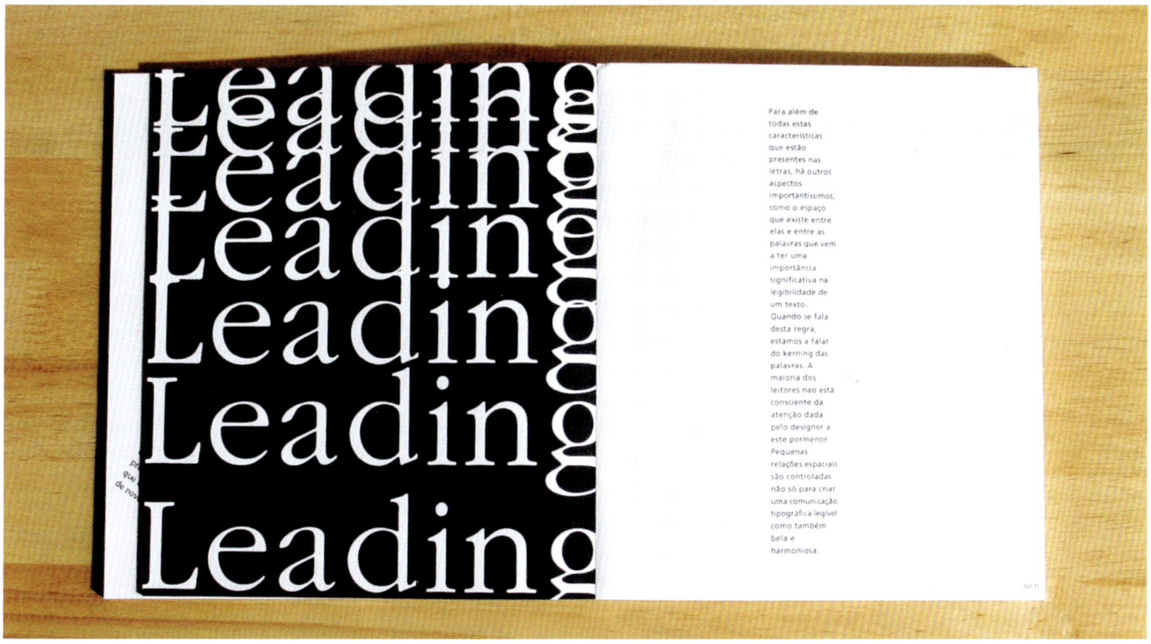
Leading
Leading
Leading
Leading
Leading
Leading
Leading
Para além de todas estas características que estão presentes nas letras, há outros aspectos importantíssimos, como o espaço que existe entre elas e entre as palavras que vem a ter uma importância significativa na legibilidade de um texto. Quando se fala desta regra, estamos a falar do kerning das palavras. A maioria dos leitores nao está consciente da atenção dada pelo designer a este pormenor Pequenas relações espaciais são controladas não só para criar uma comunicação tipográfica legível como também bela e harmoniosa.

«A noite já ia longa quando uma senhora, magnificamente vestida e adornada pelas mais belas jóias que os dois jovens alguma vez tinham visto, interrompeu a conversa. Esta seria a patrocinadora de Tipo. Deveriam partir juntos. Gutemberg presenciou, a cuidada distância, a abrupta separação dos dois jovens e ainda a mais cuidada distância, elegante distância, a tristeza que invadiu os olhos de Grafia nos dias que se seguiram. Conhecedor da razão que enchia de tristeza e apatia a sua antes tão prestável e alegre ajudante, prontificou-se a procurar a condessa que albergava Tipo, decidido a juntar de novo os dois jovens
A condessa não reagiu bem à visita de Gutemberg, tão agradada estava com os serviços de Tipo. A explicação que ouviu fê-la compreender o olhar vago e a ausência de sorrisos na face do seu protegido. Ainda assim não estava disposta a prescindir dos seus serviços. Gutemberg ofereceu-se para encontrar outro jovem que pudesse preencher a vaga deixada por Tipo, um jovem igualmente bem preparado e suficientemente educado para o substituir, e ainda assim foi relutantemente que a condessa aceitou a partida do seu empregado.»

«Numa destas deslocações conheceu um jovem órfão, Tipo. Comoveu-o particularmente a forma como este jovem vivia. A sua casa ficava no extremo norte de uma aldeia nos arredores de Estrasburgo. Nesta casa, não obstante a visível pobreza, tudo estava imaculado, perfeitamente limpo. E a organização da pequena sala, uma minúscula divisão que era também quarto, saltava à vista. Tudo estava organizado de maneira a que a divisão proporcionasse o maior espaço e conforto possível ao seu único habitante. A inteligência de Tipo impressionou de tal forma Gutenberg que este o levou para Estrasburgo nesse mesmo dia.»

Typographic - Mimesis

Designer:
Hyoun Youl Joe
Production Date:
2008
Description:
A 16x16 book for typographic re-presentation of sixteen students. This book takes a form of copying typographic and editorial systems ranging from the design of Jan Tschichold in the 1930s to contemporary graphic design to re-present texts and images of sixteen students.

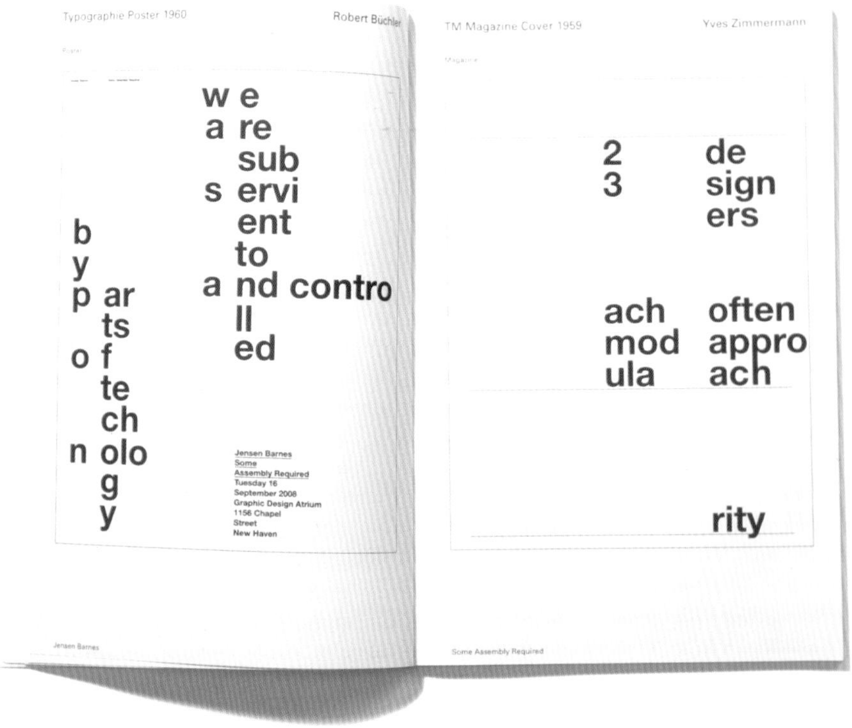

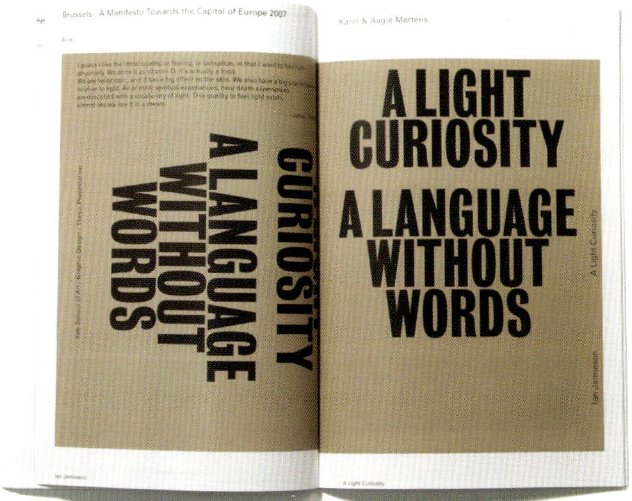
Brussels – A Manifesto Towards the Capital of Europe 2007
Karel & Aagje Martens
A LIGHT CURIOSITY
A LANGUAGE WITHOUT WORDS
CURIOSITY
A LANGUAGE WITHOUT WORDS
Yale School of Art | Graphic Design | Thesis Presentation
A Light Curiosity
Ian Jamieson

My Way to Typography 2000
Wolfgang Weingart

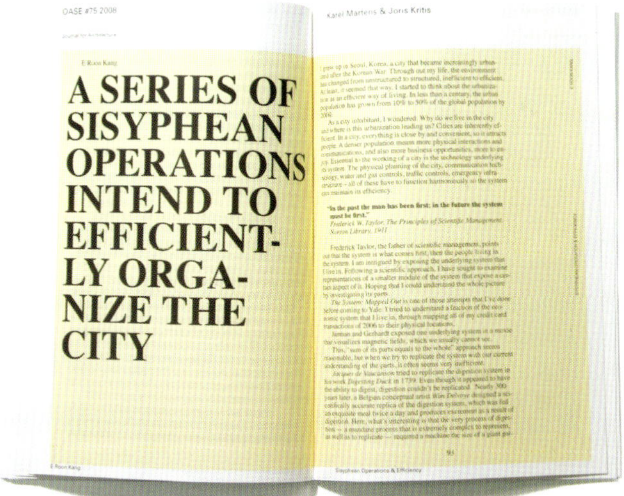
OASE #75 2008
Karel Martens & Joris Kritis
A SERIES OF SISYPHEAN OPERATIONS INTEND TO EFFICIENT-LY ORGA-NIZE THE CITY
Sisyphean Operations & Efficiency

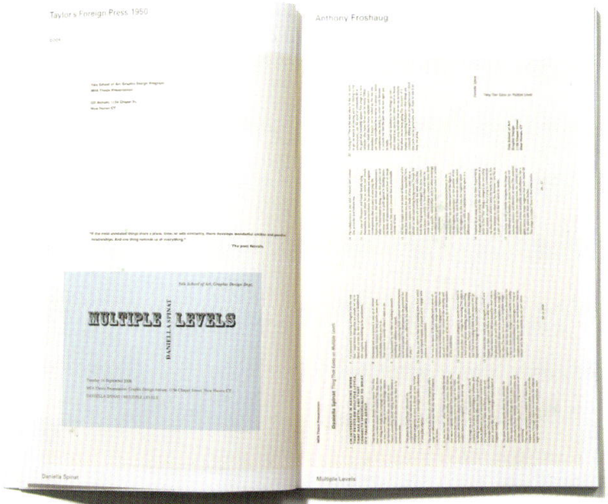
Taylor's Foreign Press 1950
Anthony Froshaug
MULTIPLE LEVELS
Daniela Spinat
Multiple Levels

process

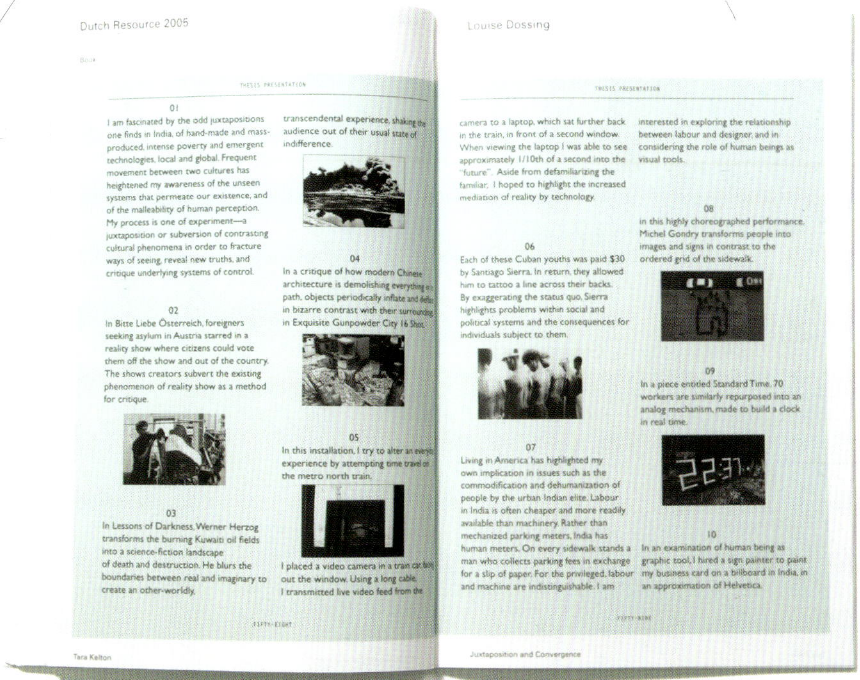
Dutch Resource 2005
Louise Dossing
THESIS PRESENTATION
01
I am fascinated by the odd juxtapositions one finds in India, of hand-made and mass-produced, intense poverty and emergent technologies, local and global. Frequent movement between two cultures has heightened my awareness of the unseen systems that permeate our existence, and of the malleability of human perception. My process is one of experiment—a juxtaposition or subversion of contrasting cultural phenomena in order to fracture ways of seeing, reveal new truths, and critique underlying systems of control.
02
In Bitte Liebe Österreich, foreigners seeking asylum in Austria starred in a reality show where citizens could vote them off the show and out of the country. The shows creators subvert the existing phenomenon of reality show as a method for critique.
03
In Lessons of Darkness, Werner Herzog transforms the burning Kuwaiti oil fields into a science-fiction landscape of death and destruction. He blurs the boundaries between real and imaginary to create an other-worldly
transcendental experience, shaking the audience out of their usual state of indifference.
04
In a critique of how modern Chinese architecture is demolishing everything in its path, objects periodically inflate and deflate in bizarre contrast with their surroundings in Exquisite Gunpowder City 16 Shoes.
05
In this installation, I try to alter an everyday experience by attempting time travel on the metro north train.
I placed a video camera in a train car, facing out the window. Using a long cable, I transmitted live video feed from the
FIFTY-EIGHT
camera to a laptop, which sat further back in the train, in front of a second window. When viewing the laptop I was able to see approximately 1/10th of a second into the "future". Aside from defamiliarizing the familiar, I hoped to highlight the increased mediation of reality by technology.
06
Each of these Cuban youths was paid $30 by Santiago Sierra. In return, they allowed him to tattoo a line across their backs. By exaggerating the status quo, Sierra highlights problems within social and political systems and the consequences for individuals subject to them.
07
Living in America has highlighted my own implication in issues such as the commodification and dehumanization of people by the urban Indian elite. Labour in India is often cheaper and more readily available than machinery. Rather than mechanized parking meters, India has human meters. On every sidewalk stands a man who collects parking fees in exchange for a slip of paper. For the privileged, labour and machine are indistinguishable. I am
interested in exploring the relationship between labour and designer, and in considering the role of human beings as visual tools.
08
In this highly choreographed performance, Michel Gondry transforms people into images and signs in contrast to the ordered grid of the sidewalk.
09
In a piece entitled Standard Time, 70 workers are similarly repurposed into an analog mechanism, made to build a clock in real time.
10
In an examination of human being as graphic tool, I hired a sign painter to paint my business card on a billboard in India, in an approximation of Helvetica.
22:31
FIFTY-NINE
Tara Kelton
Juxtaposition and Convergence

Steppe Stories

Design Agency:
iji-design
Designer:
Dmitry Galsan
Client:
Publishing Project "Buryad-Mongol Nom"
Production Date:
2010
Description:
This book is a collection of both ancient and contemporary stories, amusing legends and tales that are still living among the people of Buryat-Mongolia (Buryatia), Oirat-Mongolia (Kalmykia), Mongolia and Inner Mongolia Regions. This book is a dedication to everyone who is interested in history, folklore, life and traditions of the Mongol people. Written in Russian, with titles translated into classical Mongolian script.

СТЕПНЫЕ
БЫЛИ
И НЕБЫЛИ
ЦЫ
Улан-Удэ / 2010
Буряад-Монгол
Ном

ГОНЕЦ
ЭРЛИКА
36
37

АМАР-
БАТА
106
107

The Best Dutch Book Designs 2007

Design Agency:

Ingeborg Scheffers

Client:

The Best Dutch Book Designs

Production Date:

2008

Description:

First there was one original book made, this was then photographed and these images have been placed in a book again. By doing this all elements exist like threads on threads. The spreads reproduced of the prize-winning book has the same page number as in the catalogue. This is how the decision is made which spread to choose. Special editions for prize winners. The prize winners got an extra reproduction of their book on glossy paper. The designer was inspired by early full-colour reproductions of paintings in art books which where pasted in later after being first printed in black & white.

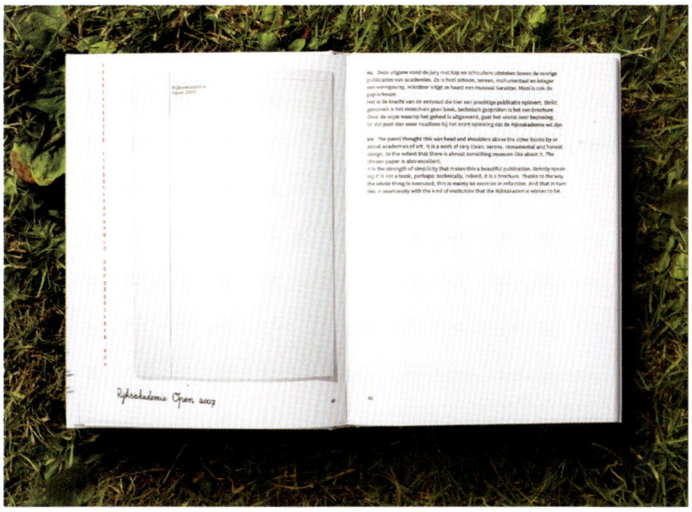
Rijksakademie Open 2007

De vernuftige edelman Don Quichote van La Mancha

De vernuftige edelman Don Quichote van La Mancha

Eva Besnyö

Inside Outside
Petra Blaisse
EVA BESNYÖ
CO-OPs
BATIA SUTER
PARALLEL ENCYCLOPEDIA
FORTIS
C.B. VAN DER TAK
Nieuwsgierigheid 114–117
Douala in Translation 134–137
Lachspiegel 110–113
Rozenteelt in Nederland 94–97
Without and within 106–109
Man van twee wegen 98–101
De leeglopers 130–133
berlin_nl 46–49
Mondriaan Stichting. Jaarverslag 2006 50–53
Cornelius Quabeck. Hood 90–93
Ad Schouten 1:1 62–65
Bloedmooi 30–33
Petra Blaisse. Inside Outside 78–81
Krijn de Koning 82–85
Subjective Atlas of Palestine 54–57
Schapen tellen 34–37
OFOFFJOFF. ONE TO ONE 122–125
Aap, vis, boek 66–69
Eva Besnyö 150–153
CO-OPs 138–141
Hoe komt wie vliegt ooit tot bedaren 86–89
High resolution 26–29
VMX Architects. Agenda 142–145
Parallel Encyclopedia 146–149
Ringel Goslinga. Family Tree 74–77
Sur place 58–61
Letterdromen met Do 22–25
Pages 38–41
Rijksakademie Open 2007 42–45
C.B. van der Tak 126–129
Niels Stomps. Mist 70–73
De vernuftige edelman Don Quichot van La Mancha 118–121
Geschiedenis van de Koninklijke Shell 102–105
21

Ruimte Voor Verdieping

Design Agency:

Ingeborg Scheffers

Client:

Plat form Interieur architecture

Photography:

dirkwolf.com

Production Date:

2008

Description:

"Ruimte Voor Verdieping" details the importance of having a masters' programme in interior architecture. The report addresses the differences between the advanced study of architecture and that of interior architecture. Nowadays both qualifications overlap one another in certain aspects. As a result, there deserves to be an increase in both the quality and intensity of interior architecture education. The book is designed inside-out. The front (cover) of the book is on the inside. The pages of the book are folded together and bound along the spine of the book. To be found on the inside of these pages are pictures of the facades of buildings designed by interior architect. The pages are printed on thin paper enabling the silhouettes of these facades to shine through, while on the front of the page is text about interior architecture and an explanation about what the interior architect has designed for that building.

I
Een breed
gedragen
master-
opleiding
Interieur-
architectuur

Inhoud

Voorwoord

IV
Uitgangs-
punten van
de nieuwe
opleiding

Proefkoken voor de Koningin (Testcooking for th Queen)

Design Agency:
Ingeborg Scheffers
Client:
Cuisine Culinaire Nederland (CCN)
Production Date:
2008
Description:

This is a cookbook for CCN. The design of this book is based on this fact. This book has been made specifically for the semi-professional. The pages in the book have a special line to fold the page along. Using this, a cook can choose if he wants to cook without the detailed steps and only have the list of ingredients. If he decides to make a particular dish it is easy to fold the pages in a unique way. In this way, a very hardworking cook will end up with a book which has this special shape. This way of folding (dog-ear) will get you quick to your favourite dishes. Also, this cookbook has measurements in the back of the book. Different cooks were asked several things like what a pinch of salt or a hand of capers amounts to. By using photographs it is attempted to make the size of these measurements clear. In the recipes of the book you get directed to this measurements chapter.

Award: Bronze prize OUTPUT 10 (International Contest in Graphic Design; 900 participants from 38 different countries)

II Salade van tarbot met as
roomkaas, nootmuskaat,
zachtgekookt ei

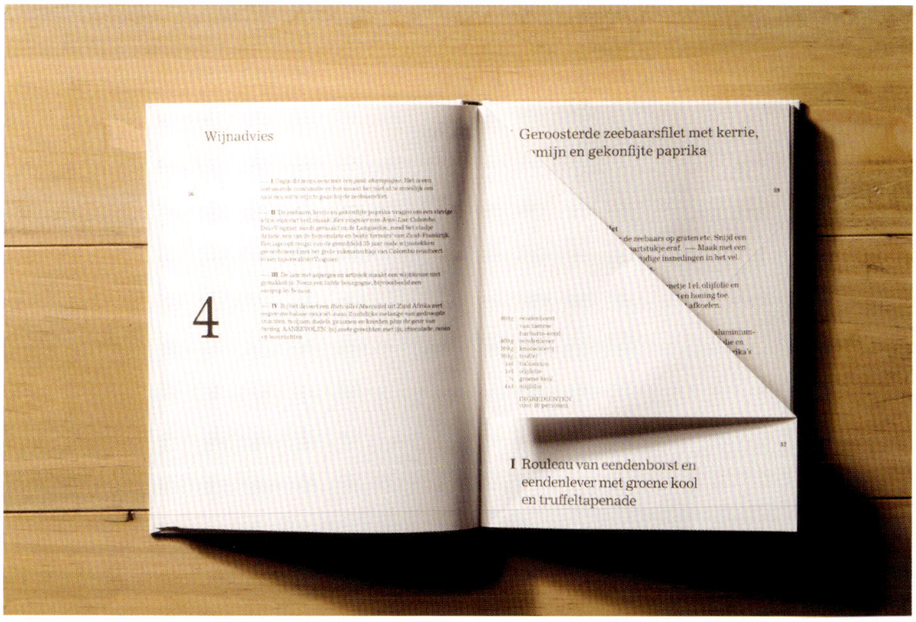
Wijnadvies
4
Geroosterde zeebaarsfilet met kerrie,
I Rouleau van eendenborst en
eendenlever met groene kool
en truffeltapenade

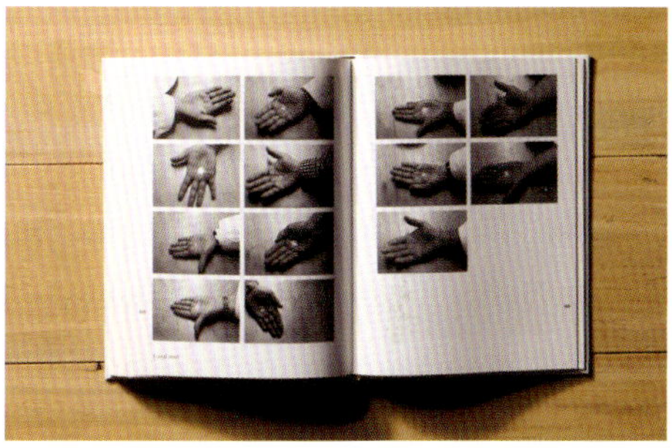

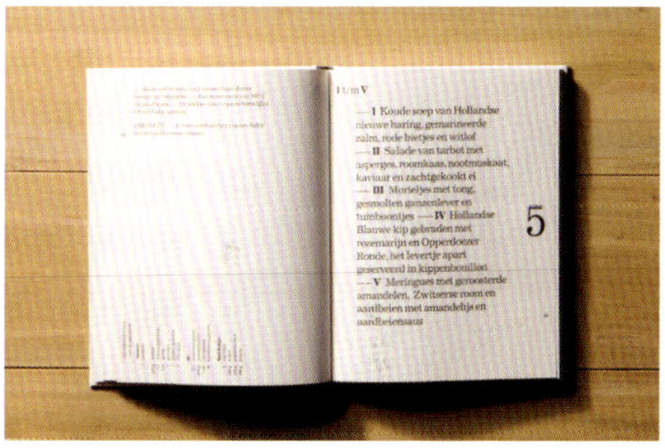
5

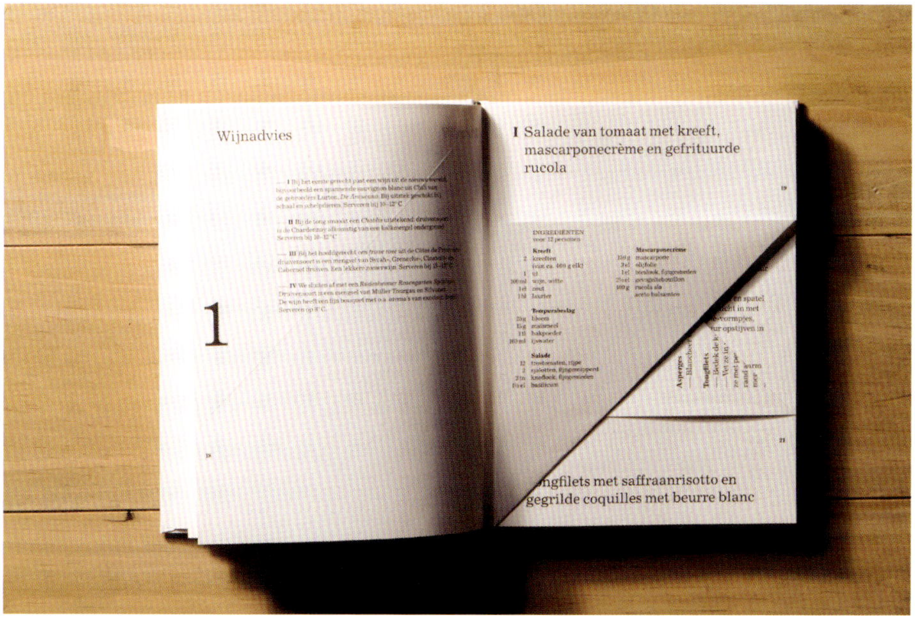
Wijnadvies
1
I Salade van tomaat met kreeft,
mascarponecrème en gefrituurde
rucola
gegrilde coquilles met beurre blanc

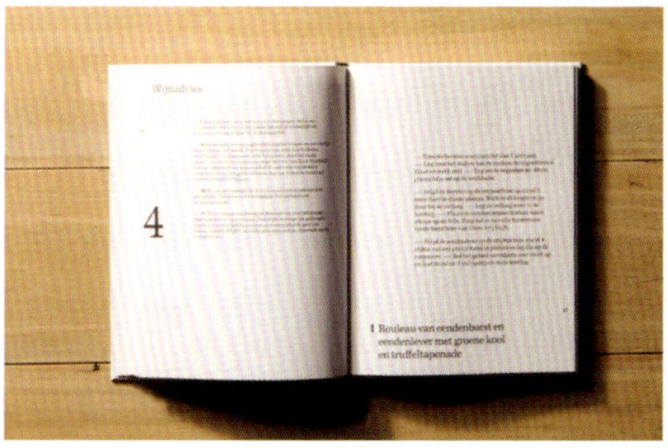
4

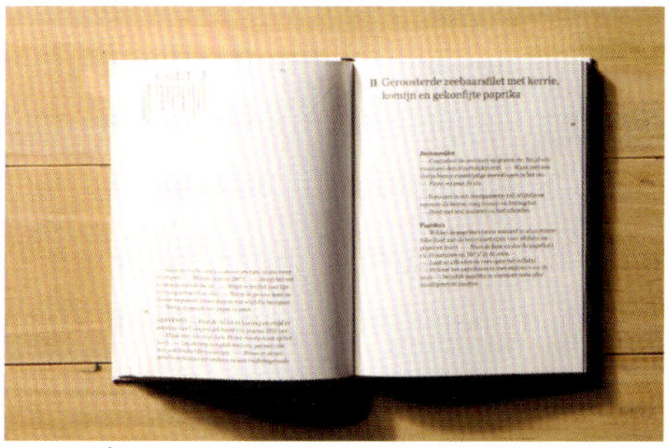

40 Stories

Designer:

James Kuo and Profis

Client:

40 Stories

Production Date:

2009

Description:

In 2009, Toronto Christian Resource Centre (CRC) published 40 Stories. In design perspective, the designer chose typefaces for the body text and headline allowing for a maximum word count per page within the layout golden section grid. In overcoming the design challenge, art direction chose to make the text-heavy book appealing and universal by balancing words with contemporary, full-bleed photography, as well as by using a golden section grid design for the book structure and content presentation.

Lettering System for Paris Airport

Designer:

Javier Melon Gil

Client:

Savannah College of Art and Design

Production Date:

2010

Description:

Lettering System for Paris Airport is a typographic book based on Frutiger's work at Charles de Gaulle International Airport. The designer took the shape of an airline ticket and created interesting layouts with a European design style. After learning different typographic treatments the designer was assigned to create a book, and this is the result.

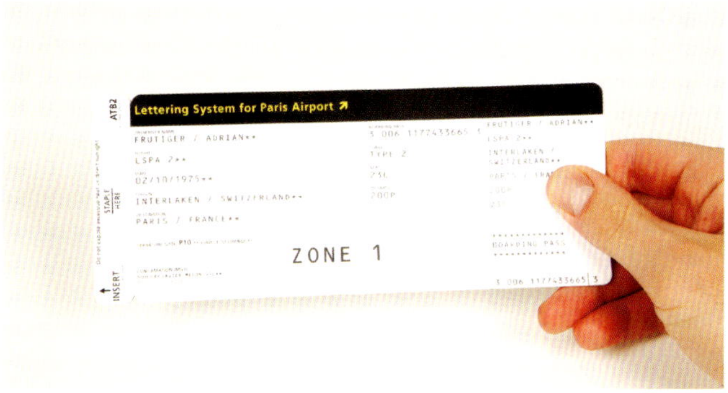

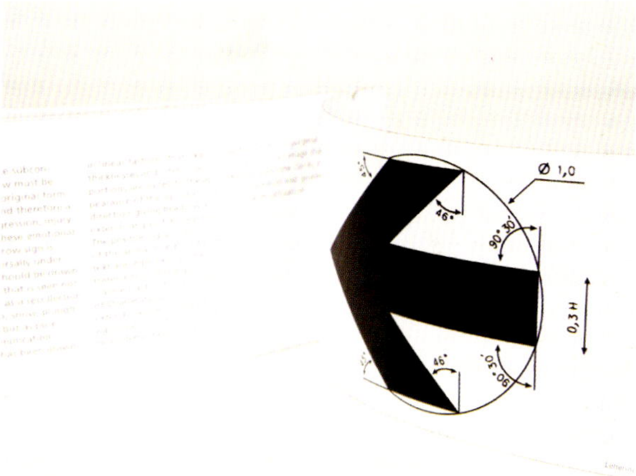

Guggenheim's Hugo Boss Prize

Design Agency:
Karlssonwilker Inc.
Designer:
Jan Wilker, Hjalti Karlsson
Client:
Guggenheim Museum, NYC
Production Date:
2006
Description:
The book features the winners of Hugo Boss' Bi-Annual Art Prize 2006.

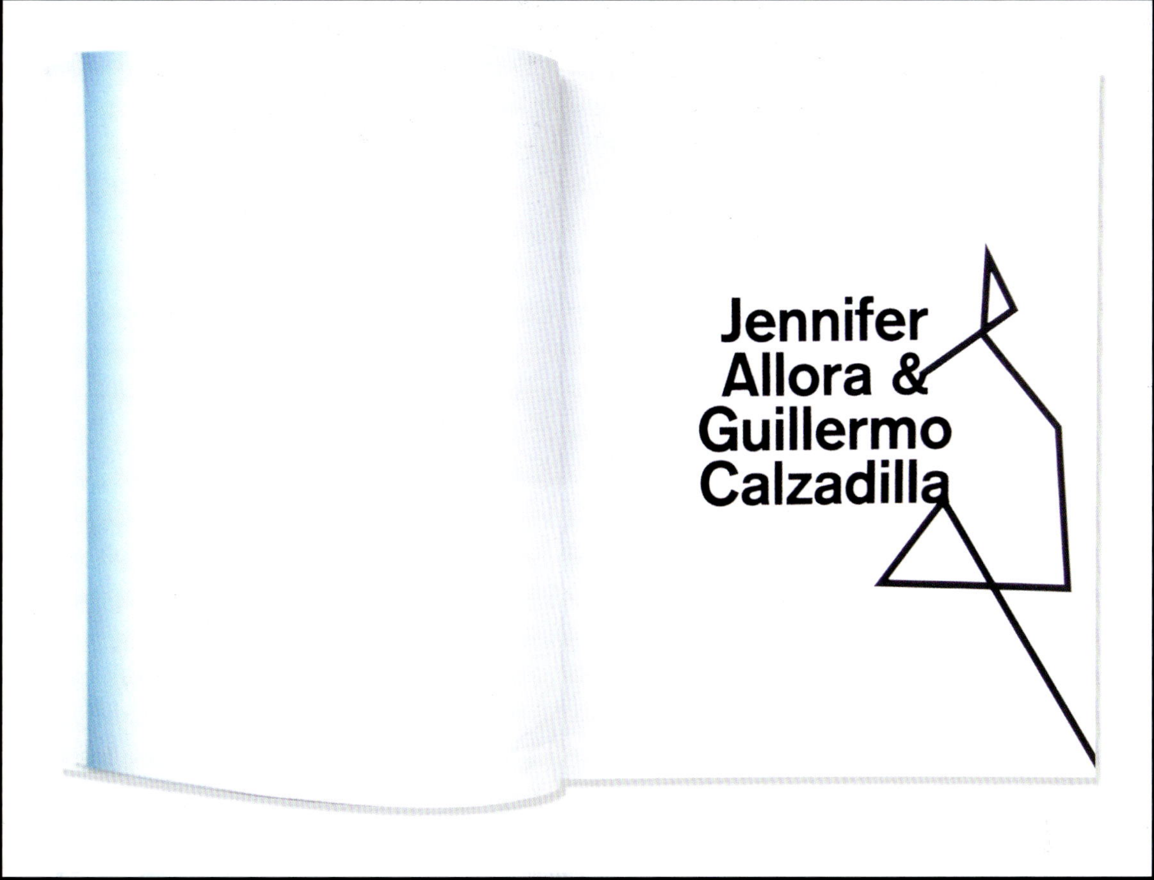
Jennifer
Allora &
Guillermo
Calzadilla

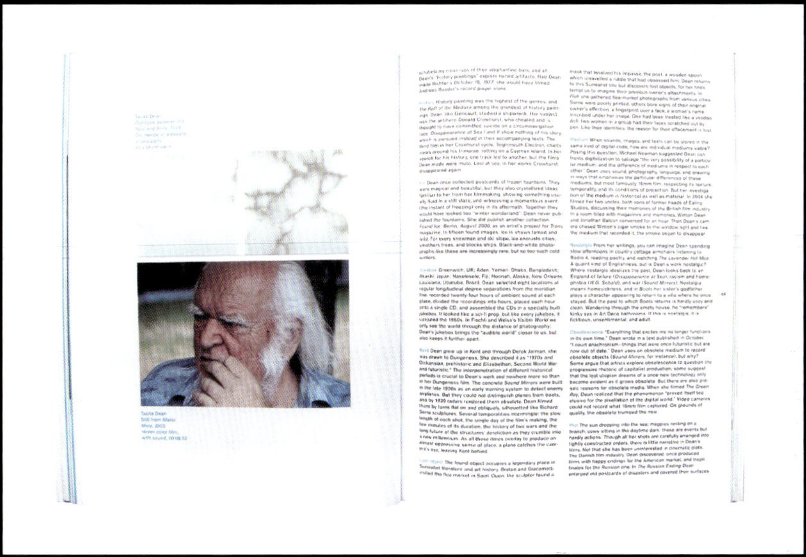

THE ABC OF TCD

120—121

Curious Boym Book

Design Agency:

Karlssonwilker Inc.

Designer:

Jan Wilker, Hjalti Karlsson

Client:

Princeton Architectural Press / Boym Partners Inc.

Production Date:

2004

Description:

It is a monograph on New York-based product designer Duo Boym.

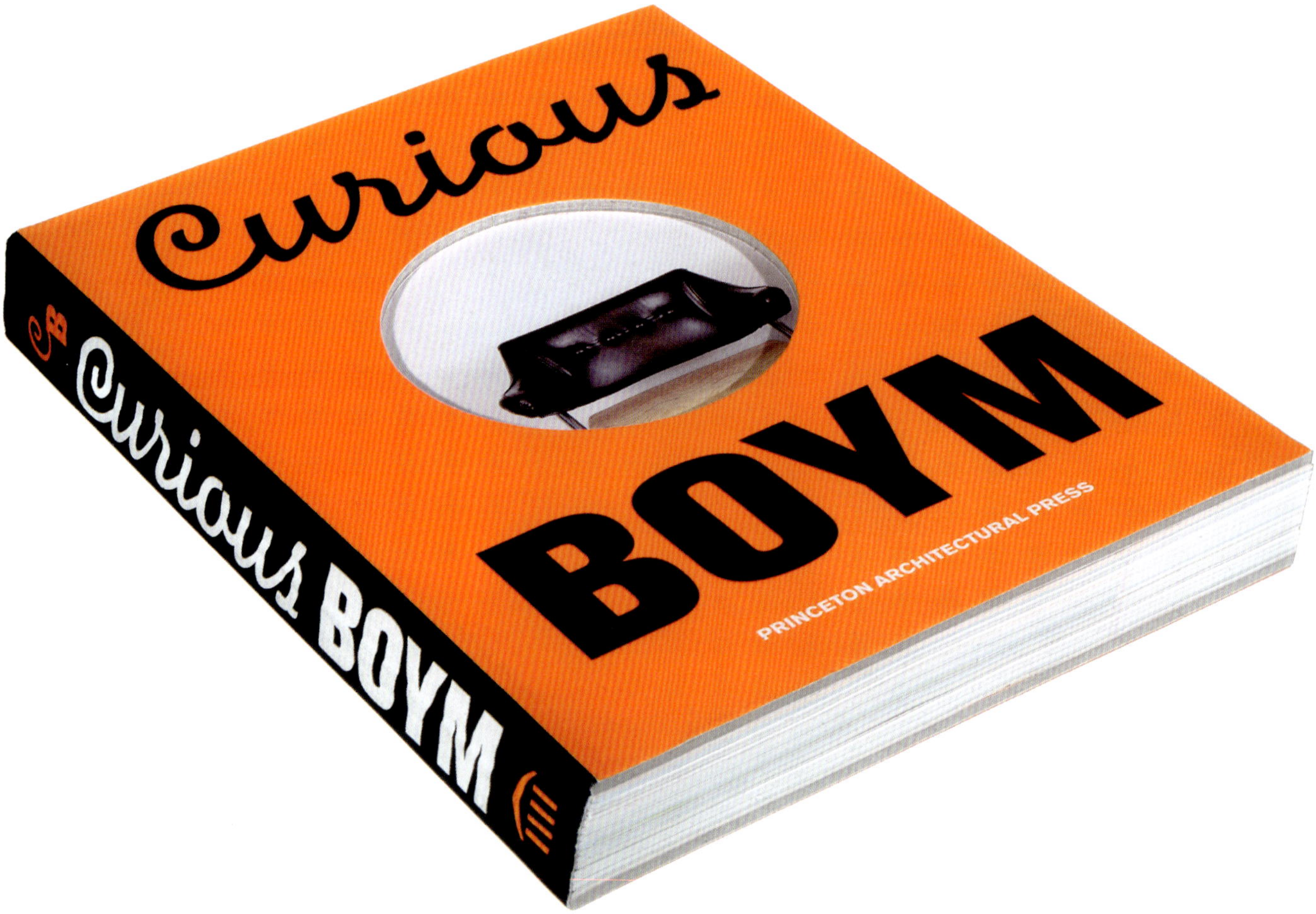

RE-
DECORATION
In the beginning of 2001, decoration seemed like a timely topic to address. "At the outset of a new century, Minimalism appears to be strangely out of place. The economy, technology, culture, and fashion all seem to have reached the boiling point. This time of high tide asks for a new design attitude: more intense, more inclusive, and a bit more fun," we argued in the call for a show.
In an attempt to signal a new direction we decided to assemble a small group of New York designers who all agreed to contribute new works on the subject of decoration. While the exhibition fell short of starting a new movement, the opening events in May 2001 were certainly memorable. In order to transform an impersonal space in little time and with minimal expense, we covered the entire floor with thick layers of confetti. A visual manifestation of decoration itself, the confetti also provided an instant party spirit.
Taxicab chair—one of our own contributions for the exhibition—took inspiration from beaded seat covers favored by taxicab and van drivers. Instead of being placed on a chair, our seat cover became a chair. Oversized wooden balls played the role of functional decoration. Not surprisingly, the chair was comfortable and pleasant to sit on.

DESIGN WORKS

PRODUCTS

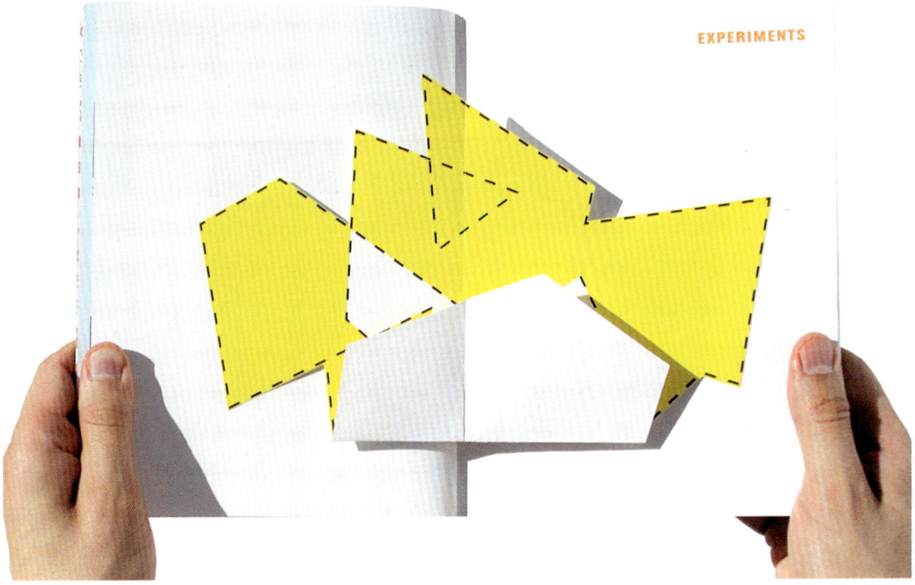
EXPERIMENTS

Tell Me Why

Design Agency:

Karlssonwilker Inc.

Designer:

Jan Wilker, Hjalti Karlsson

Client:

Princeton Architectural Press

Production Date:

2003

Description:

It is a monograph on Karlssonwilker, a New York-based design studio.

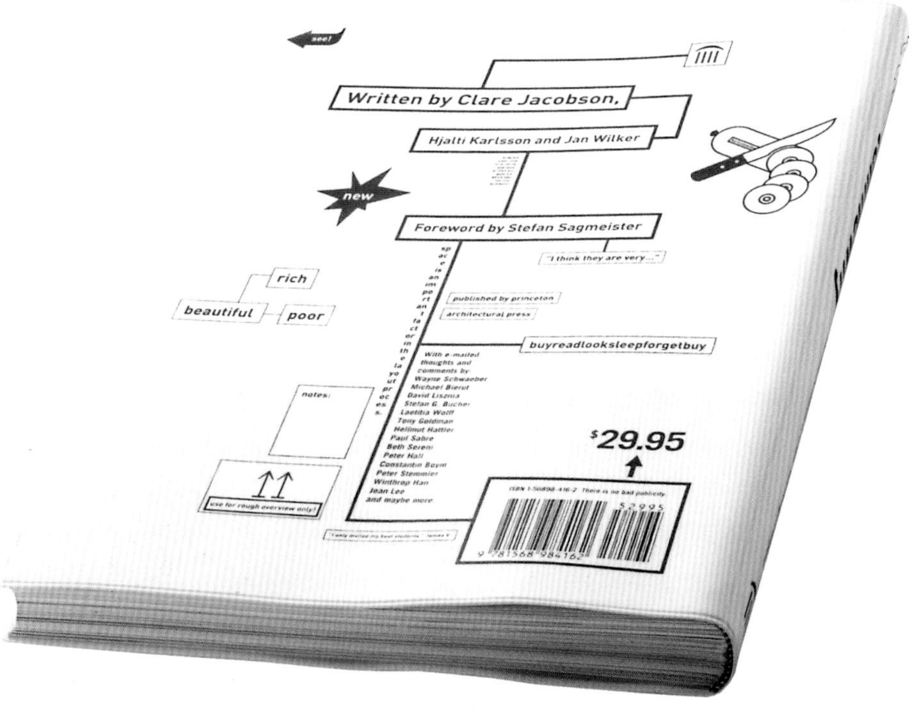

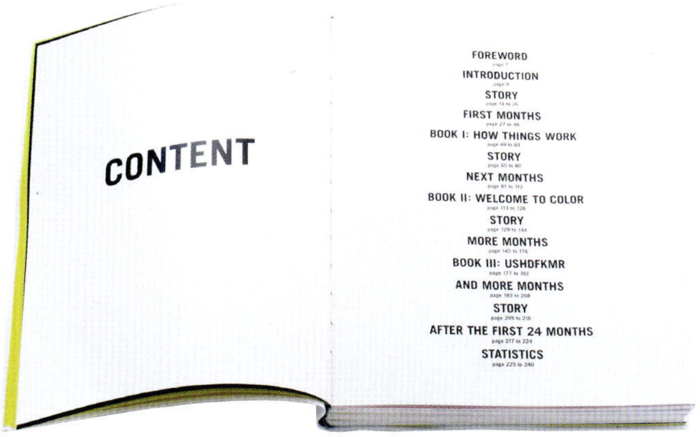
CONTENT
FOREWORD
INTRODUCTION
STORY
FIRST MONTHS
BOOK I: HOW THINGS WORK
STORY
NEXT MONTHS
BOOK II: WELCOME TO COLOR
STORY
MORE MONTHS
BOOK III: USHDFKMR
AND MORE MONTHS
STORY
AFTER THE FIRST 24 MONTHS
STATISTICS

DECIPHERING THE OFFICE (1).

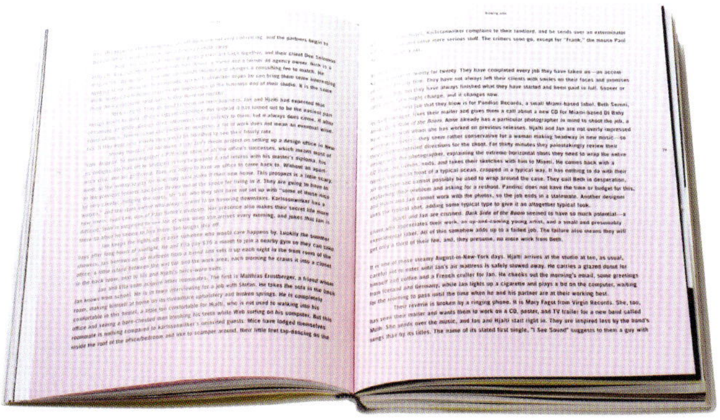

TOTAL PLAYING TIME OF ALL THREE DISCS: 3:18:17
2001 COMPOSERS RECORDINGS, INC. 73 SPRING STREET, SUITE 506, NEW YORK, N.Y. 10012 PHONE (212) 941-9673 WWW.COMPOSERSRECORDINGS.COM (CRI LOGO) (BLUESHIFT LOGO) CD 2001 DDD (COMPACT DISC LOGO) THE BARCODE IS LOCATED ON THE SPINE

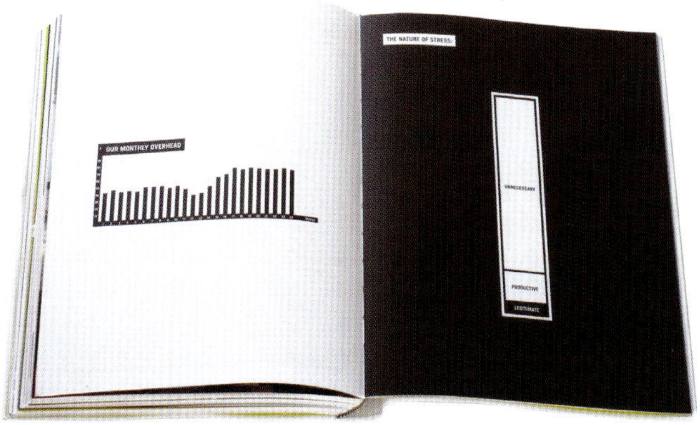
OUR MONTHLY OVERHEAD
THE NATURE OF STRESS.
UNNECESSARY
PRODUCTIVE
LEGITIMATE

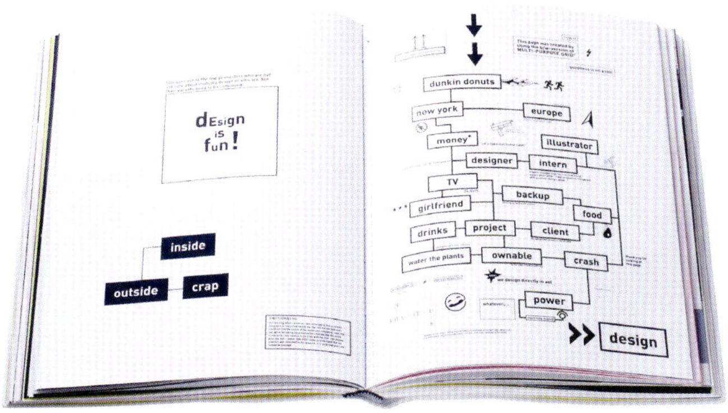
dEsign is fun!
inside
outside
crap
dunkin donuts
new york
europe
money
illustrator
designer
intern
TV
backup
girlfriend
food
drinks
project
client
water the plants
ownable
crash
power
design

Save Game Book

Design Agency:
Kolektiv Studio
Designer:
Michal Krul
Production Date:
2008
Description:
This is a concept book as personal project.

SAVE

Borkebjs-The Return of the Monsters

Design Agency:

KOREFE

Client:

Borkebjs

Production Date:

2009

Description:

The Borkebjs are the origin of all monster stories. Invisible to those humans lacking in imagination, they live in Helfjlaf Forest in the far North. After humans destroyed their home, they were forced to leave the forest. With the exception of one: Frejlif Borkebie. 300 years later, the final survivor decides it is time to fetch the Borkebjs back home. But he needs your help in waking the spirits and bring the forest back to life.

Awards:

Cannes Gold, Eurobest Silver, NY Festivals Gold, London International Awards Silver

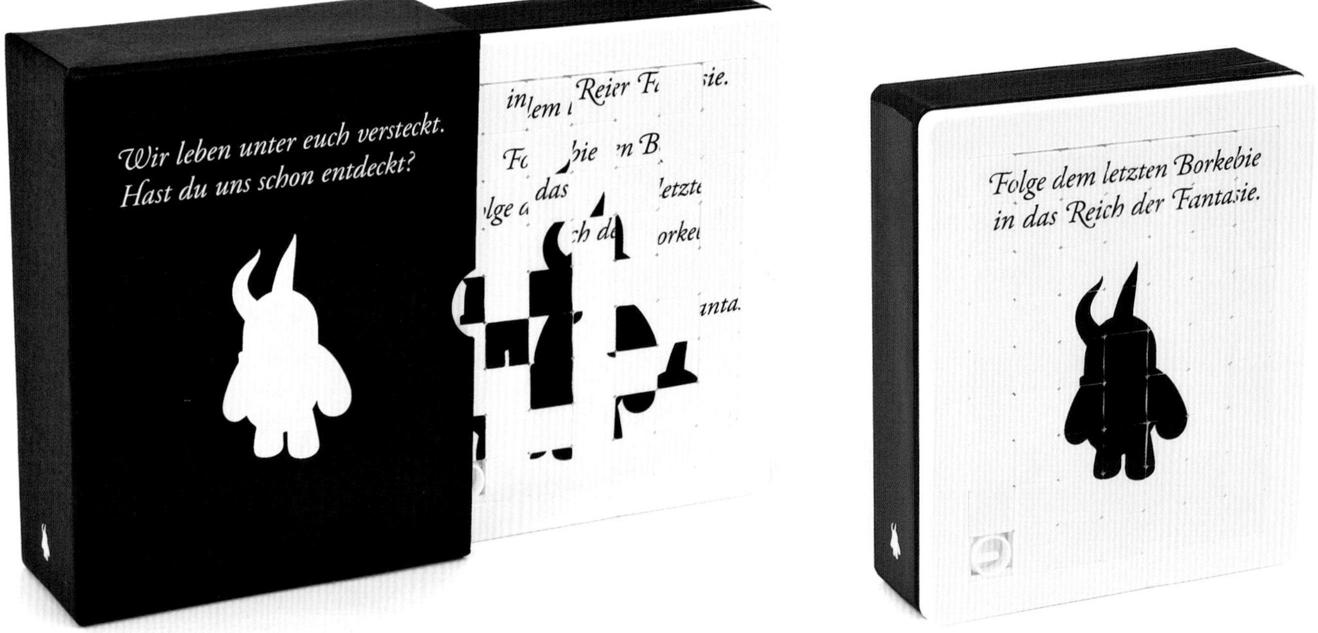

KJARTAN.
Kjartan Borgendjs, der Anführer der legendären Zehn. Nach seiner fehlgeschlagenen Mission, diese zusammenzuhalten, zieht er auf die andere Seite der Welt, um dort alleine zu sein. Das fehlende Horn hat er in einem Zwergentunnel verloren, was seine Stimmung noch verschlimmerte.
Den Namen Kjartan hat er von den Trollen bekommen, und er bedeutet so viel wie „Krieger".

FREJLIF.
DIE GROSSE
ÜBERFAHRT.

Fibre Art Wales

Design Agency:

Kutchibok

Designer:

Alwyn Thomas, Sion Dafydd

Client:

Fibre Art Wales

Production Date:

2010

Description:

Fibre Art Wales is a selected group of professional fibre artists. As well as exhibiting fibre art members work to commission, they have won international awards and prizes and have their work included in many public and private collections worldwide.The brief was to design a publication comprised of Fibre Art Wales' latest work, promoting the development and growth of the group and celebrating their 10th year anniversary.

Artistsaid ___
Featured Artists
Bethan Ash
Helen Foroughi
Michelle Griffiths
Ruth Harries
Ruth McLees
Alison Mercer
Alison Moger
Lisa Porch
Laura Thomas

BEUYS

Designer:

Lina Khesina

Client:

BEUYS

Production Date:

2006

Description:

It's on student's projects on the University of Applied Sciences Potsdam. Text, idea, design, layout and publication are subjective discourse to the quotations of Joseph Beuys.

Look Book Informations Design

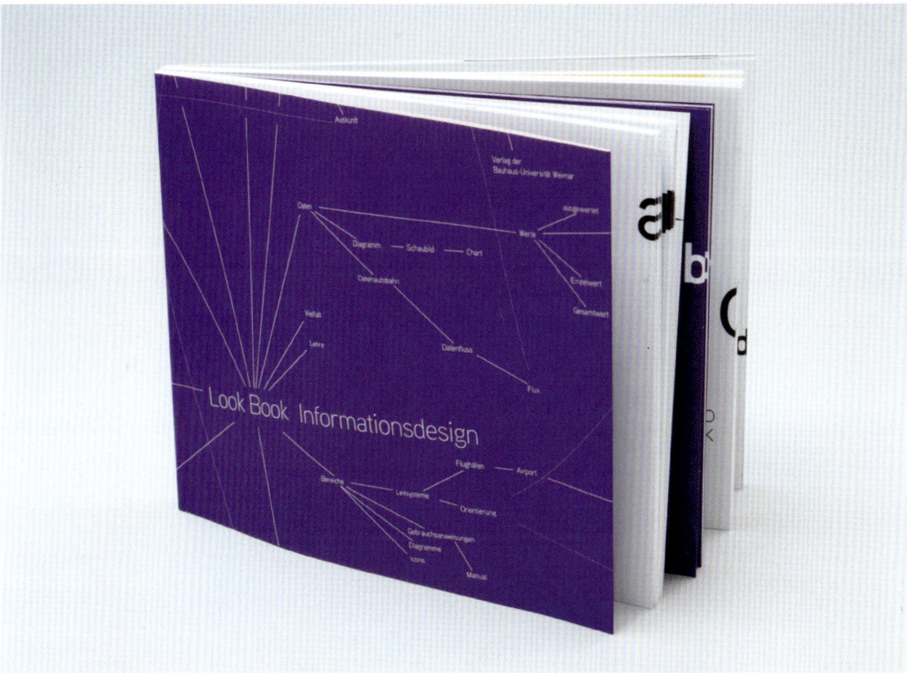

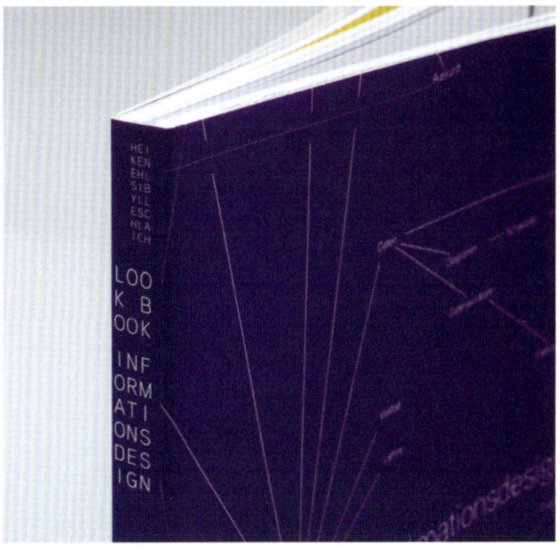

Design Agency

Moniteurs GmbH

Production Date:

2008

Description:

Under the supervision of Heike Nehl and Sibylle Schlaich, a group of students were challenged to research the potentials of information design. The brief was to critically examine this particular topic for its spectrum of possible applications, to explore the everyday and multiple uses. The students' results emphasise the importance of systematic information graphics for all areas of our life and society. In this context, scientific data, instruction manuals, calendars, along with interactive programmes and experimental films have been visualised.

The Origins of Film - Catalan Film Producers

Design Agency:
LeCool Publishing
Client:
LeCool Publishing & Catalan Films
Production Date:
2009
Description:
It is the Catalan Film directors' directory.

The Origins Of Film
70 Catalan film producers
Sharing their stories from where it all began

Catalan film producers
The Origins Of Film

Jordi
Llompart

Denit Hotel Guide

Design Agency:
LeCool Publishing
Client:
Grupo Majestic
Production Date:
2010
Description:
It is the art direction and design for Denit Hotel's notebook. The particularity of this project is the idea to show the contents of the notebook (city tips, comments, places to go, to eat and to visit) on the walls of the hotel itself. The illustrations and text decorate discreetly the surroundings of the interior building.

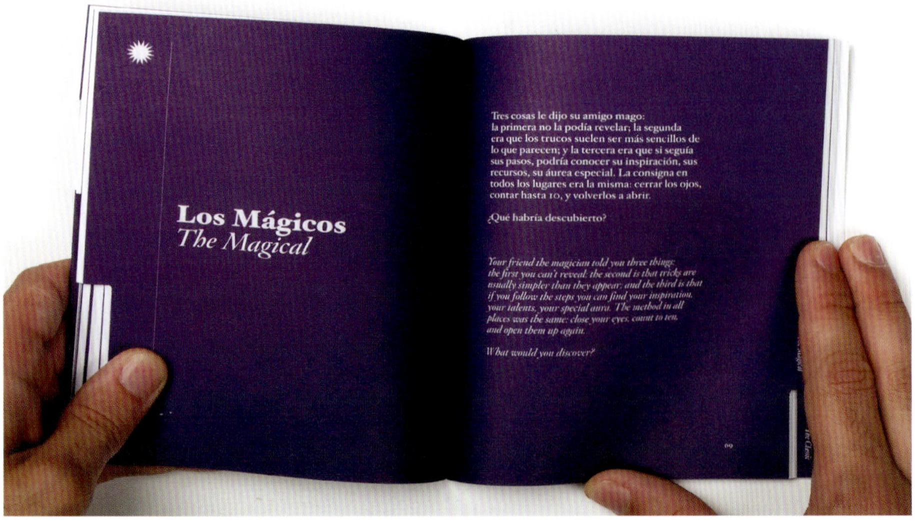

Rompeolas
Las mejores ideas surgen mirando al mar. Las palabras más bonitas se dicen delante del mar. Un buen recuerdo siempre lleva al mar. Y lo tienes muy cerca, casi a tocar...
The best ideas are born while watching the sea. The most beautiful words are said alongside the sea. A fond memory always has a hint of the sea. And you have it close by, almost close enough to touch...
Los Mágicos
The Magical
Los Clásicos
The Classic
Plaça de la Rosa dels Vents, 1
93

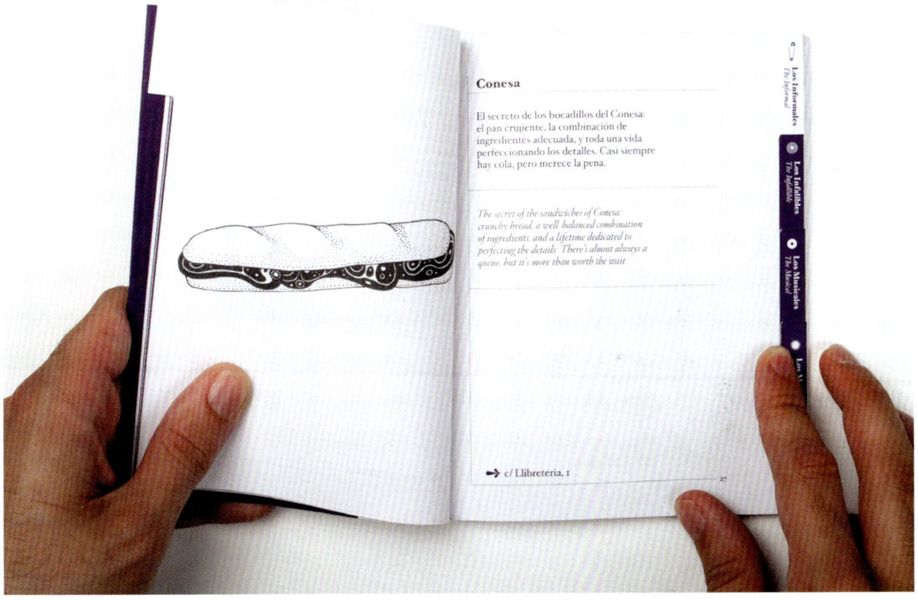
Conesa
El secreto de los bocadillos del Conesa: el pan crujiente, la combinación de ingredientes adecuada, y toda una vida perfeccionando los detalles. Casi siempre hay cola, pero merece la pena.
The secret of the sandwiches of Conesa: crunchy bread, a well-balanced combination of ingredients, and a lifetime dedicated to perfecting the details. There's almost always a queue, but it's more than worth the wait.
Los Informales
The Informal
Los Infalibles
The Infallible
Los Musicales
The Musical
c/ Llibreteria, 1
27

Vinçon
Una lámpara te da los buenos días, un sillon te cuenta el resultado del partido de ayer, y una cómoda charla amigablemente con una sartén de chef.
Los objetos de diseño cobran vida en Vinçon, y les da igual si te los llevas a casa o sólo curioseas.
A lamp greets you with a good morning, a chair tells you the score from yesterday's match, and a chest of drawers casually chats with a chef's pan. Designer objects take on a life of their own in Vinçon, and they couldn't care less if you take them home or are just here to browse.
Los Infalibles
The Infallible
Los Musicales
The Musical
Passeig de Gràcia, 96
33

Notes from Barcelona

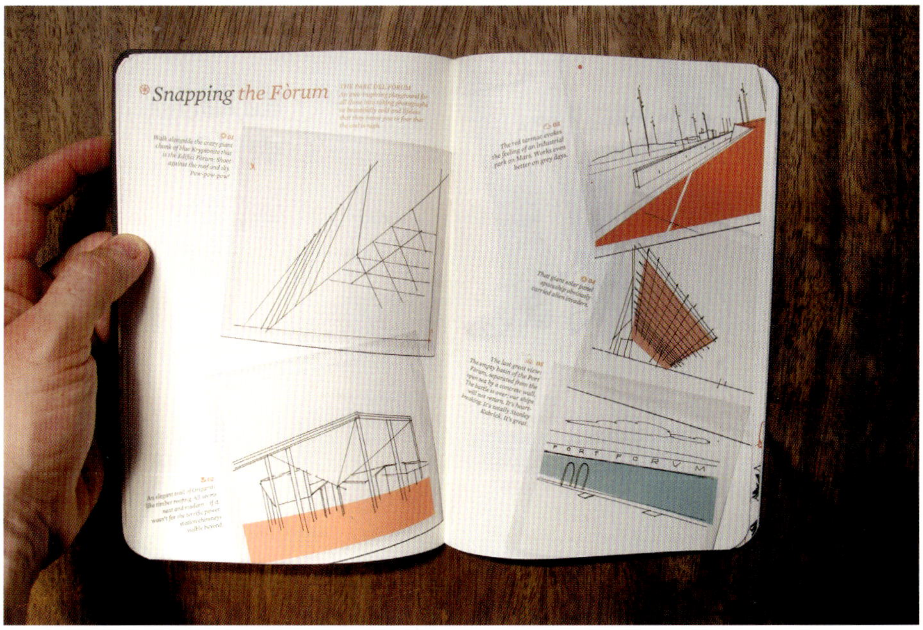

Design Agency:

LeCool Publishing

Client:

Grupo Majestic

Production Date:

2008

Description:

It is an illustrated guide of nice places of Barcelona.

Led-a-porter Catalogue

Design Agency:

LeCool Publishing

Client:

Led-a-porter

Production Date:

2009

Description:

Led-a-porter is a firm that manufactures LEDs and also takes over lighting projects. The alphabet for this project has been designed using only the light given by LEDs. With a colour bar and a long photographic exposure, the whole alphabet was created. It was used to illustrate the brand's catalogue and stationery.

Not Just a Notebook

Design Agency:
LeCool Publishing
Client:
Pullitzer Hotel
Production Date:
2009
Description:
This guide and notebook has been conceived and designed for the Regina Hotels clients. Its main feature is the way it combines a practical guide with the personal and interactive experience. Also, each section and city has a different and personal language. The final result expects to be a soft and poetic notebook that gives the visitor the opportunity to create his private and customised way to understand the guide.

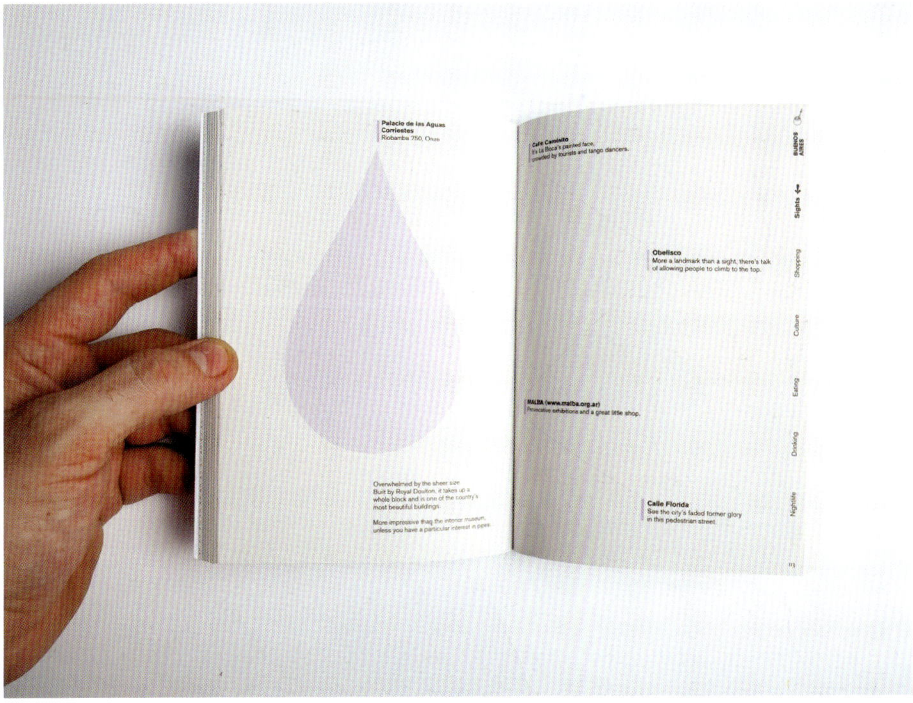

Sing for Darfur

Design Agency:
m-m design
Client:
Sing for Darfur
Production Date:
2009
Description:
"Sing for Darfur" is a non-profit movie. Being attached to the movie, this book with 64 pages mainly reflects the content of the movie.

Nuria Soler

25.26.27. 28.29.30.

LOVE!

NOT FUNNY

ESTO NO TIENE GRACIA

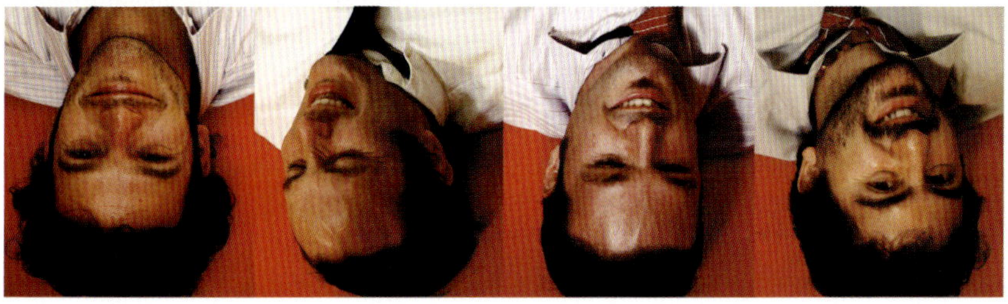

Porno Para Mujeres

Design Agency:

m-m design

Client:

Porno Para Mujeres

Production Date:

2009

Description:

This book advocates feminist, and for the reason that pink is always used to represent for the female, hence, the book choses pink colour as the main tune.

Synopsis

YUKO is a dreamy, young Japanese woman. She does not like her job at a bank, nor does she look forward to her marriage with a conservative, wealthy Japanese boyfriend.
On her free time, she likes to practice Flamenco dancing. She loves Spanish culture, she thinks flamenco and Spain symbolize something very exotic to Japanese: freedom, passion, individuality. After a few days in Spain, she is dreading going back to Tokyo, to her fiancée, to her boring job.

JOSELE is a young Spanish from Sevilla. After encountering some problems with the law, he is advised to leave Spain for a few months. A good friend tells him he could easily find a job in Japan, teaching flamenco. Although Josele has never really liked to dance, he can't think of a better plan, so he decides to follow his friend's advice. Bitter about his past, full of doubt about his future, he boards a flight to Tokyo.

In Tokyo, **JOSELE** is to dance at a Spanish Restaurant, managed by an arrogant Spaniard. He will also work at a Flamenco School. A few months before, the previous teacher at the School, another young Spaniard, was found dead in his apartment. Everyone thinks a jealous female student killed him. At the School, **JOSELE** will direct the end-of-the-year show. He will also take the main male role. The main female role will be played by **YUKO. FEDERICO**, one of the best male students, will be the stage director.

JOSELE feels Lost In Translation, doesn't like the situation he is in, can't understand Japanese people, doubts he could ever find a home in Tokyo. Still, after a few weeks of rehearsals, **JOSELE** starts falling for **YUKO**. When he dances with her, he even enjoys himself, and is able to understand why some people in Sevilla are so passionate about Flamenco. Meanwhile, Federico, a repressed gay, falls for **JOSELE**. Both him an **YUKO** show **JOSELE** a side of Tokyo he could have never discovered through other foreigners: a more refined, unexpected, authentic Tokyo. Not only does he learn to appreciate Japan, he also becomes aware of fond memories

3

Closed loop recycling · Cluster verde · Regreening
Win-win-win business

From cardboard to caviar: un ciclo de reciclaje perfecto

Experiencia detectada en Wakefield, Reino Unido: creación de un cluster de empresas que tiene su razón de ser en el hecho de que cada una se nutre de los desechos de la anterior: de una fábrica de cartón al cultivo de caviar, un producto resultante de alto valor añadido que incluye además una línea educativa sobre reciclaje y un programa de contratación de colectivos discapacitados.

+ Explorar más

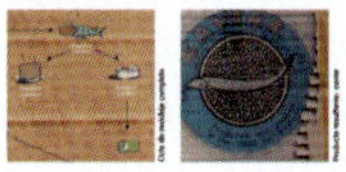

The caracters

It is no wonder that our main female character is YUKO, a young Japanese woman who studies flamenco and ultimately falls in love with JOSELE, a young Spanish, who accidentally finds himself working in Tokyo as a flamenco dancer.

Japanese corporate culture is tailored after men rather women. Women are expected to interrupt their careers to raise their children, they are forced to look for ways of personal fulfillment outside the office, and as a consequence, it is women rather than men who learn foreign languages or exotic art forms, in the hope of finding a way to be who they choose to.
YUKO is bored with her day job, she is not looking forward to the life she is expected to lead as a conventional Japanese woman, and fantasizes about an art –Flamenco- and a land –Spain- where people are supposed to live a freer, happier life.

However, there are two sides to our story. YUKO is not alone in her attraction to a distant culture. JOSELE never planned to work or live in Japan, but after a while starts appreciating Japan's hidden beauty, and eventually falls for our heroine.

Across the movie, YUKO and JOSELE will meet foreigners which will help us understand what makes some non-Japanese move to Tokyo in the first place, and then become long-term residents. Some of them were outcasts in their past life. They came to a country where nobody knew them, where it was easy to reinvent themselves, where they experienced a success they could have never attained back home.

Tokyo is full of individuals straight out of the famous Alphaville song "Big In Japan": they can experience happiness "as long as they are big in Japan". Meanwhile, male or female Japanese fall in love with them, unaware that they would never be considered "ordinary" in their own countries of origin, be it Canada, USA, Australia, Italy or Spain. Simultaneously, foreigners in Japan are seldom conscious of the fact

5

Distancia mínima negocio-ciencia · Nuevos estudiantes
Nuevas capacidades para aprender · Economía del conocimiento

El futuro de las universidades

La educación superior pasa por un momento extraordinario: Los jóvenes llegan a la Universidad con un cableado distinto en el cerebro, porque han pasado miles de horas interactuando en Internet, el teléfono móvil, o la Play Station. Hay que potenciar estas habilidades e invertir en ellas. Las universidades deberán reinventarse, teniendo en cuenta los nuevos segmentos de población potencialmente interesados (formación continua de adultos, séniors, colectivos de inmigrantes, antiguos alumnos, universidad corporativa), y reinventar sus formas de financiación, aprovechando todas las oportunidades de la economía del conocimiento.

+ Explorar más

Treatment

A young Spaniard called JOSELE leaves Sevilla. He has been hanging out the wrong kind of people, and is now running away from some legal trouble. He has been told to leave town for a few months, so he accepts an offer to work in Japan as a flamenco dancer. We follow him as he leaves his hometown by taxi, we see the Triana Bridges and the Guadalquivir river. He is bitter about the past he is leaving behind, and full of doubts about the months ahead. He doesn't consider himself a flamenco dancer at all, doesn't even like flamenco particularly, and feels like an imposter about the whole trip.

A group of Japanese tourists take photographs of a street sign. We are at Calle Amor de Dios, a street in Madrid where there is a very popular Flamenco Dance School. We spot YUKO, a pretty Japanese girl, who keeps some distance from the group. She is taking longer to take the photo, since it means a lot to her. When the whole group enters the school, and watches a few students practicing their dancing steps, she stands in awe, as if inside a temple.

We can see images of JOSELE in Tokyo and YUKO in Spain. They both feel like small fish in big ponds, she is mistaken by a cabdriver for a Korean or a Chinese. He sits alone in the subway. Nobody will sit next to him, out of fear he might come up with a question in English. He wrongly believes he is being a victim of racism, and it hurts him.

YUKO is shopping for a fan and a pair of Flamenco shoes in a small shop in Sevilla. She bargains with her limited Spanish, and smoothly but firmly refuses to pay the prize. We get to know her a bit better. She is clumsy and a bit naive, but also very determined. She loves Spain, and against all odds, she is willing to get to the heart of Spanish culture. Although she is engaged to a Japanese young man, she rebels against the idea, she is not willing to conform to the Japanese conventional way of doing things.

JOSELE tries to walk through a crowded street in Tokio. He is carrying a big bag, and a small map, with a couple of phone numbers written on it. He goes inside a telephone booth, but can't manage to make the call. A recorded voice speaks to him in Japanese, he doesn't understand a word.

7

Hotel · Mínimo · Instantáneo · Confort · Lowcost
Check in/out · Flexible

Yotel: Máximo confort, mínimo espacio

Romper la lógica del mercado hotelero. Prestaciones de 5 estrellas en una habitación de 10 m2 que se alquila por horas en la misma terminal de un aeropuerto (Gatwick, Heathrow, Schiphol). Su target son pasajeros que desean descansar en condiciones confortables entre vuelos o que deben estar en el aeropuerto a una hora muy temprana o tardía del día, o bien que quieren un espacio reservado y con todas las comodidades. Check in y out automático.

+ Explorar más

Living Identity

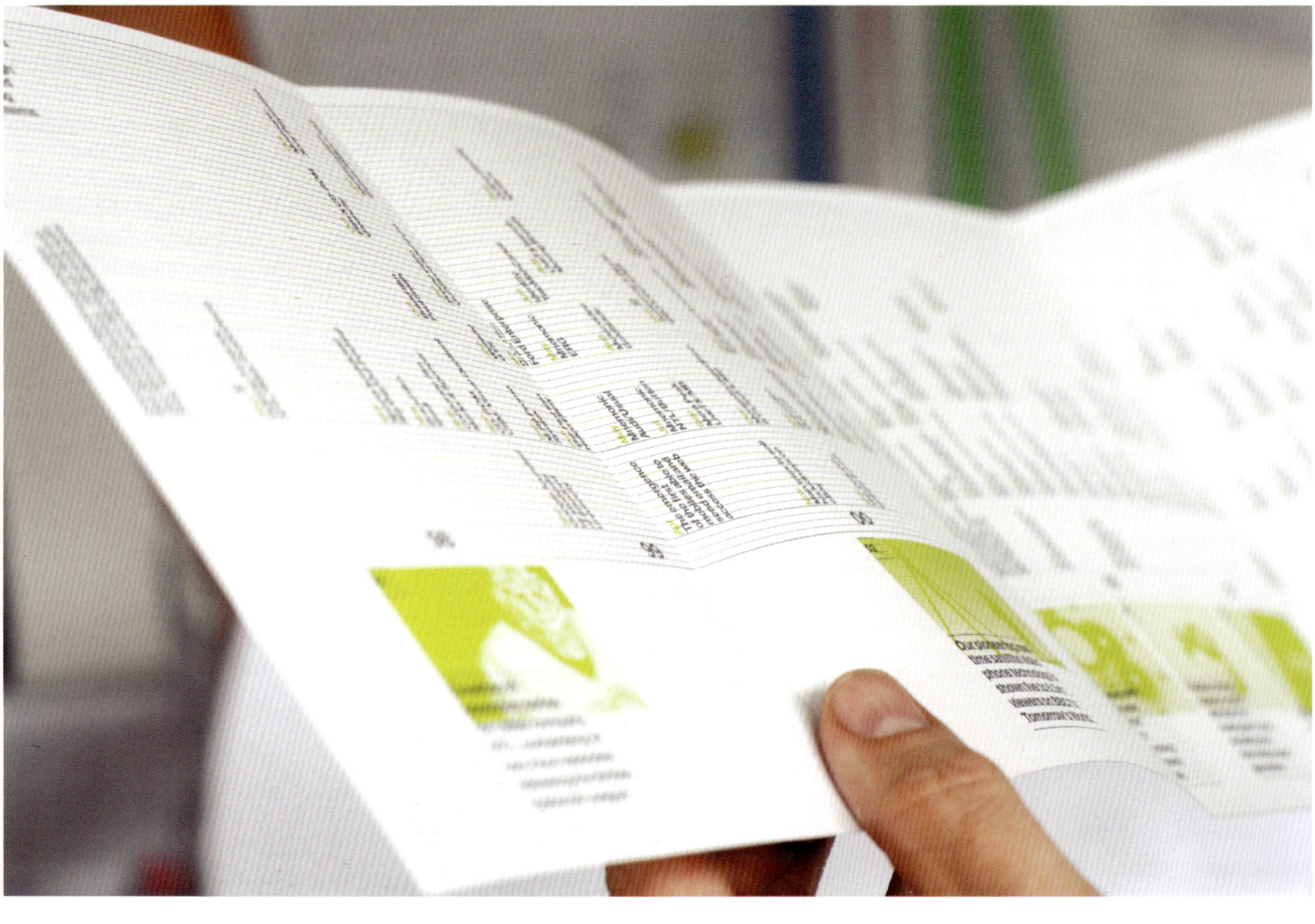

Design Agency:

Moving Brands

Client:

Self-initiated project

Production Date:

2009

Description:

"Living Identity" is the first self-initiated paper from the Moving Brands' studio. To help the book "live" beyond its printed form, the designer made their logo – featured on the book's cover – into a marker for Augmented Reality (AR) technology. The book is divided in to two sections, both in content and paper. The designer wanted to place their written views up front, so the first section was printed on Cyclus, uncoated stock to give it the feel of notepaper. In the second section, which showcases the work, the designer used a gloss stock with spot varnish for the images. The cover is a 12-page gate fold and acts as a "reveal" for their project timeline, spanning eleven years of the studio's history.

De Pasar Malam van Tong Tong, Een Indische Onderneming

Design Agency:

M-Space / Making Waves

Designers:

Marcel van den Berg, Sabrina Luthjens

Client:

Stichting Tong Tong

Nationality:

The Netherlands

Production Date:

2007

Description:

This book tells the history of the 50-year existence of the Pasar Malam Besar (the largest Eurasian festival in the world) in the Hague, The Netherlands.

Der Große Wurf - Faltungen in Der Gegenwartskunst

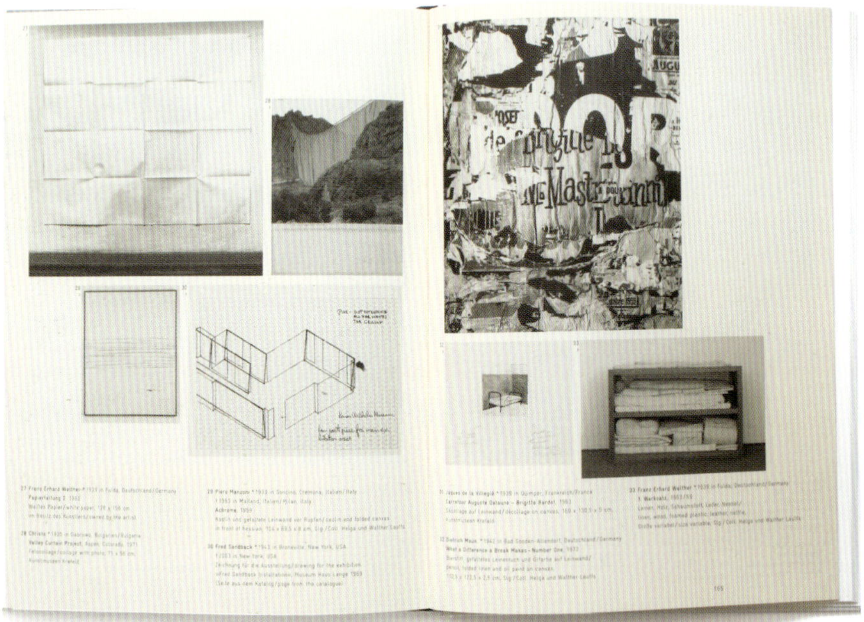

Design Agency:
nowakteufelknyrim

Creative Director:
Petra Knyrim, Stefan Nowak

Designer:
Carla Meurer

Client:
Self-initiated project

Production Date:
2008

Description:
This catalogue is published on the occasion of the exhibition "Falling Right into Place - The Fold in Contemporary Art", Kunstmuseum Krefeld / Museum Haus Lange.

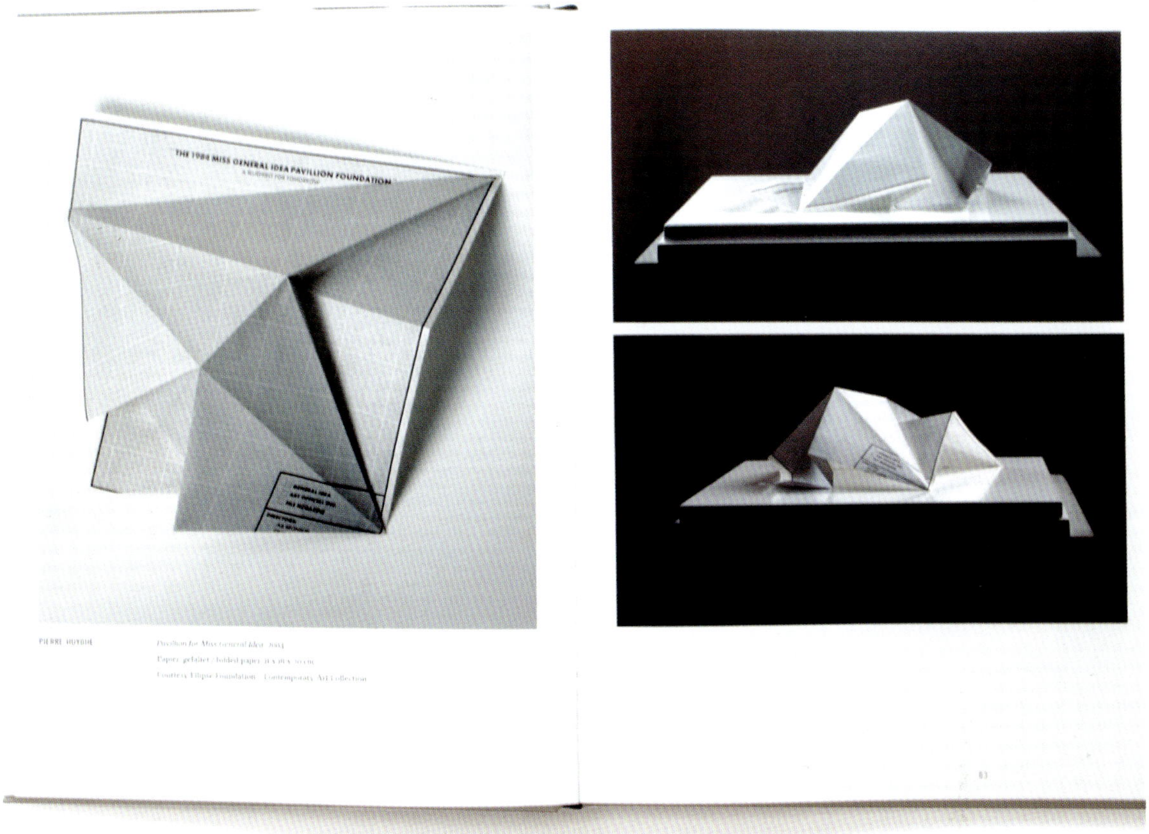
THE 1984 MISS GENERAL IDEA PAVILLION FOUNDATION
PIERRE HUYGHE
Courtesy Ellipse Foundation – Contemporary Art Collection

ALBERT WEIS
Rasterfolien auf Papier / screentone sheet on paper, 21 x 29,7 cm
Im Besitz des Künstlers / owned by the artist
C-Prints, je / each 21 x 29,7 cm
Im Besitz des Künstlers / owned by the artist

Folio Book

Art Director:

Mark Pernice

Design:

Mark Pernice, Eriko Yahiro

Production Date:

2007

Description:

The designer contracted the lovely and talented Eriko Yahiro to make this beautifully crafted book and slipcase. Black leather bound with aluminium inlays and a solid walnut slipcase.

154—155

“ ”

Design Agency:

Oezlen Sagir

Client:

Georg Simon Ohm University of Applied Sciences

Production Date:

2007

Description:

"It is not until limitations are put on him that the master really shows himself," said Goethe about the relationship between the artist and his materials. Against the background of a clearly reduced layout, the work can completely concentrate on the portrayal and interpretation of individual quotations, of which some are presented typographically and others in combination with illustrations. The content of the chosen quotes is tailored to the situation of (design) students, who are at the start of their professional career and still have a lot ahead of them and hand employing different printing techniques and bound with great skill using high quality paper.

Comment:

When the designer came up with the idea about manual printing a complete illustrated book, he was scared to make mistakes hard to repair. But in the end he was amazed about how this imperfections could inspire him so much to solve further pages, as well as how these unforeseeable accidents made this book a unique one and full of new ideas.

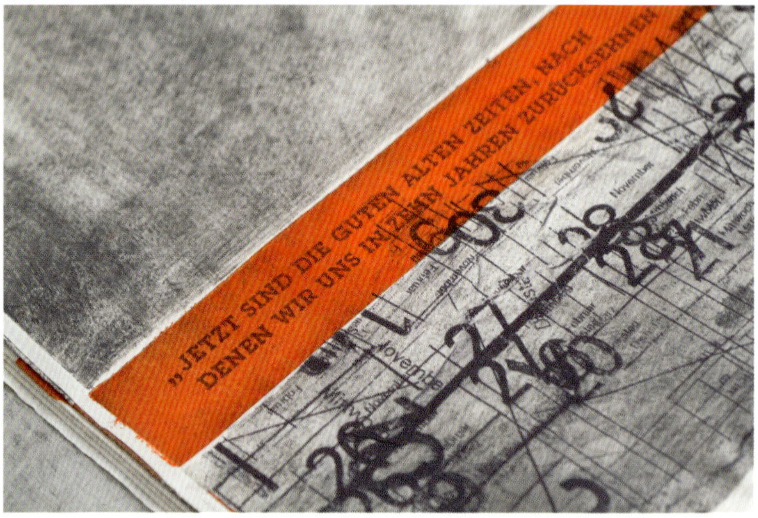

»CARPE DIEM, MACHT ETWAS
UNGEWÖHNLICHES AUS EUREM LEBEN«

„WENN EINEM DAS
WASSER BIS ZUM

UNSC/R

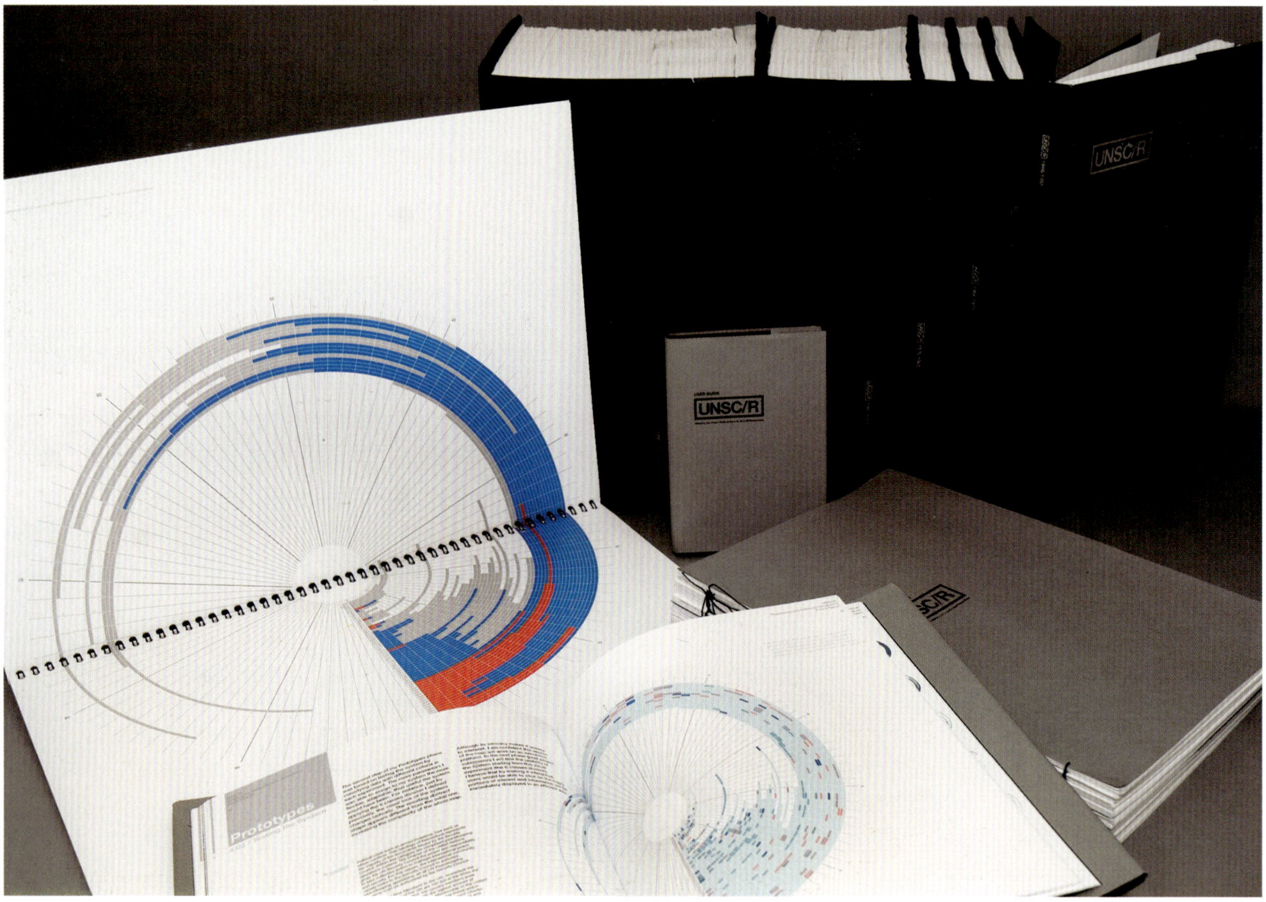

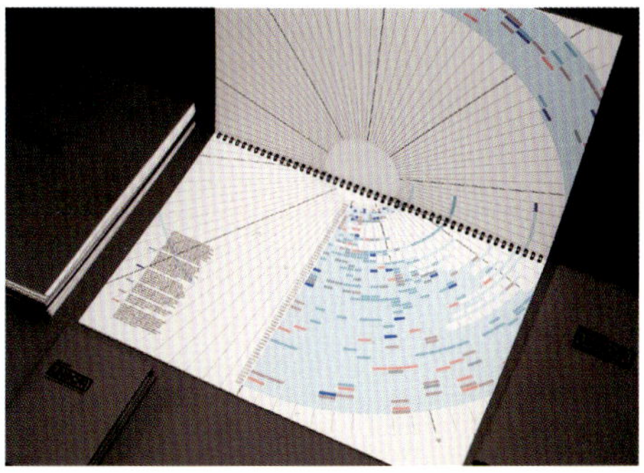

Design Agency:

Piero Zagami

Client:

UNSC/R

Production Date:

2010

Description:

This is the abbreviation for the United Nations Security Council Resolutions. These documents represent the decisions of the UN's executive body. This massive amount of data (more than 1700 documents) doesn't come in any organised form. The purpose of this project is to apply information design strategies to create visual maps of the Resolutions to help students in politics approach the subject of the UN.

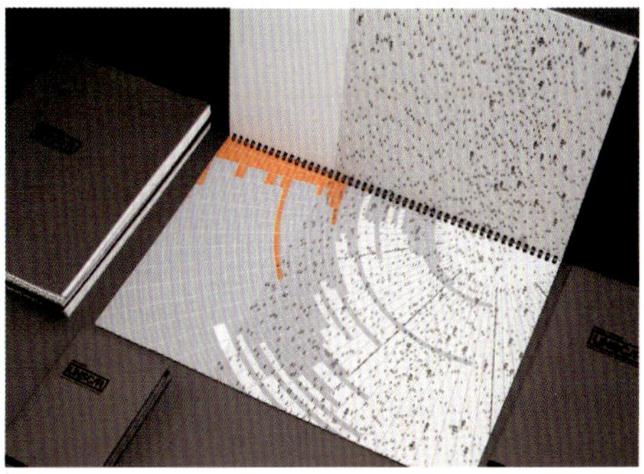

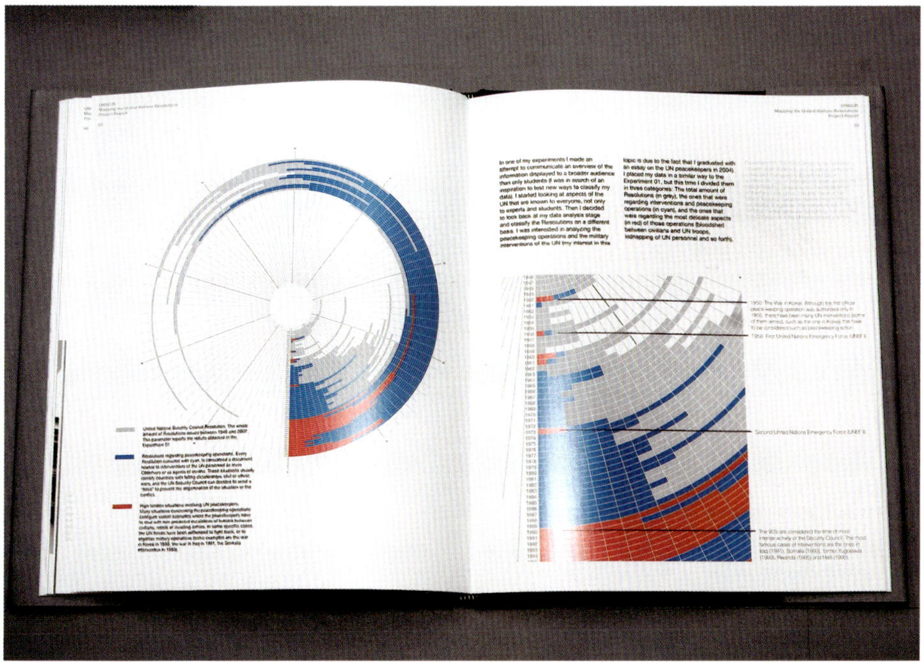

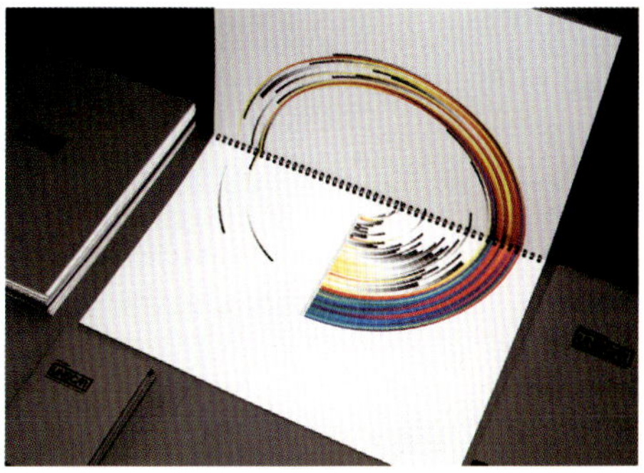

Volume

Design Agency:

Poero Zagami

Client:

Volume

Production Date:

2008

Description:

MA Final Show Catalogue was produced for the MAGD 2008 course at the London College of Communication. In charge of collecting visual material of each of the 70 students' projects. In charge of the photography of several content images in the book. Cover design and catalogue layout were produced in collaboration with E. Hoffmann, D. Naegele and N. Di Costanzo.

BRANDING AGNOSTICISM
Branding Agnosticism
Edgar Hofmann
T. S. Eliot's The Waste Land: an animated interpretation
Thomas Howey
This animated interpretation is an abridged version of T. S. Eliot's 1922 modernist masterpiece 'The Waste Land', and is based on his 1934 reading of the poem. With the intention of expressing the 'music' of the poetry, the animation contains within its structure aspects of both the poem itself and Eliot's reading of it. These are: the loudness of Eliot's voice, shown by the distance words travel across the screen; the pitch, shown by the height of words; stressed and unstressed words, shown by their size; rhythm, shown by the timing of words as they appear; the characters in the poem, shown by the differing typefaces; and the conversation between characters, shown by the opposing direction of words on screen. Eliot conceived of the poem as an expression of what he termed the 'objective correlative': common emotions that can be found in disparate experiences.
The picture shown here; of all the words from the abridged poem shown at once, could be seen as a visualisation of this 'objective correlative'; or as a bleak vision of The Waste Land itself.

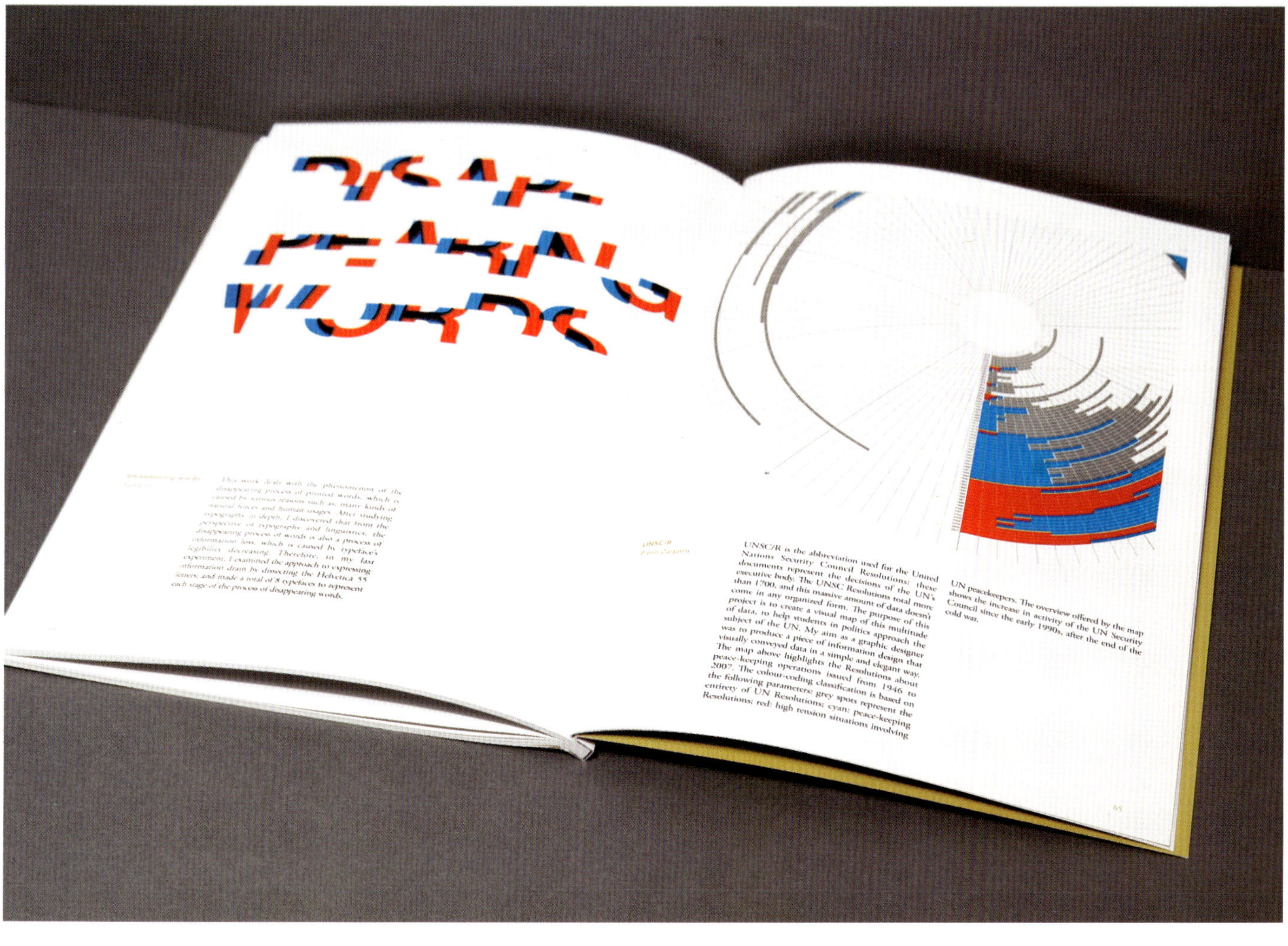
UNSC/R
UNSC/R is the abbreviation used for the United Nations Security Council Resolutions: these documents represent the decisions of the UN's executive body. The UNSC Resolutions total more than 1700, and this massive amount of data doesn't come in any organized form. The purpose of this project is to create a visual map of this multitude of data, to help students in politics approach the subject of the UN. My aim as a graphic designer was to produce a piece of information design that visually conveyed data in a simple and elegant way. The map above highlights the Resolutions about peace-keeping operations issued from 1946 to 2007. The colour-coding classification is based on the following parameters: grey spots represent the entirety of UN Resolutions; cyan: peace-keeping Resolutions; red: high tension situations involving UN peacekeepers. The overview offered by the map shows the increase in activity of the UN Security Council since the early 1990s, after the end of the cold war.

Denkmalpflege in der Stadt Bern

Design Agency:

Pirol, Büro für Visuelle Gestaltung

in cooperation with Bern University of Arts Atelier

Designer:

Ruth Amstutz and Simone Farner

in cooperation with Franco Bonaventura (BUA)

Client:

Denkmalpflege der Stadt Bern

Production Date:

2009

Description:

The book starts with a series of orthophotos of the city of Berne, where all the monuments mentioned in the book are marked. The map-pages and the colour photos at the end of the book build a frame around the four-year report: A documentation of 70 projects of preservation of monuments in pictures and texts, grouped according to the districts of the city.

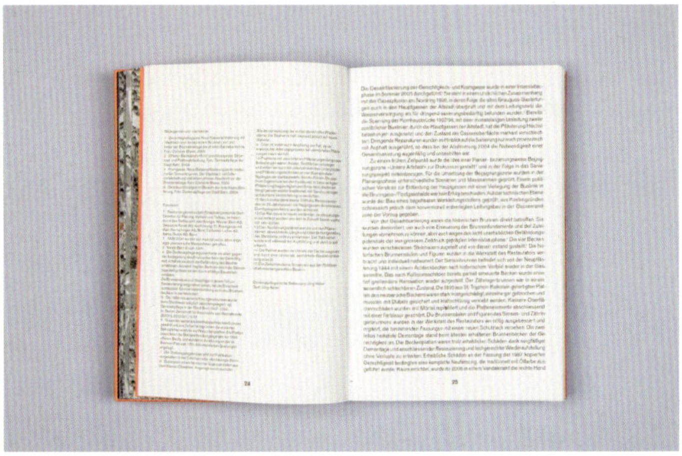

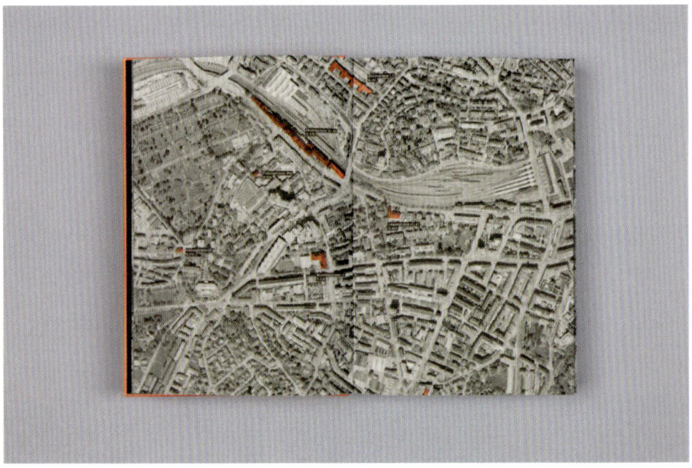

Be
rich
te

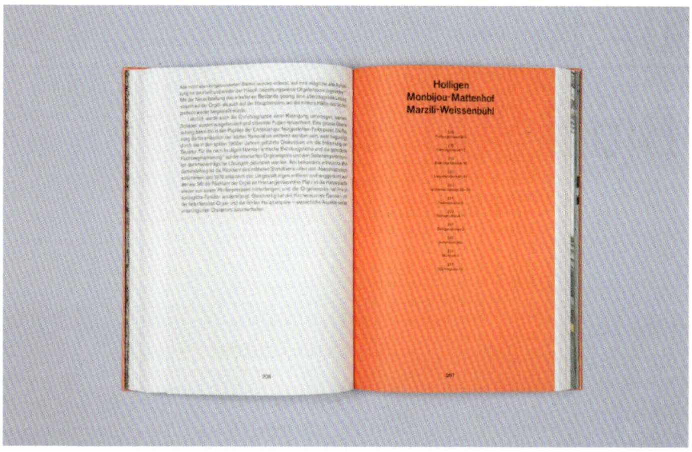
Holligen
Monbijou-Mattenhof
Marzili-Weissenbühl

Herrengasse 10

Bremgartenstrasse 131–137

Block800

Art Director:
Pitertsev Mikhail
Designer:
Pitertsev Mikhail
Client:
LZID Ltd.
Production Date:
2009
Description:
Block800 is the new type of finishing work material by LZID Ltd. Block800 is an artificial decorating stonelike material specially created for cladding surfaces. Capability of unique colouring is avaliable.

04
05
Применение декоративного камня в качестве отделочного материала при строительстве и ремонте зданий стало показателем высокого качества. Искусственный или натуральный декоративный камень обладает эстетичным внешним видом, высокой прочностью и долговечностью. Декоративный камень характеризуется устойчивостью к неблагоприятным воздействиям. Разнообразие форм, фактур и оттенков декоративного камня обуславливают его широкое применение в дизайне интерьеров, наружной отделки и ландшафтном дизайне. Современное производство декоративного камня позволяет получать искусственный декоративный камень, который внешне не отличим от своего природного аналога. Более того, производство декоративного камня выполняется из экологически чистых природных материалов. Наша компания предлагает декоративный камень в Краснодаре в самом широком ассортимент
искусственный камень
артикль SDB 800-07

14
16
Предел прочности
при сжатии, не менее,
МПа
33,7
искусственный камень
артикль SDB 800-07

03
Содержание
О камне 04
Производство 06
Характеристики 10
Формы 28
Колористика 30
Компоненты 34
Оборудование 38
Каталог камня 40
искусственный камень
артикль SDB 800-07

ESPN - Ultimate Highlight Reel

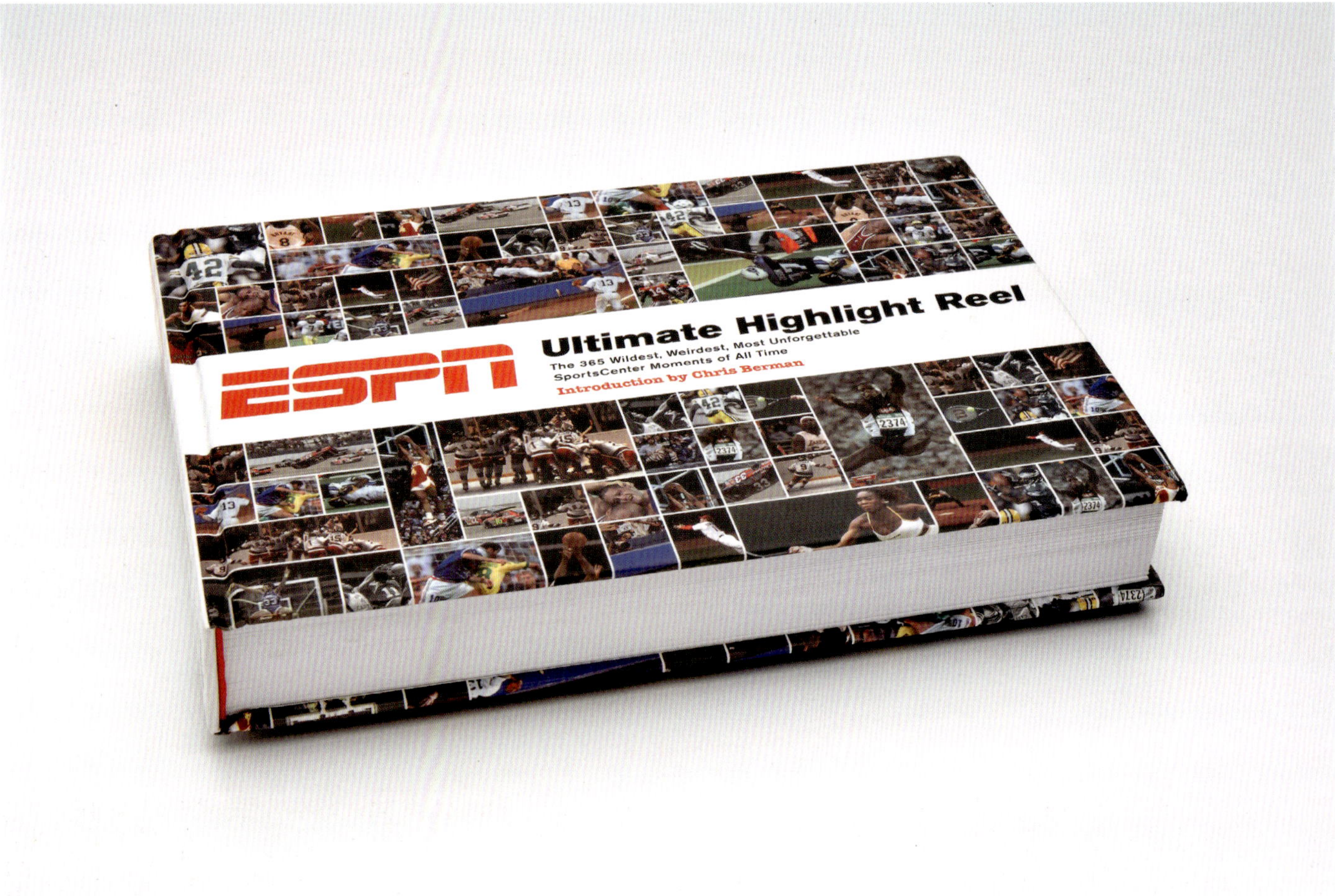

Art Director:

Joshua Berger

Designer:

Joshua Berger, Todd Houlette

Client:

ESPN Books / Melcher Media

Production Date:

2009

Description:

This nearly 400-page coffee table book was produced as part of the 25th anniversary of ESPN's SportsCentre. It contains 365 of the "wildest, weirdest, most unforgettable SportsCentre moments of all time".

Home
Schoole
Onward
Christian's
Soldiers
March 28, 1992
DUKE
32

Toothless
Shark
April 14, 1996
Bull
Market
April 16, 1996

Perfectly
Seasoned
March 21, 2002
April

$241,758
per Second
June 27, 1988
Mike Tyson vs. Michael Spinks
A Hawk Soars

Velvet Gloves
March 16, 1996
Christy Martin vs. Deirdre Gogarty
There was just one thing that saved the 1.1 million suckers who paid-per-view to see Mike Tyson beat a trembling Frank Bruno into submission in a stinker of a fight: Christy Martin. Martin hammered Deirdre Gogarty in a bloody bit of business that made up for the Tyson-Bruno yawn at the top of the card. Gogarty broke Martin's nose early in the fight, but Martin scored the only knockdown in the second and won the six-round fight by decision. Afterward, her husband/trainer said, "The key to our success is that she's 100% female—she wears high heels, fingernail polish, everything." And packs a powerful right.
Trading Paint
March 16, 2003
Kurt Busch vs. Ricky Craven
After two laps of neck-and-neck racing between Ricky Craven and Kurt Busch at the end of the Carolina Dodge Dealers 400, it came down to the final turn at Darlington. Exiting the corner, Craven slid down below Busch and the pair roared down the last straightaway, bumping each other—hard—all the way to the checkered flag. Craven took the win by inches—a
-second margin of victory, the closest since NASCAR started using electronic timing a decade earlier.

Liza Ryan: SPILL

Art Director:
Joshua Berger
Designer:
Joshua Berger
Client:
Reed College Cooley Gallery
Production Date:
2009
Description:
It is the catalogue published on the occasion of the exhibition Liza Ryan: SPILL, on view at the Cooley Gallery in winter of 2009. The exhibition was curated by gallery director, Stephanie Snyder. Subsequent exhibition and release party were held at Griffin Gallery, Los Angeles. SPILL was recently acquired by the Getty Museum.

Liza
Ryan

Liza
Ryan

Amplificador

Design Agency:

qubo + Scheps Workshop

Client:

Scheps Workshop, Architecture University of Uruguay

Production Date:

2010

Description:

Amplificador gathers a series of conferences and workshops that took place between 2005 and 2009, addressing various issues, each viewed from different disciplines.

It is a low circulation, low cost book, printed only in two inks, and its design attempts to exploit the most of these restrictions. Format, materials and finishes are decisions that follow from this.

The two inks are used as an expressive resource; they are visible from the outside, existing two variants of the same book cover. Inside they alternate, separating sections, creating textures, stopping at margins or bleeding. The result is a delicate, diverse and powerful object.

La "carpeta" en Debate

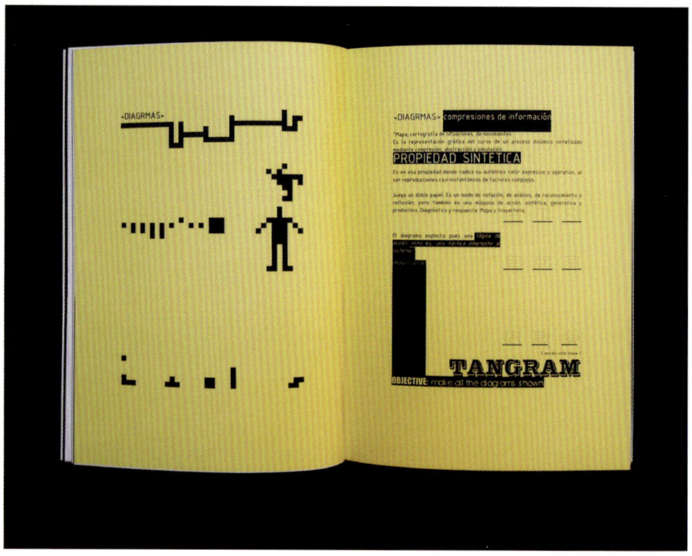

Design Agency:

qubo

Client:

Architecture University of Uruguay

Production Date:

2009

Description:

Interior and cover design for a book containing the result of the national contest of the best graduation projects from the Architecture University of Uruguay planed to select a winner to send to Archiprix 2009.

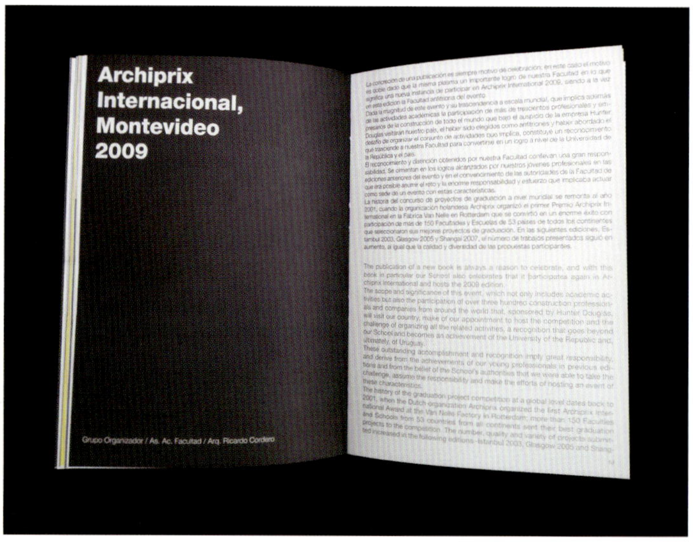

Nomadismo

Design Agency:

qubo

Client:

ArquitecturaRifa gen. 2001/2002

Production Date:

2008

Description:

It is interior and cover design of a booklet containing a special selection of the Literary Contest of ArquitecturaRifa Travel Groups, the Third Edition.

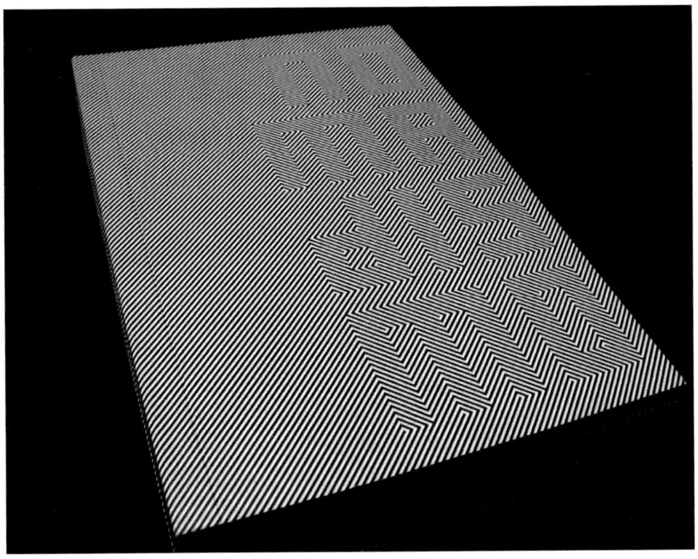

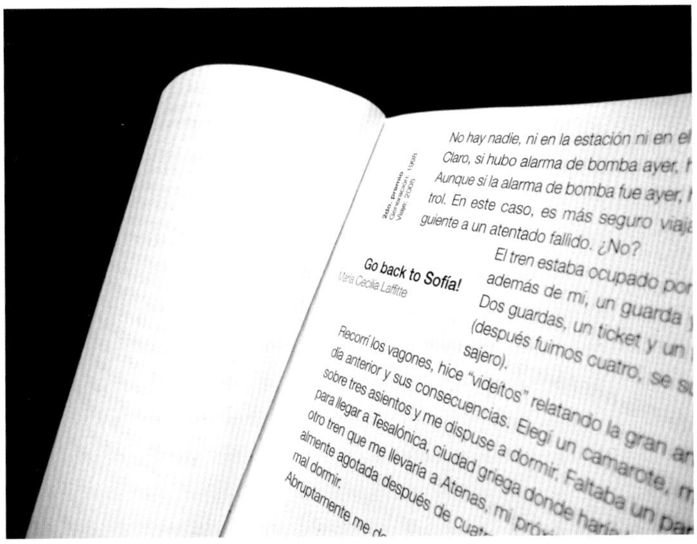

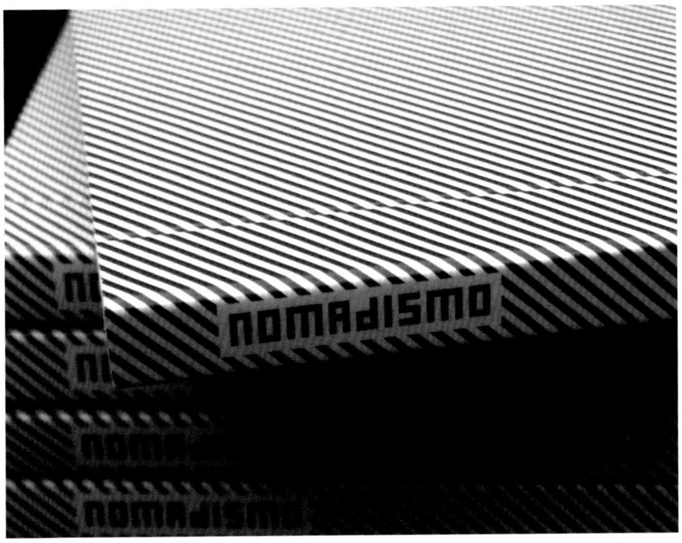

My Dream

Design Agency:

Redstorm

Designer:

Alexander Kalachev

Client:

Uralsib Bank & "Share Your Knowledge" Charity Foundation

Production Date:

2009

Description:

As a part of charity project "Share Your Knowledge" by Uralsib Bank Written-contest for Children was initiated. Participants from orphanages all over Russia sent their short stories where they shared intimate dreams. As a result of the contest in addition to various prizes for the participants 50 stories were chosen to be published in "My Dream" book. The main goal was to make the book as good for children as for adults. Just before final approval the designer decided that the book turns boring and added childish drawings on some spreads.

УЧАСТНИК ЛИТЕРАТУРНОГО КО
Оля Ильина
15 лет. Зырянский детский дом, Томская

Максим Востряков

Катя Масальцева

D&AD: Annual 2008

Designer:
Neville Brody, Nick Hard, George Sheldrake

Production Date:
2008

Description:
Neville Brody and Research Studios have designed the 2009 D&AD Annual. Invited to undertake the prestigious annual by the president, Simon Waterfall, 2009 was the first time that "the book" also went online.

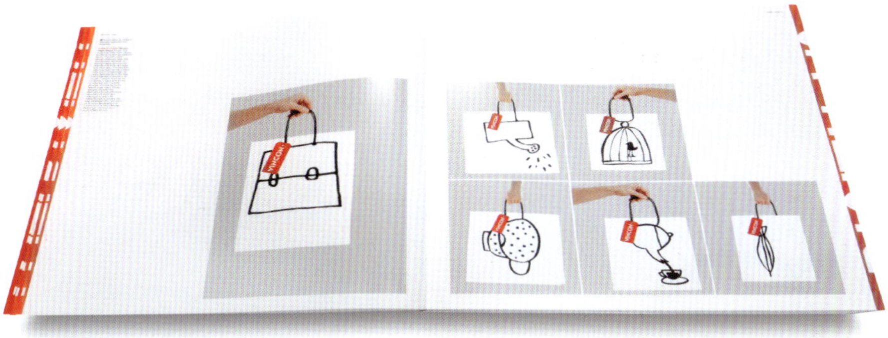

PICASSO
ACNE PAPER

Simon Waterfall
President
This book sits around for a hell of a long time. If you read this in 2008 you will remember seeing the work and spit teeth when you recognise the talent who did it under a silly haircut in Hoxton. If it's 2012, then the London Olympics are about to start, Great Britain is going for gold and no one will give a toss about design for a couple of months. Anything after that, and it's research for my epitaph – 'He was a... and here you can insert an appropriate adjective... I'd hope for 'good' president, swore a lot and wore flamboyant suits'.
But, look at this book. Hold it in your hands. Flip that spine and thumb through the juries – the weight of work contained in it is frightening isn't it? When you look back at all the annuals, everyone has a favourite. I've been incredibly lucky to have Neville Brody in my corner for this brave, brash and different book. It represents so much of my year as the first digital president. Digital is no longer about the type of work it's about the access to it, the old adage of looking through a window rather than staring at the glass. This annual I hope breaks new ground, we have included hyperlinks throughout the book to contextual video interviews with the judges, interviews with key creatives on the future of the sector and the industry as a whole, and most importantly links that take you straight to the moving image work online, so you can see the work yourself and in its correct format. These are the beginnings of our archive, of insights and work which we hope to share with all our members and communities. The theme of Digital vs Anti Digital represents the evolution of the digital industry – moving away from 'Can we do this technically?' to 'Should we do this for the brand?'. digital work is not new media – it's just media. But people expected many things of the new creative set, and through the highs and the lows of an industry, and world, on the brink of a slow down, we have come out a stronger, more fun and I hope more rounded body. No one said our jobs would be easy, but I can honestly say that it's always a pleasure.
As president you worry about 'your year', the work that is entered (over 25,000), how the judges (304) are going to find it, and how many from the nominations (143) will make it to a Pencil (63) and praying for a black... (6 record-breaking ones). The figures are UP they are always UP, the work across the board is more integrated, whether you come from digital towards advertising or brand into packaging design, it's all working together. As a general trend, there was a lot of 'make work together'. Collaboration with the customer or audience, from Sony's 'Music pieces' and 'Colour Tokyo!' in digital to the user interaction and exchange in HBO's 'Voyeur'. Also a rise of time consuming craft with appropriate budgets, see 'Wave' from Big Yellow Storage Company, Skoda's 'Cake' for branded and Samsung's 'How We Met' for underground. The guilty pleasure of eating chocolate was beautifully illustrated with the equally embarrassing admission of listening, and enjoying Phil Collins, so perfectly portrayed by Fallon in 'Gorilla'. 'I can feel it coming in the air tonight' is now a karaoke epidemic.
I gave the President's Pencil this year (see page 14) to a husband and wife team, who, like D&AD, have been working for decades to promote, educate and champion the endeavour of creative excellence – Sir John and Frances Sorrell. Their hand-in-hand walk to the stage to accept the award, at a brand new ceremony staged at the Royal Festival Hall, reminded me how much we rely upon each other – whether it be our partners, colleagues or peer group. The ones that make winning such a ludicrously small wooden award worth it, because they all know how hard you worked to achieve it – it's recognition from the people who really matter. If you are in this book, then that's fantastic, well done and thank you for sharing your talent with us.
I would like to thank all MY significant others – all the executive team, but especially my VICE President, Garrick Hamm and all the staff at D&AD HQ, who have made the year possible. You really are the engine behind it all. The Education teams who tirelessly train, encourage and award the next generation of upcoming talent. And, let's not forget the moneymen, the sponsors, who've bought us both cash and credentials, and have been so supportive throughout the year. Thank you.
I guess that only leaves me to sign off by saying, one last time 'D&AD – it's all about the Work.'
'The theme of Digital vs Anti Digital represents the evolution of the digital industry – moving away from 'Can we do this technically?' to 'Should we do this for the brand?', digital work is not new media – it's just media'

AKV | St. Joost Prospectus

Designer:

Roosje Klap

Client

Akademie voor Kunst en Vormgeving St. Joos

Production Date:

2010

Description:

Each bachelor and master study at the Academy for Art and Design St. Joost has its own colour and build-up. In this prospectus is shown in pictures, texts and pie charts what studying at St. Joost looks like.

A two-sided printed dustjacket with all the pie charts surrounds the book. Inside the book there are little post-its with quotes the designer distilled from interviews they did with students. This gives colour to the plain texts about the curriculum. Out of photographs of the academy the designer made sequences, like stop motions, to show the real everyday feeling inside the school.

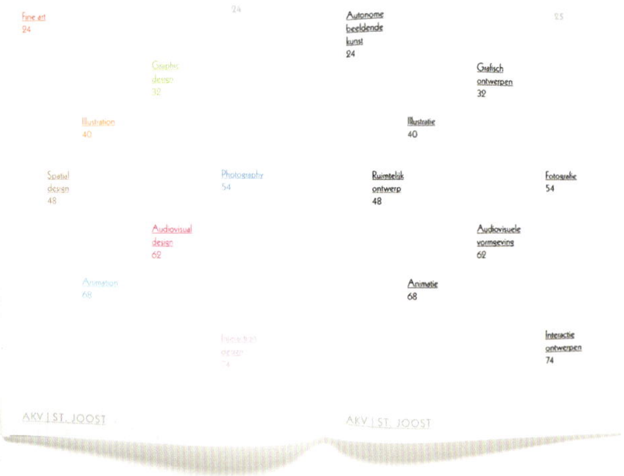

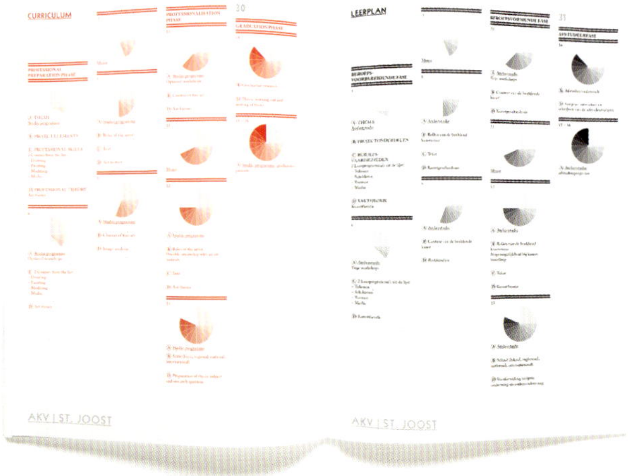

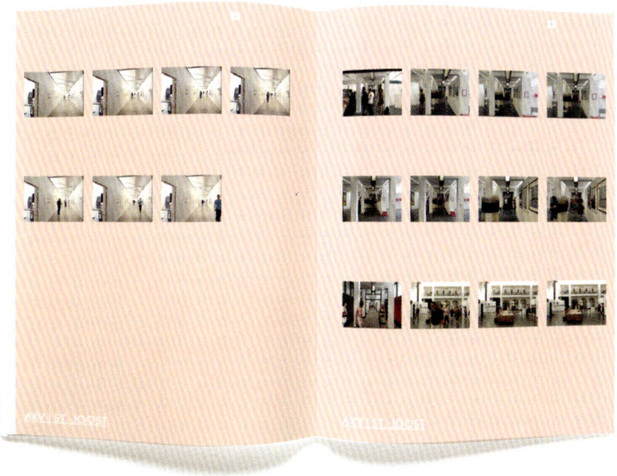
AKV | ST. JOOST
AKV | ST. JOOST

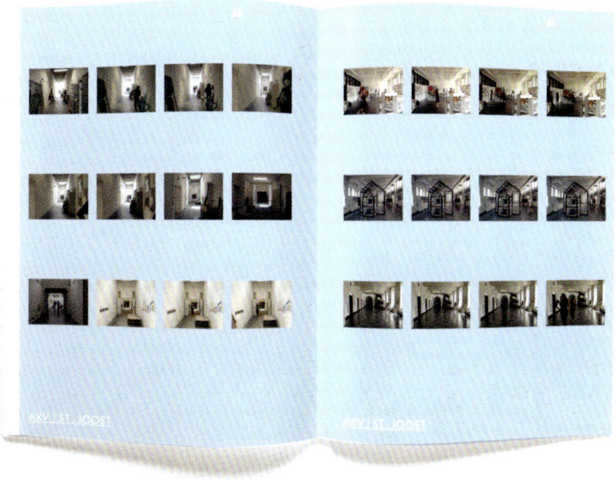
AKV | ST. JOOST
AKV | ST. JOOST

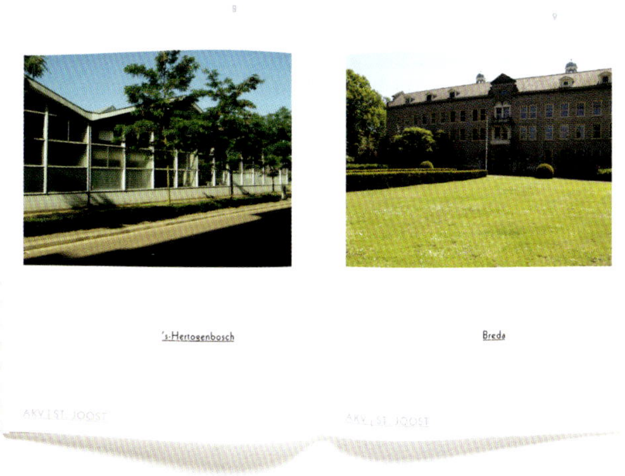
's-Hertogenbosch
Breda

108
109
This is the best school
there is. My mother
never understood why
I went to school
in the holidays.
Breda
AKV | ST. JOOST
AKV | ST. JOOST

Alles voor de Kunst, De Bemiddelaar in de Kunst

Designer:
Roosje Klap
Client
Fonds BKVB, Amsterdam
Production Date:
2009
Description:
The book "Alles voor de Kunst" focuses on the role and position of the mediator (bemiddelaar) in art. As the mediator comes in many shapes and forms, the designer created a publication in different sized cahiers for each chapter and bound it together.

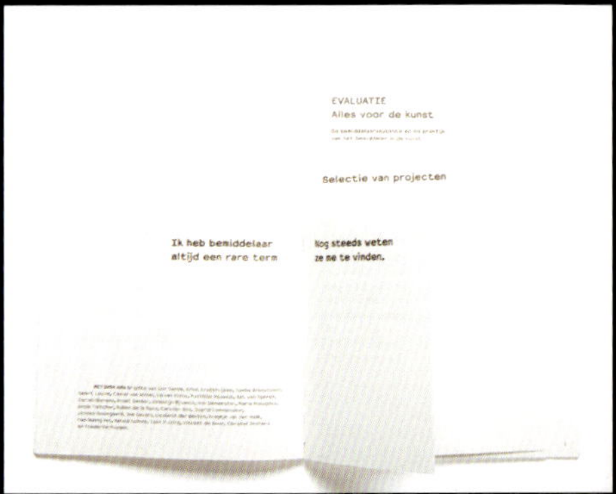

De Zachte Atlas Van Amsterdam

Designer:
Roosje Klap
Client:
Jan Rothuizen
Production Date:
2009
Description:
Artist Jan Rothuizen walks in cities all over the world. He notes down everything he sees, thinks and feels while walking - resulting in drawings that are not only a view on things the way they are but also reveil the way he experiences the city.

The design puts a firm finger on an itchy problem that small drawings usually have in the middle of a spread: things disappear in the centre.

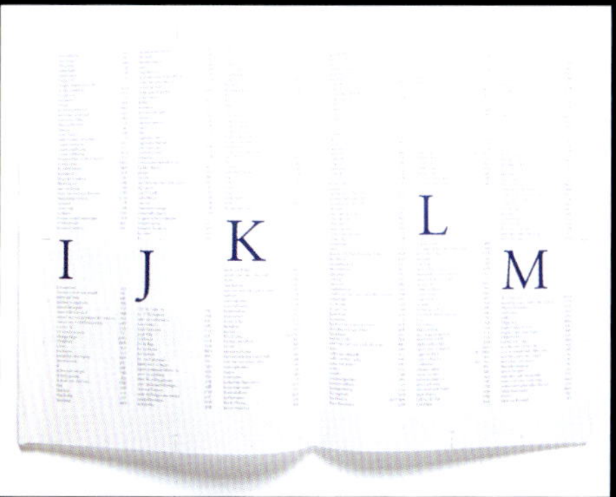

Exquisite Gunpowder City 16 Shot

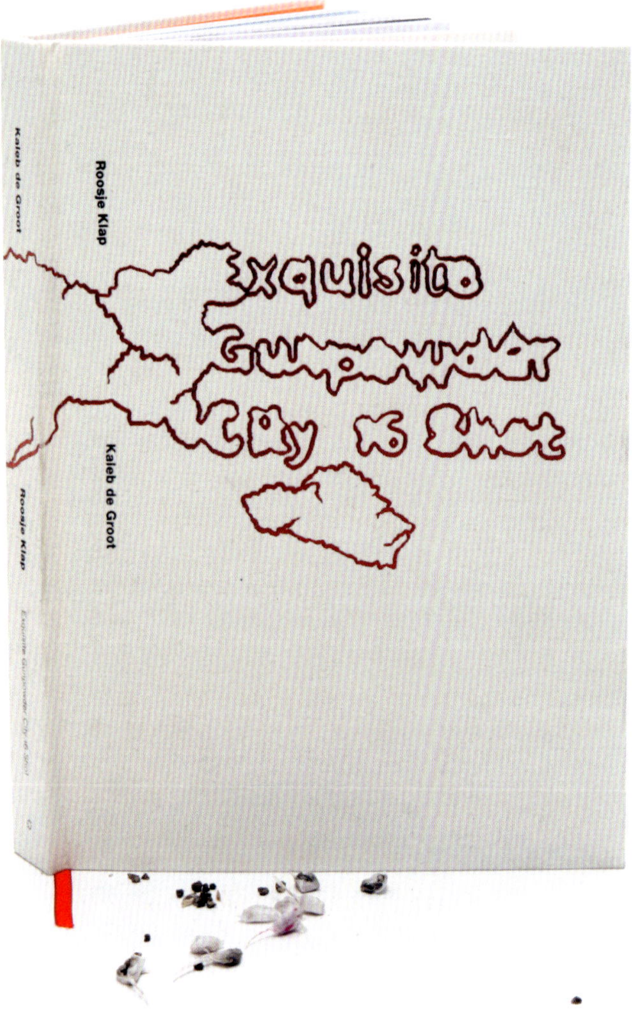

Designer:

Roosje Klap

Client:

Own Commission

Production Date:

2010

Description:

Pop-up book, also containing drawings, photographs and several texts about the idea of destruction versus construction. The book was made during a residency project with the same name in Xiamen, China.

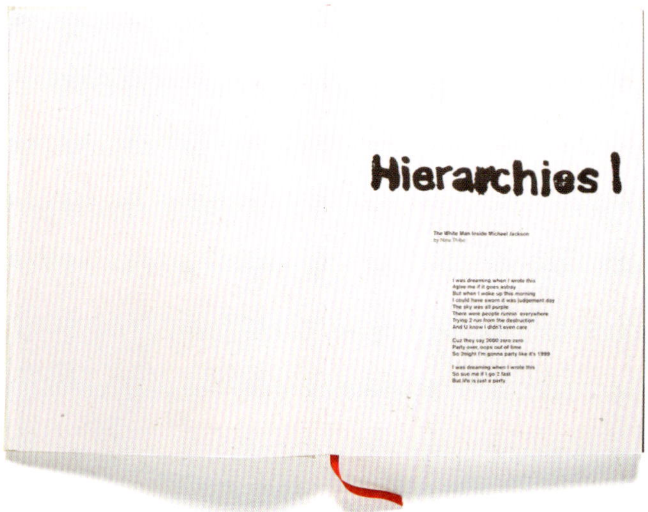

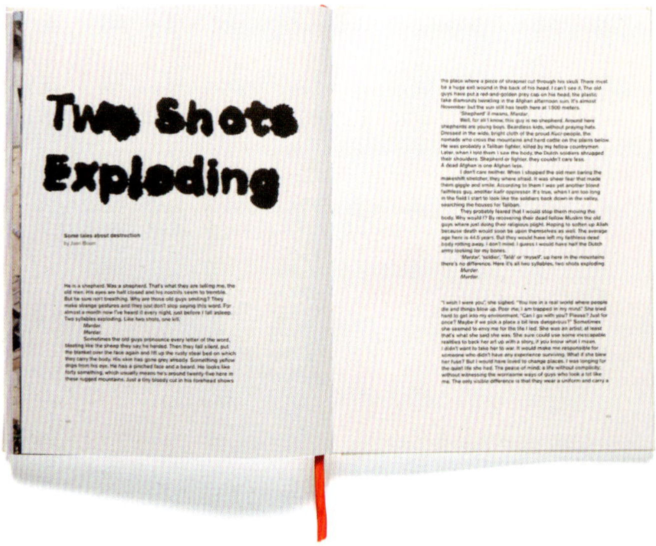

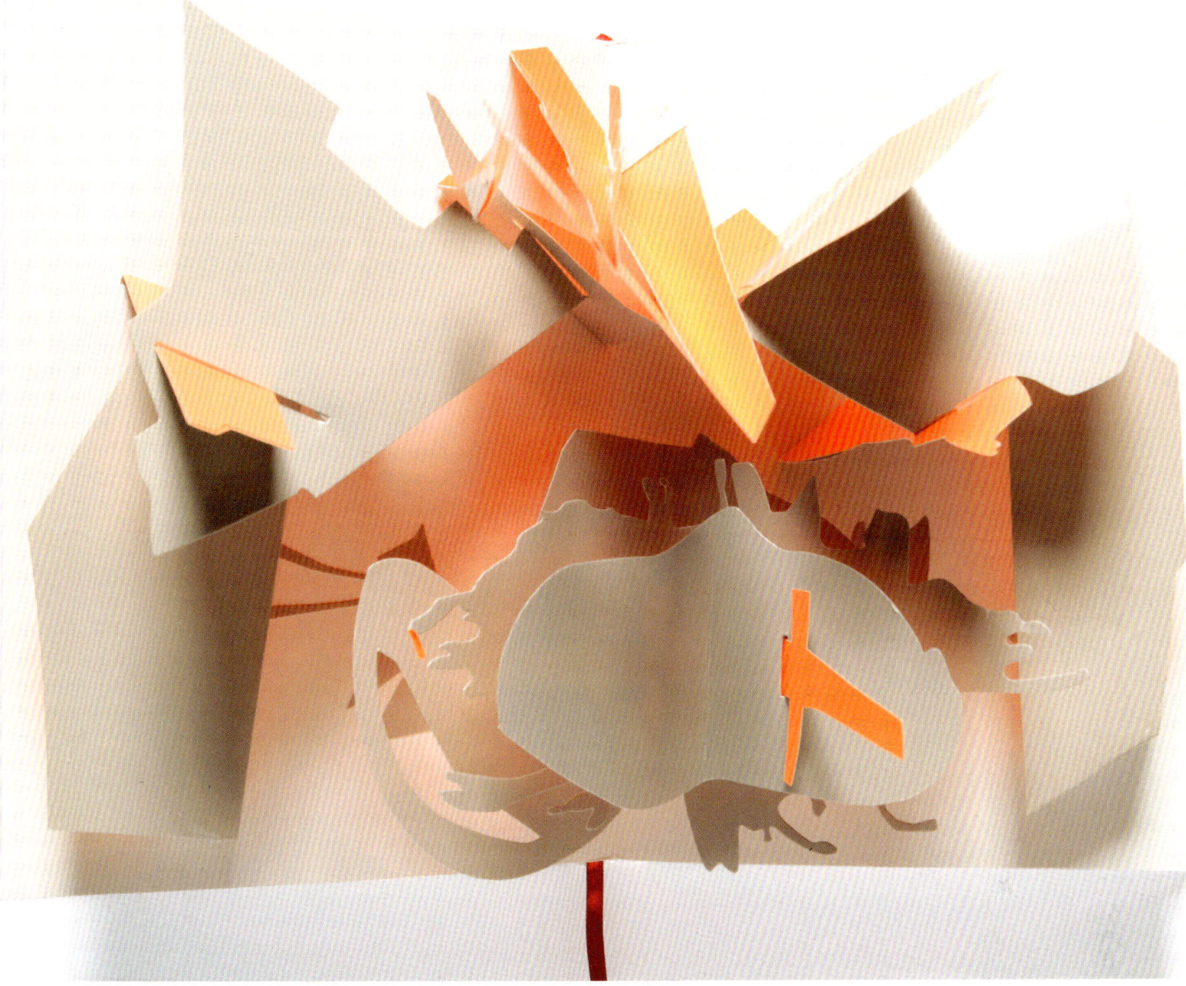

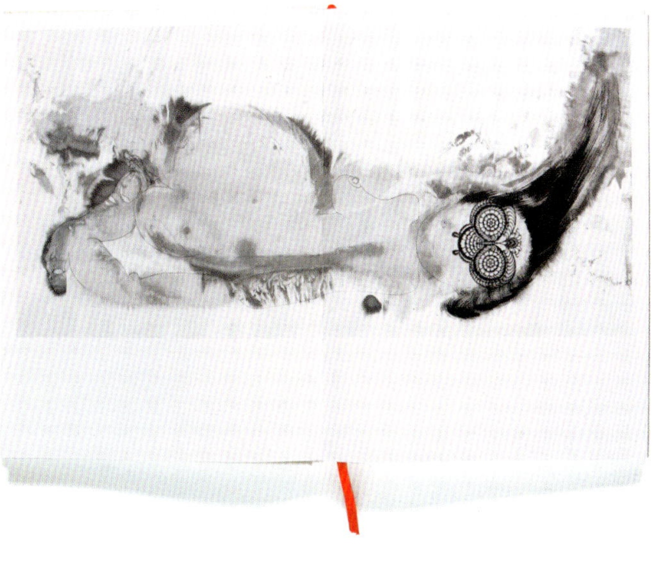

The Encyclopedia of Fictional Artists / The Addition

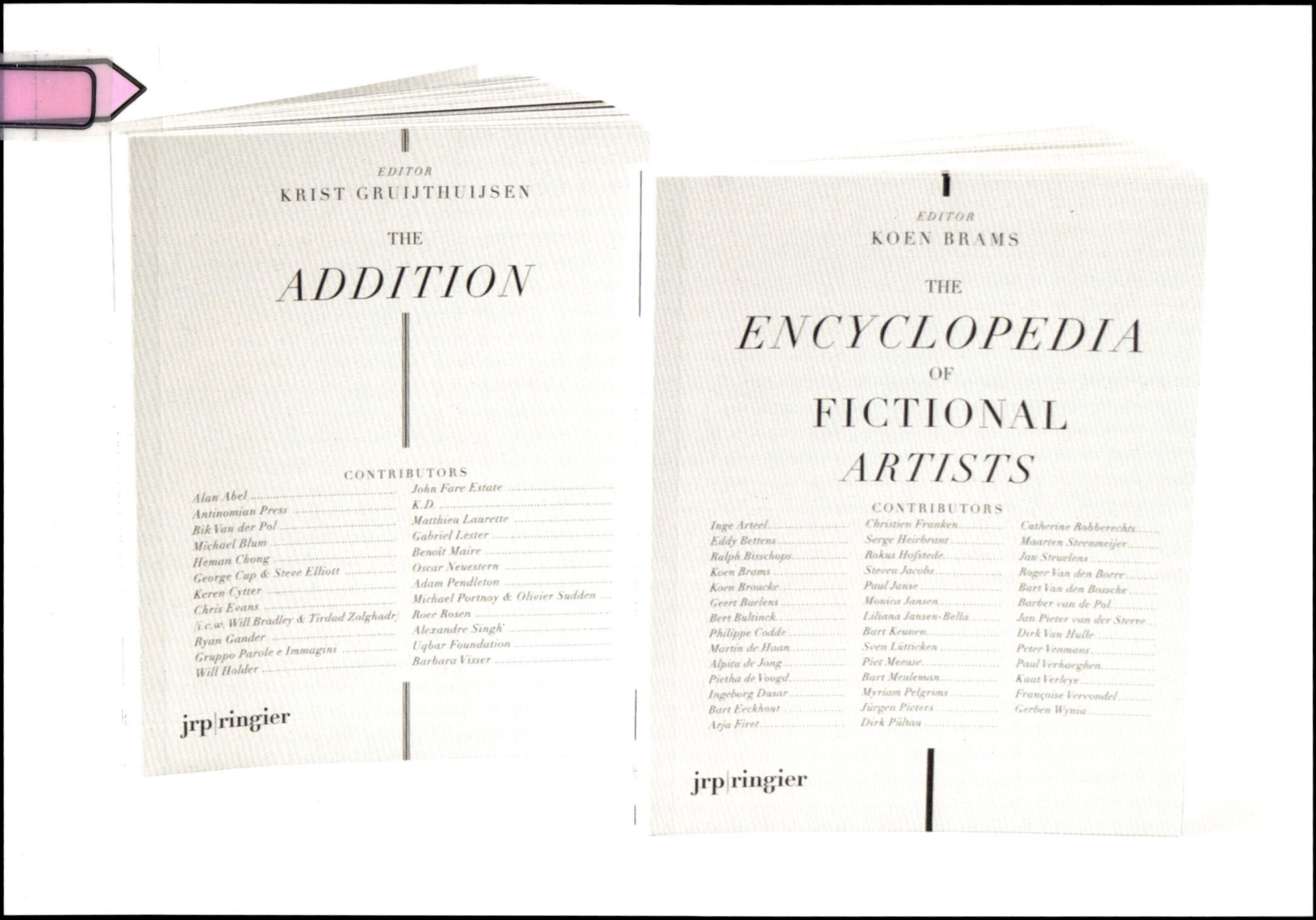

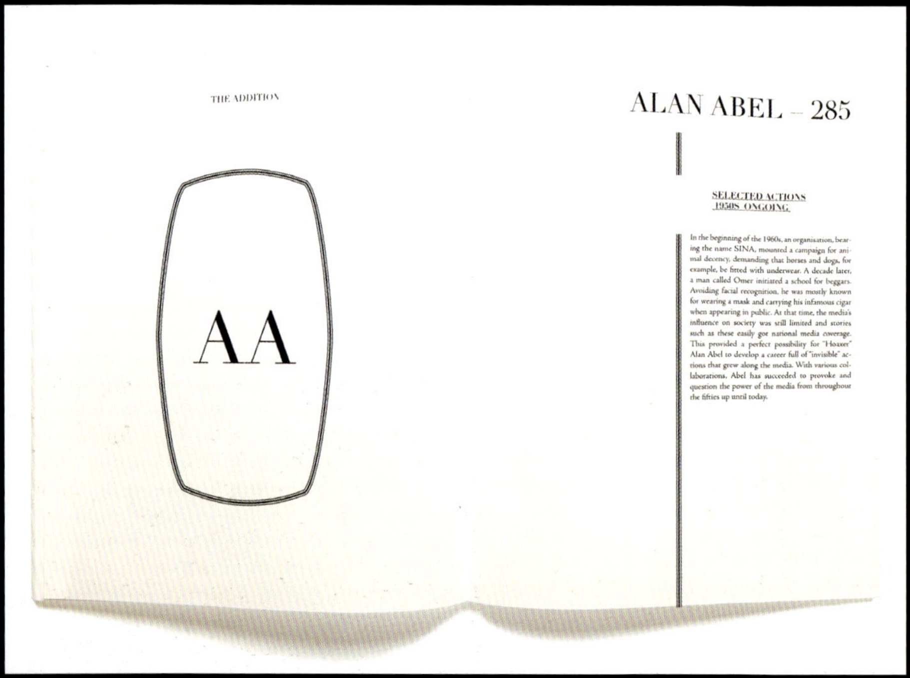

Designer:

Roosje Klap

Client:

JRP Ringier, Zürich (Switzerland)

Production Date:

2010

Description:

First published nearly a decade ago, and here translated into English for the first time, "The Encyclopedia of Fictional Artists" is a projec by author and editor Koen Brams, for which he commissioned and compiled an anthology o imaginary biographies based on the numerous artists invented by writers across the centuries from the beginning of the seventeenth century to the present. The imaginary artist is, of course, a supremely seductive figure to readers, writers and artists alike, being a sort of screen upon which the most astounding imaginary creations may be projected, without need of them ever being visible to the eye. As such, "The Encyclopedia of Fictiona Artists" constitutes a trove of inspiration for al manner of creative endeavor. The Addition is Kris Gruijthuisen's editorial answer to the Encyclopedia in which he invites more than 30 artists to reflect on the aspirations and ideals of encyclopedias.

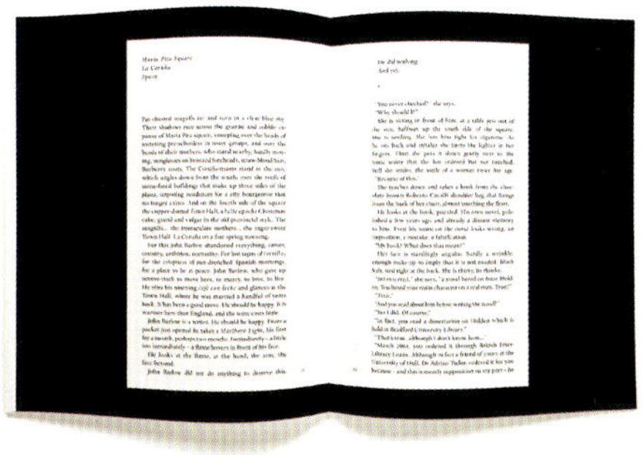

Designer:

Roosje Klap

Client:

Stedelijk Museum Bureau Amsterdam (SMBA) & Platform Garanti, Istanbul

Production Date:

2007

Description:

Following exhibitions at Stedelijk Museum Bureau Amsterdam (SMBA) and Platform Garanti in Istanbul this is the third and last presentation formed under the title "We All Laughed at Christopher Columbus". It was realised in the form of a publication, and presented at the Turkish Pavillion during the opening of La Biennale di Venezia in 2007.

269
Q. How long had you been in the Army before you went on to this security work?
A. About 8 minutes.
Q. What was your rank when you started out?
A. First Lieutenant. I was a reserve officer in the field artillery by reason of graduation from VMI.
Q. After your interview of September 12, 1943, with Dr. Oppenheimer did you submit a copy of that to General Groves?
A. The record so shows. I have no present recollection of it.
Q. You have no doubt that you did?
A. I have no doubt that I did.
Q. Did you have any doubt that prior to doing that you read it over to make sure it was an accurate reflection of what had been said in your interview?
A. I have no doubt that I read it over and I would have made any changes that I felt were erroneous in substance, but as I remember that was a recording I would have made no attempt to correct English or reconstruct garbled portions.
Q. But had you found anything in there which was not in accord with what had been said? In other words, had the stenographer not correctly transcribed the recording, you would certainly have made the correction, would you not?
A. I can only say I am sure I would. We are reconstructing now. I have no present recollection.
Q. I don't expect you to recall now independently, Mr. Lansdale. But as your past memory recorded, you have no doubt that transcript was accurate, do you?
A. No; I really don't.
Q. Mr. Garrison asked you some questions about the scientific mind in relation to that interview that you had with Dr. Oppenheimer and you responded, I think, that Dr. Oppenheimer's attitude might well have been a manifestation of the workings of a scientific mind; is that correct?
A. Oh, yes; of which I came up against many examples.
Q. Dr. Oppenheimer has testified here before this board that he lied to you in that interview. You would not say that lying was one of the manifestations of a scientific mind, would you?
A. Not necessarily, no.
Q. It is not a characteristic——
A. It was certainly a characteristic to decide that I didn't need to have certain information.
Q. No. But the question is, Mr. Lansdale, you would not say that scientists as a group are liars, would you?
A. No. I don't think persons as a group are liars.
Q. No.
A. I certainly can't over emphasize, however, the extremely frustrating, almost maddening, let me say, tendency of our more brilliant people to extend in their own mind their competence and independence of decision in fields in which they have no competence.
Q. You were undertaking at the time you interviewed Dr. Oppenheimer to investigate what you believed to be a very serious attempt at espionage, is that right?
A. Yes. Let me put it this way. No. "Yes" is a fair answer.
Q. And Dr. Oppenheimer's refusal to give you the information that you asked him for was frustrating to you?
A. Oh; certainly.
Q. You felt that it seriously impeded your investigation, didn't you?
A. Certainly. But he wasn't the first one that impeded my investigation, nor the last.
Q. Mr. Lansdale, do you have any predisposition or feeling that you want to defend Dr. Oppenheimer here?
A. I have been trying to analyze my own feelings on that.
Q. I notice you volunteered that last remark, and I wondered why.
A. I know, and it was probably a mistake. I have attempted as nearly as I can—as nearly as it is possible—to be objective.
Q. Yes, sir.
A. I do feel strongly that Dr. Oppenheimer at least to the extent of my knowledge is loyal. I am extremely disturbed by the current hysteria of the times of which this seems to be a manifestation.
Q. You think this inquiry is a manifestation of hysteria?
A. I think——
Q. Yes or no?

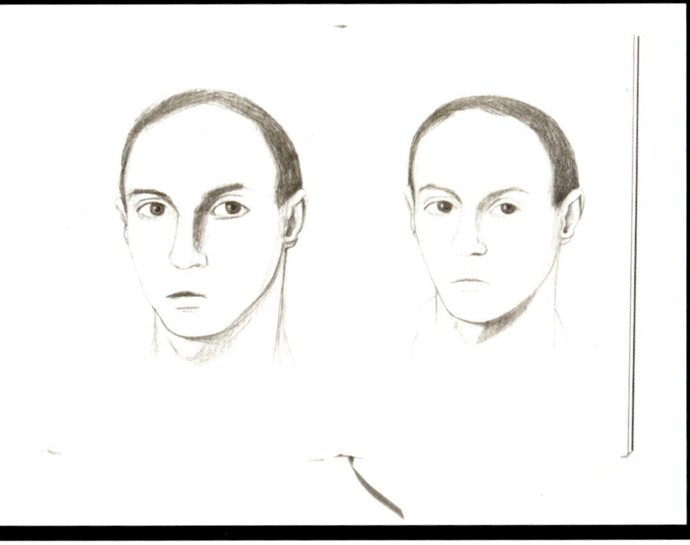

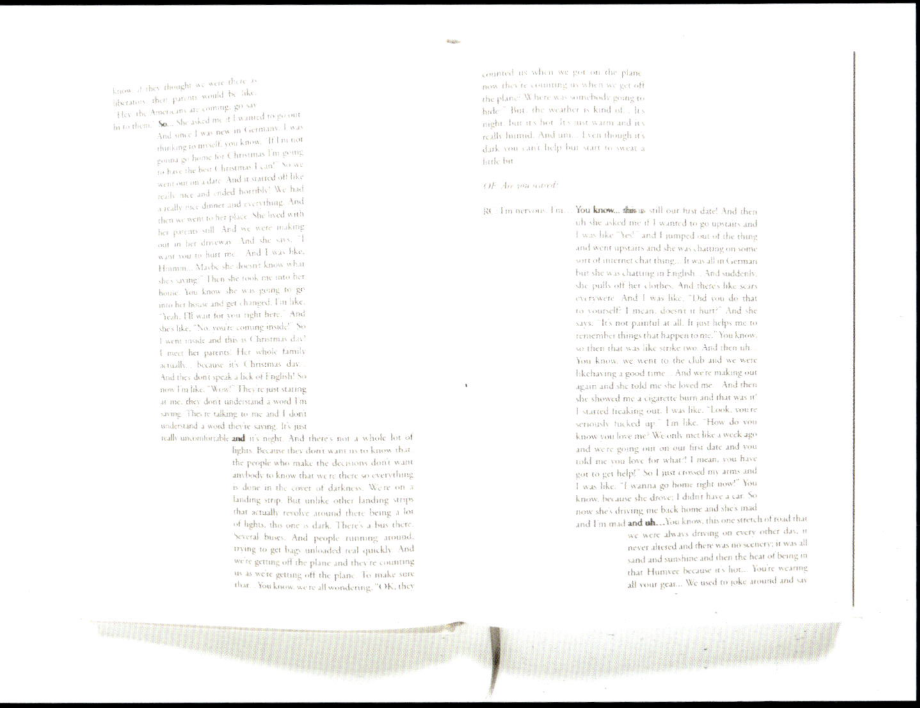
So... She asked me if I wanted to go out. And since I was new in Germany, I was thinking to myself, you know, "If I'm not gonna go home for Christmas I'm going to have the best Christmas I can!" So we went out on a date. And it started off like really nice and ended horrible! We had a really nice dinner and everything. And then we went to her place. She lived with her parents still. And we were making out in her driveway. And she says, "I want you to hurt me." And I was like, Hmmm... Maybe she doesn't know what she's saying." Then she took me into her house. You know she was going to go into her house and get changed. I'm like, "Yeah, I'll wait for you right here." And she's like, "No, you're coming inside!" So I went inside and this is Christmas day! I meet her parents! Her whole family actually... because it's Christmas day... And they don't speak a lick of English! So now I'm like: "Wow!" They're just staring at me, they don't understand a word I'm saying. They're talking to me and I don't understand a word they're saying. It's just really uncomfortable and it's night. And there's not a whole lot of lights. Because they don't want us to know that the people who make the decisions don't want anybody to know that we're there so everything is done in the cover of darkness. We're on a landing strip. But unlike other landing strips that actually revolve around there being a lot of lights, this one is dark. There's a bus there. Several buses. And people running around, trying to get bags unloaded real quickly. And we're getting off the plane and they're counting us as we're getting off the plane. To make sure that... You know, we're all wondering, "OK, they
counted us when we got on the plane now they're counting us when we get off the plane? Where was somebody going to hide?" But, the weather is kind of... It's night but it's hot. It's just warm and it's really humid. And um... Even though it's dark you can't help but start to sweat a little bit.
You know... this is still our first date! And then uh she asked me if I wanted to go upstairs and I was like "Yes!" and I jumped out of the thing and went upstairs and she was chatting on some sort of internet chat thing... It was all in German but she was chatting in English... And suddenly, she pulls off her clothes. And there's like scars everywere. And I was like, "Did you do that to yourself? I mean, doesn't it hurt?" And she says: "It's not painful at all. It just helps me to remember things that happen to me." You know, so then that was like strike two. And then uh... You know, we went to the club and we were likehaving a good time... And we're making out again and she told me she loved me. And then she showed me a cigarette burn and that was it! I started freaking out. I was like, "Look, you're seriously fucked up." I'm like, "How do you know you love me? We only met like a week ago and we're going out on our first date and you told me you love for what?! I mean, you have got to get help!" So I just crossed my arms and I was like: "I wanna go home right now!" You know, because she drove; I didn't have a car. So now she's driving me back home and she's mad and I'm mad and uh... You know, this one stretch of road that we were always driving on every other day, it never altered and there was no scenery; it was all sand and sunshine and then the heat of being in that Humvee because it's hot... You're wearing all your gear... We used to joke around and say

Give for Good - The Story of GiftCardGiver.com

Design Agency:

Russell Shaw Design

Designer:

Russell Shaw

Client:

Gift Card Giver

Production Date:

2010

Description:

Gift Card Giver is a revolutionary non-profit idea that collects unused or partially used gift cards and redistributes them as resources to people and organisations in need. This book is a promotional piece the designer created explaining the organisation's history, strategy, and goal.

Comment:

Gift Card Giver has a very clean and modern branding as well as a vibrant colour scheme. So this book was designed to match: to feel fresh and hopeful, a deliberate direction to differ - in style and imagery - from how many other non-profit organisations' marketing materials emphasise sympathy for despair. The designer wanted people to walk away from the book with positive feelings about the organisation and how they can get involved.

57 PERCENT OF ALL BIRTHDAY GIFTS ARE GIFT CARDS.

THE HOUSE PARTY

PHOTOGRAPHY BY: MICHELLE MARIE PHOTOGRAPHY

THE RESPONSE

"I am particularly moved by the generosity and downright friendliness of the people at Gift Card Giver. From all of us at the Evanston Children's Choir, thank you for reaching out to us and for doing what you do. The world needs more of this kind of thing!"

GARY GEIGER - DIRECTOR, EVANSTON CHILDREN'S CHOIR

"The Shining Stars Celebration Dinner celebrates the children we serve as well as the volunteers who love and mentor them. We could not have had this event this year (an event that impacts our children for years to come) without the Wal-Mart gift cards provided to us by our Gift Card Giver Campaign. Thank you!"

BIG BROTHERS BIG SISTERS

"With the gift cards provided, we were able to purchase all of our paint supplies for our next set of canvases... these canvases will allow us to raise a total of $50,000 and provide for 200 children in South Africa this year. The gift cards really will help change the lives of 200 children in Africa this year!"

LINDSEY TARQUINIO - FOUNDER, LUO

"Because of you, the Moving in the Spirit Apprentice Corporation experienced an extraordinary summer tour that they will never forget."

LORI TEAGUE - MOVING IN THE SPIRIT

$60,000 GIVEN TO PEOPLE IN NEED.

106 ORANIZATIONS SUPPORTED.

84 HOUSE PARTIES HOSTED.

26 NATIONAL MEDIA STORIES.

"I can't begin to tell you how much these gift cards will help on my daughter's medical travel expenses. They will pay for gas and food for many days! It is such a humbling experience to be on the receiving end of such a blessing. Gift Card Giver has helped so much more than you could know. It may help keep us from sleeping in the car!"

THE TRAEGER FAMILY, ALABAMA

"When we discovered giftcardgiver.com it was a true blessing! The need is on the rise for food and giftcardgiver.com came through with many needed gift cards."

REV. BETH DICKINSON - VININGS UNITED METHODIST CHURCH

"Thank you so much for the gift cards... With Gift Card Giver's donation, we were able to buy supplies for making bracelets, art/watercolor activities, and hygiene supplies."

JODY ELSLAGER - GUATEMALAN MISSION TRIP LEADER

"In a world where needs seem to be so great, Gift Card Giver has found a unique way of taking care of the small needs that often seem to get overlooked by the big picture. I am extremely thankful to Gift Card Giver for enabling us to remove several of the obstacles from establishing our neighborhood garden."

JEFF DELP - EXECUTIVE DIRECTOR, FCS COMMUNITY ECONOMIC DEVELOPMENT

PHOTOGRAPH BY: MICHELLE MARIE PHOTOGRAPHY

THE FOUNDERS

When Andre and I were preparing for marriage eight years ago, we dreamt of creating a fund to help others in great need. If a friend needed to fix a car, we could pitch in. If a homeless neighbor needed a meal, we could provide. If a house in our community caught on fire, we could aid in the restoration process. Our dream for a fund to help others in need has since grown into something that looks a little different than what we first imagined. We started Gift Card Giver, a non-profit organization that collects unused gift cards and gives them to people and organizations in need. We began small, giving only to unique needs in our Atlanta neighborhood. But as our dream continued to grow, Gift Card Giver has turned into a national community of donors, contributing gift cards from all across the nation, and we are currently giving directly to various national and international organizations in great need. From sex trafficking to natural disasters, stolen goods to needed supplies, we have been able to provide hope and love to many in the midst of their suffering through the donation and collection of gift cards. On behalf of the individuals and organizations touched by your generous giving, thank you for your continued and loving support.

Jeff & Andre Shinabarger
GiftCardGiver.com

Across Singapore

Design Agency:
sciencewerk
Designer:
Octavia S.
Client:
sciencewerk
Production Date:
2010
Description:
Across Singapore is a visual publication project visualising the hustle and bustle of Singapore, from the city, MRT, to suburb areas.

ATTENTION please,
FOR YOUR SAFETY,
PLEASE HOLD THE HANDRAIL
WHEN USING THE ESCALATOR

Street Corner Symphony

sorry
[watch your step!]
[hel!]

Unspoken conversation. Is it exist? It is. During peak hour morning, lunch time, evening, noone talks each other while crossing the platform or moving to another line, mostly, just for being fast to reach their destination. There is a mute conversation. Communicating in mute. Conversing by stepping on the floor, they want to say something.
Something like an alert to give them a way because they are in a hurry. Some steps move to the side to give a way, but not all. Conversation through step

Hipsters : A World Without Them

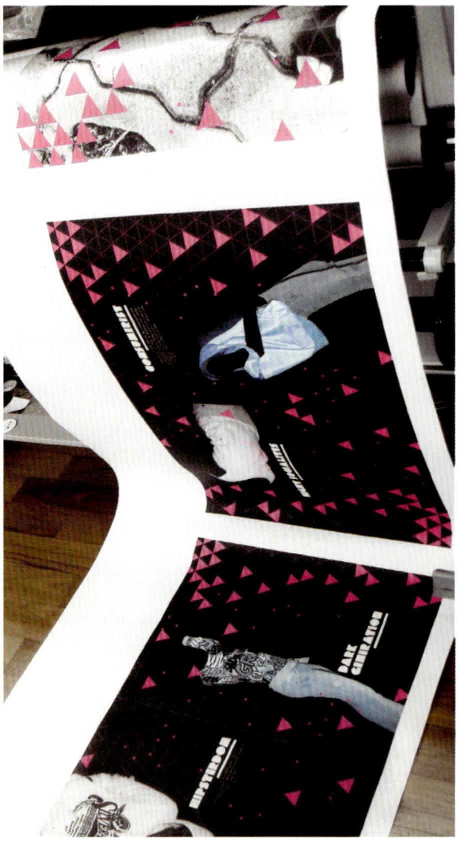

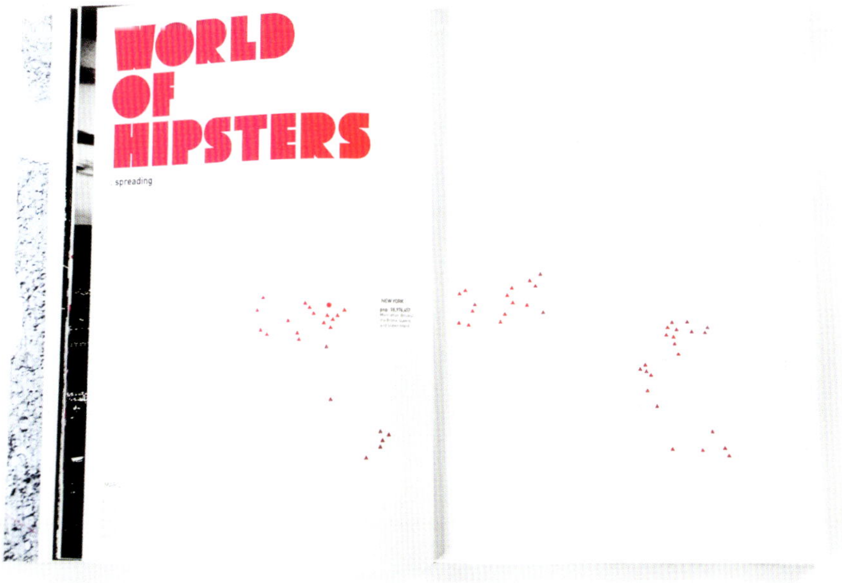

Design Agency:

sciencewerk

Designer:

Octavia S.

Client:

sciencewerk

Production Date:

2010

Description:

It is a publication that explores about Hipster. "Hipster" has been used in sometimes contradictory ways, making it difficult to precisely define "hipster culture" because it is a "mutating, trans-Atlantic melting pot of styles, tastes and behaviour[s]."

Comment:

One commentator argues that "hipsterism fetishises the authentic" elements of all of the "fringe movements of the postwar era—beat, hippie, punk, even grunge", and draws on the "cultural stores of every unmelted ethnicity", and "regurgitates it with a winking inauthenticity". Others, like Arsel and Thompson, argue that hipster is a cultural mythology, crystallisation of a mass mediated stereotype generated to understand, categorise and marketise the indie consumer culture rather than an objectified group of people.

Tranquility

Design Agency:

sciencewerk

Designer:

Octavia S.

Client:

sciencewerk

Production Date:

2009

Description:

Tranquility is a visual book portraying moment of free from disturbance. Visuals at every page that illustrate images sound louder than words.

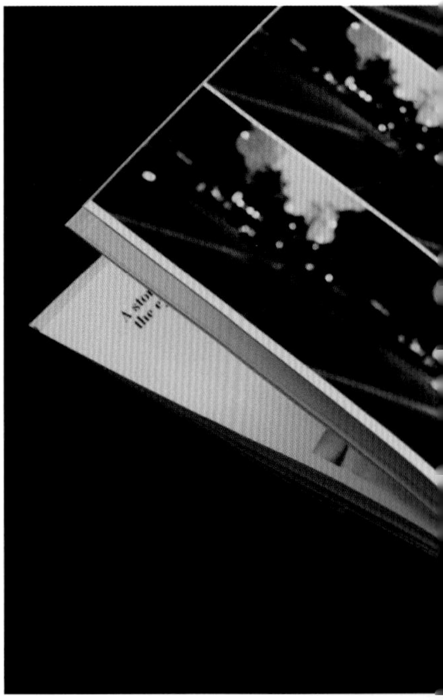

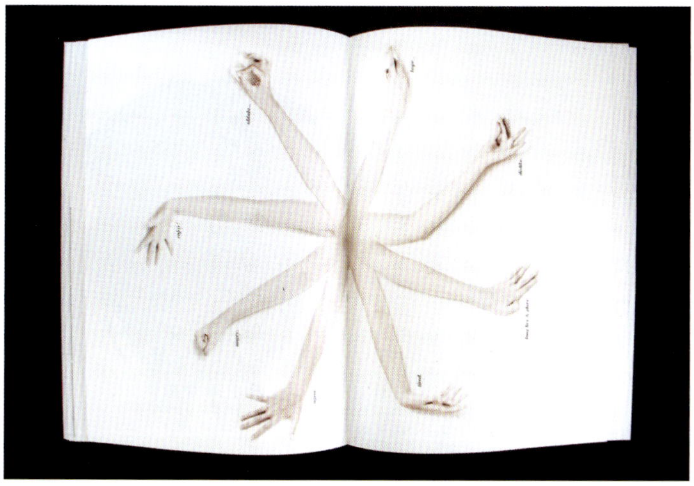

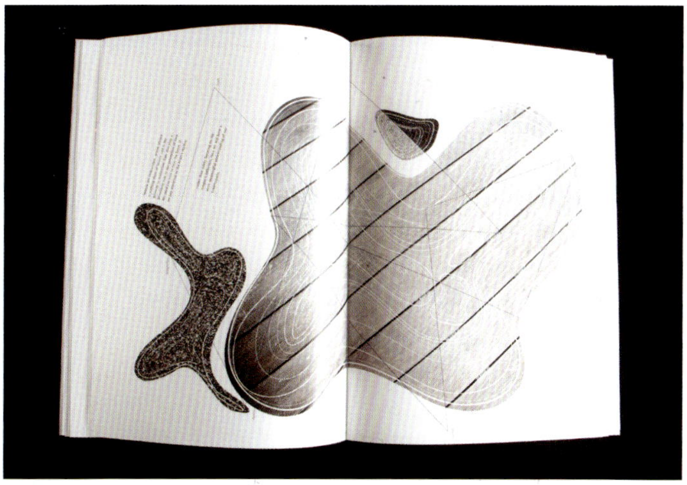

One to Ten

Designer:

Sergio Alves

Client:

self-promotion

Production Date:

2009

Description:

Book where Sergio Alves joins his ten best projects of 2008. The book was made for him manually, since the cover was made with cloth, until the stitching. This project reflects how design is ephemeral, because in a year the works patient there are no longer goods for him.

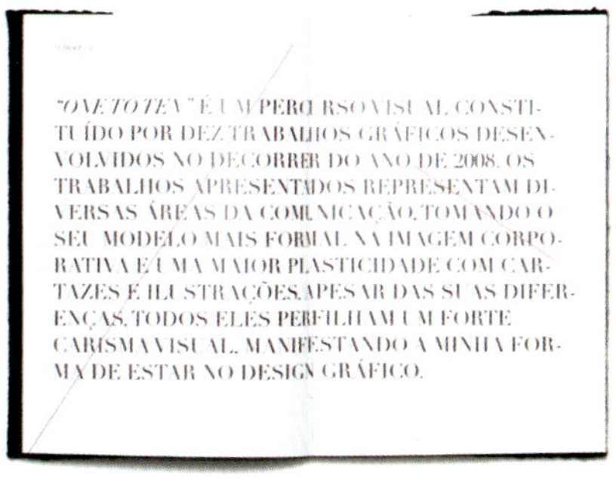
"ONE TO TEN" É UM PERCURSO VISUAL CONSTITUÍDO POR DEZ TRABALHOS GRÁFICOS DESENVOLVIDOS NO DECORRER DO ANO DE 2008. OS TRABALHOS APRESENTADOS REPRESENTAM DIVERSAS ÁREAS DA COMUNICAÇÃO, TOMANDO O SEU MODELO MAIS FORMAL NA IMAGEM CORPORATIVA E UMA MAIOR PLASTICIDADE COM CARTAZES E ILUSTRAÇÕES. APESAR DAS SUAS DIFERENÇAS, TODOS ELES PERFILHAM UM FORTE CARISMA VISUAL, MANIFESTANDO A MINHA FORMA DE ESTAR NO DESIGN GRÁFICO.

Shapeshifters: Shaping Fashion Silhouettes

SELMA
BERISALIC

Born in Sarajevo, Bosnia-Herzegovina, Selma Berisalic's work explores the modern female experience, appropriating both feminine and masculine elements in her designs. Her award-winning collection Starfinger is a combination of both the hard and soft; the austere and luxurious; the impenetrable and plaint. The eye-catching, almost bizarre outer shape is offset by the delicate inner lining of the outfit.

Inspired by ancient Chinese philosophy and the history of silk in China, the moody, mysterious and dramatic silhouettes hint at the secretive cocoon of a silkworm, or a rough-edged yet bulbous oriental fan, contributing further to the abstract chinoiserie references.

Using mainly material with sturdy, metallic properties on the outside to hold the structure and soft silk on the inside, lined with down for cushioning, Berisalic combines two disparate fabrics in Starfinger, complementing each other in perfect harmony like *yin* and *yang* elements of the culture that inspired it. The garments emphasise the sensual with the flowing texture of silk and exaggerated womanly contours, yet embrace harder, more masculine elements in their colour, severity in shape, and hardwearing black material.

From Starfinger,
Autumn/Winter 2009/2010

Designer:

Shiwei Ng

Client:

Page One Publishing Pte Ltd

Production Date:

2010

Description:

In the hands of today's most experimental fashion designers, the human silhouette is being radically reshaped and the boundaries between fashion, art, sculpture and architecture, fascinatingly redrawn. Shapeshifters showcases a range of inspiring and visually-arresting designs from all over the world. From bulbous and voluminous to austere and angular, the looks presented will be provocative, exquisite and sumptuous, and will intrigue with their demonstration of the structural potential of clothing. Displaying astonishingly architectural concepts that are graphically striking and sculptural.

IRINA SHAPOSHNIKOVA

The ability of fashion to articulate an opinion, a mood, or a whole worldview underlines the Antwerp-based designer's approach to her craft. The sense of connection between the wearer and the outside world is mediated by clothing that expresses a vision of that world. While this vision may sometimes be political, they are never straightforward statements, but suggestions open to interpretations.

The architectural geometry and futuristic feel of Shaposhnikova's work articulates a modern, graphic sensibility. For the collection Crystallographica, the choice of textiles was important to achieve Shaposhnikova's goal of sharp, geometric planar surfaces. The allusions drawn are both mathematical and architectural: the garments most strongly evoke architecture with sleek, shiny facades of steel and glass as well as the strictly proportioned cut surfaces of a perfect diamond. Yet the fabrics chosen were extremely soft ones: wool, silk organza, jersey and high-tech, slippery fabrics. To create the ideal solidity, plastic was used to provide structure. Depending on the material, the thickness of the plastic varied. The final result likens an urban high-rise building, where transparency and light are built on angular structures. Already critically acclaimed, Crystallographica catapulted the young designer to the top of lists of emerging designers to watch out for.

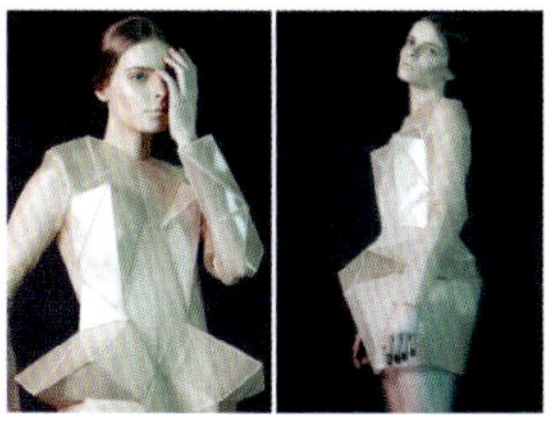

JULIA KNÜPFER

Julia Knüpfer's work expresses the current preoccupation of the fashion industry with producing clothing with a conscience. With a strong artistic vision that embraces social responsibility, Knüpfer showcases her marked affection for architecture and nature in her collections with a distinctive, dramatic style that celebrates the beauty of our fragile surroundings.

All beautifully crafted by hand, Knüpfer's work exhibits a rare harmony of structural meticulousness and earthly fluidity. Traditional handicraft, especially knitting, is a consistent feature of the collections. This has resulted in boldly beautiful items with compelling shapes, bringing with them a refreshing, modern twist to the craft technique more commonly associated with twee folk styles.

Every piece in her repertoire is carefully sculpted down to its smallest detail and made with premium organic cotton, silk, linen and wool. This is not a simple process: every fabric's fibres are first evaluated for their cultivation, processing and finishing, before deciding how they can fit harmoniously into the collection. Natural dying methods and an insistence on local production are also important aspects in Knüpfer's label, icawatermelon, making clear her firm commitment to society and the environment.

Living Rooms is inspired by natural dwellings and constructions built by birds and insects: nests, caves, nets, mussels and corals. Seeking to define natural living space and habitat, the collection focuses on techniques of weaving and braiding of fabrics. The nest was particularly interesting to Knüpfer who interpreted its forms for the collection's silhouettes and fabric treatments. This is apparent in the crocheted portions of the garments.

MASHALLAH DESIGN & LINDA KOSTOWSKI

The ubiquitous T-shirt becomes dramatically reconfigured in the hands of Mashallah Design (Hande Akcayli and Murat Kocyigit), whose collaboration with designer Linda Kostowski resulted in a fresh, visionary approach to the wardrobe staple. Embracing technology while employing an emotional, poetic sensibility, the designers rejected conventions of garment construction like the front piece and the shape of an armhole, radically opening up new arenas for artistic expression.

The T-shirt Issue is the first collaborative effort between the former schoolmates. They tapped into the unconscious of three individuals - Paul, Markus and Linda - whose memories and imaginations gave form to each jersey-knit sweater. Striving for innovation in pattern development, Mashallah Design and Kostowski first digitally scanned the bodies of their models to convert the three-dimensionality of the human silhouette to a two-dimensional sewing pattern. These were then expanded and manipulated according to the testimonies of the models. The final pieces have numbers for names.

No. 419 embodies the imagination of Markus who dreams of being raised by wolves: "The wolf would have accompanied my nocturnal wanderings, would have eagerly shared [...] my thunderous sighs." No. 378 is the digital twin of Paul, who recounts his first experience of swimming, fearing the air in his float would leak. No. 318 documents Linda's encounter with an inspiring model who changed her life as a designer.

The flat, angular surfaces of the garments are a literal interpretation of the technology of computers: the polygons represent pixilation and resolution. Executed in sweatshirt jersey (a reference to Berlin's reputation of being the city where T-shirt design is the primary sartorial output), the final fabric pieces were unfolded digitally (a function commonly employed in industrial design), cut out by lasercutter Martin Bauer and finally sewn together.

No. 419,
The T-shirt Issue, 2008

Fellowship - Collected Works

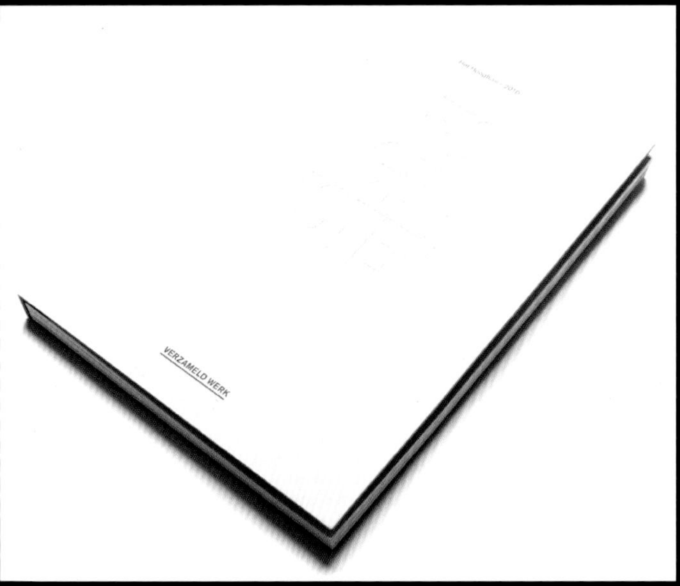

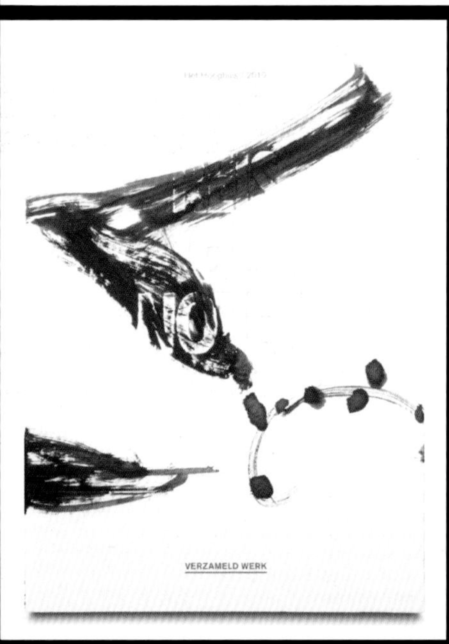

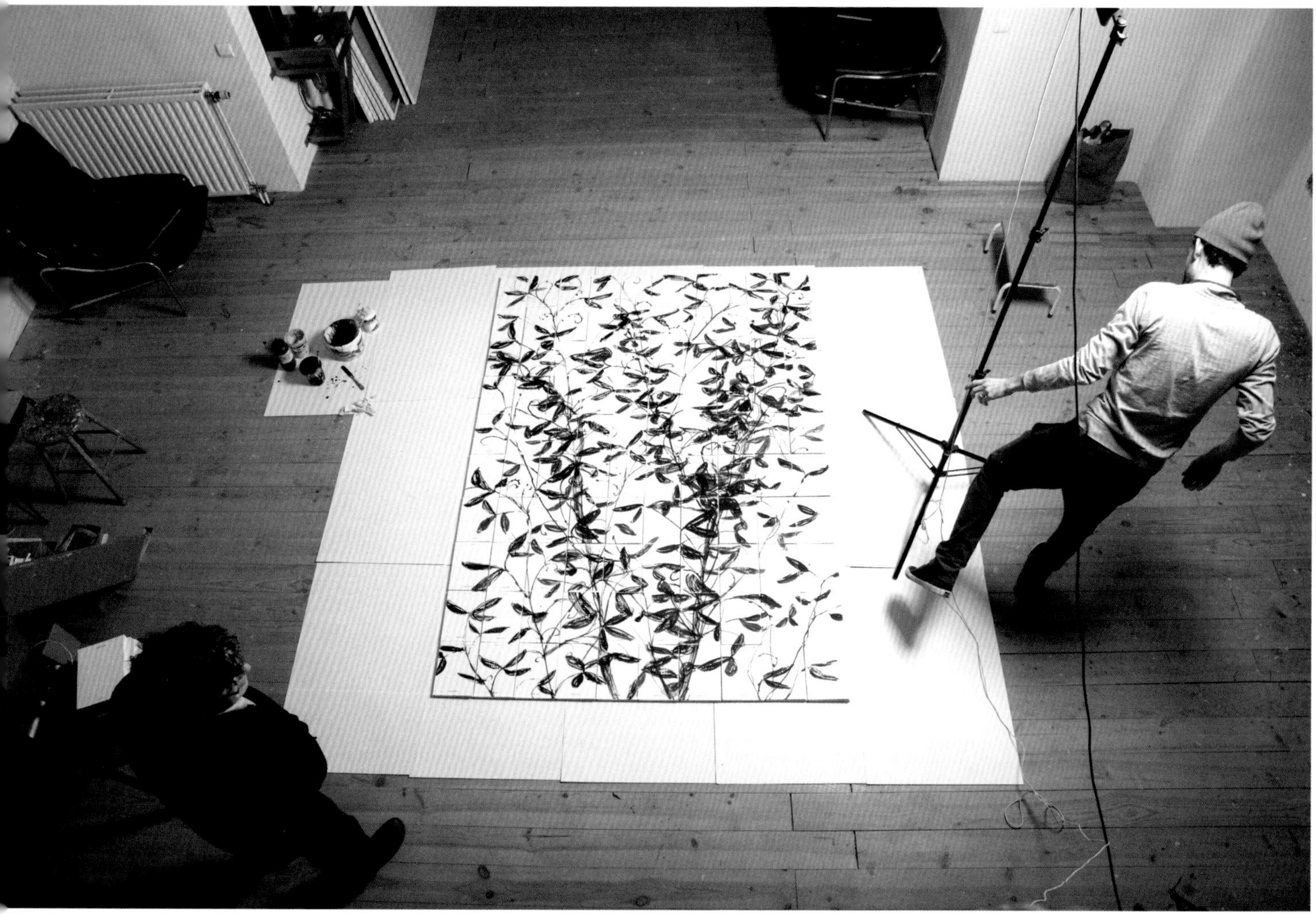

Design Agency:

Since 1416, Graphic Design & Visual Research

Designer:

Dirk Claessens, Maarten Verweij, Kees de Klein

Client:

Het Hooghuis

Production Date:

2010

Description:

In September 2009 a number of people were invited to contribute to the liber amicorum in honour of the retirement of Henk Peters, an inspiring school leader in the city of Oss, the Netherlands. The theme - collaboration & connection - has been approached from the perspective of the different authors. The diversity of the design (paper, layout, typography) is based on the diversity of the textual content. A constant factor in the book is the work of fine artist Han Klinkhamer. His work draws a trail through the book and embraces the individual texts. Besides dozens of paintings of farmer fields scattered through the publication, Klinkhamer has signed the first 100 books by a painting. In his studio 100 publications were arranged into a blank canvas, each book got a unique cover.

Het Hooghuis / 2010
REIS
GE
NOTEN
VERZAMELD WERK
Liber amicorum,
een uitgave van Het Hooghuis
ter ere van het afscheid
van Henk Peters.
Het Hooghuis / 2010

EEN GOLF EN ZIJN ZEE
60

Tekenen
van leven
Schetsboek van
een reiziger
120

Het Hooghuis · Reisgenoten
SAMENWERKEN
& VERBINDEN,
EEN SIAMESE
TWEELING
VERWACHTING
& REALITEIT
Thomas van Hees
100

Passing on the Anvil: From Smith to Industrial Metalworker

Design Agency:

Since 1416, Graphic Design & Visual Research

Designer:

Dirk Claessens, Maarten Verweij

Client:

Het Hooghuis

Production Date:

2010

Description:

It is a book about the current state of the metal industry in the historic town of Oss.

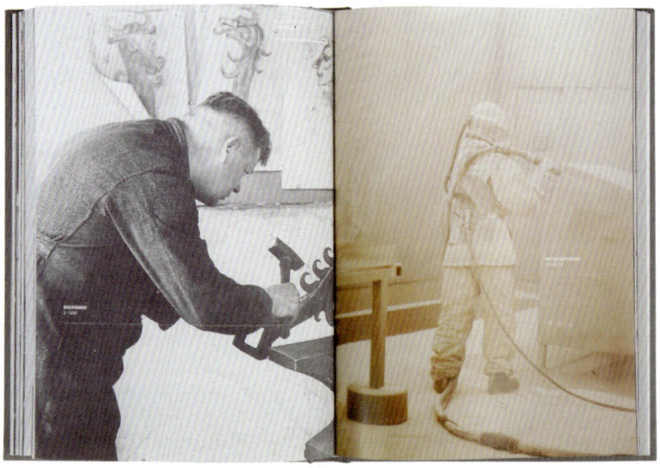

SLAGEN OP HET AAMBEELD
DE PREHISTORIE
POTJES EN PLANKJES
Gedurende de middenijzertijd (500-250 v. Chr.) verandert er niet veel in de omgeving Oss-Ussen. Naar schatting wonen er dertig mensen, waarschijnlijk allemaal familie van elkaar. Ook op het gebied van aardewerk dat men voor de dagelijkse gang van zaken gebruikt, doen zich geen schokkende ontwikkelingen voor. Het wordt nog altijd door de bewoners zelf vervaardigd en soms versierd. Wel kan uit diverse vondsten worden opgemaakt dat er een begin wordt gemaakt met zuivelproductie. Zo zijn er potten gevonden met houten plankjes als afsluiting en potten met gaten die misschien als vergiet dienden bij het maken van kaas. Een opvallende vondst is verder een driedelig schijfwiel van eikenhout, dat waarschijnlijk gebruikt werd onder twee- of vierwielige wagens, voortgetrokken door twee ossen.
DE GROEI GAAT DOOR
In tegenstelling tot in de middenijzertijd maken de bewoners van Ussen in de late ijzertijd een reeks veranderingen mee. Het aantal erven neemt licht toe tot zeven, en op elk erf wonen naar schatting rond de veertig mensen in diverse boerderijen. Ook komen er verschillende typen boerderijen, steeds dichter bij elkaar gelegen. Landbouw en veeteelt blijven nog steeds de belangrijkste bron van bestaan, maar men eet vlierbessen, bramen, hazelnoten en sleeprumen als variatie of aanvulling op het al bestaande menu. In de late ijzertijd wordt uiteindelijk het verschil kenbaar tussen de dorpjes in Ussen. De een groter en belangrijker dan de ander: het begin van wat we tegenwoordig stad en dorp zouden noemen.
SLAGEN OP HET AAMBEELD
DE PREHISTORIE
De smid is de eerste die van zijn beroep kan leven.

SLAGEN OP HET AAMBEELD
INDUSTRIALISATIE (1870-WOII)
Niet alleen het dagelijkse leven verandert aanzienlijk door de industrialisatie, ook de metaalbewerker staat aan de vooravond van een nieuw tijdperk.
SLAGEN OP HET AAMBEELD
INDUSTRIALISATIE (1870-WOII)
Industrialisatie (1870-WOII)
EEN VERSCHUIVING VAN ARBEID
Voor het tijdperk van de industrialisatie hadden de mensen in Oss, en ook in andere streken van het land, het vaak niet al te best. De opkomst van de industrie verandert de Osse samenleving echter ingrijpend. Het agrarische leven maakt plaats voor arbeid in de vele fabrieken die na 1850 ontstaan. Niet alleen het dagelijkse leven verandert aanzienlijk door de industrialisatie, ook de metaalbewerker staat aan de vooravond van een nieuw tijdperk.
In het vorige hoofdstuk bleek al dat de welvaart in Oss rond 1850 gestaag toeneemt. De meeste gezinnen uit deze tijd zijn echter groot en daardoor vaak arm. Boerenbedrijfjes zijn te klein om fatsoenlijk van te kunnen leven, dus de welvaart groeit niet zoals men eigenlijk zou willen. Aan de andere kant groeit het bedrijfsleven in deze tijd enorm. Naast de bestaande boterfabriek van Jurgens, komt ook de familie Van den Bergh om de hoek kijken. Ook in hun winkel wordt bij gebrek aan contant geld vaak met boter betaald, waardoor hoofd van het gezin, Simon van den Bergh, een gouden handel in boter kan starten. Door de stijgende welvaart in Engeland, stijgt ook de vraag naar boter. Jurgens en Van den Bergh grijpen deze gelegenheid en groeien beiden uit tot Europa's grootste boterhandelaren. Maar dit natuurproduct is in deze tijd erg kostbaar en er komt vraag naar een goedkoper alternatief. Jurgens start met de productie van kunstboter - margarine - en niet veel later komt ook de familie Van den Bergh met eenzelfde product op de markt. Overigens lijkt het erop dat de komst van deze bedrijven als inspiratiebron diende voor andere ondernemers. Niet lang na de oprichting van Jurgens en Van den Bergh ontstaan de exportslachterijen Hartog en Zwanenberg. Wederom twee bedrijven die van grote invloed zijn op het maatschappelijk leven van dat moment.
087

Startgids

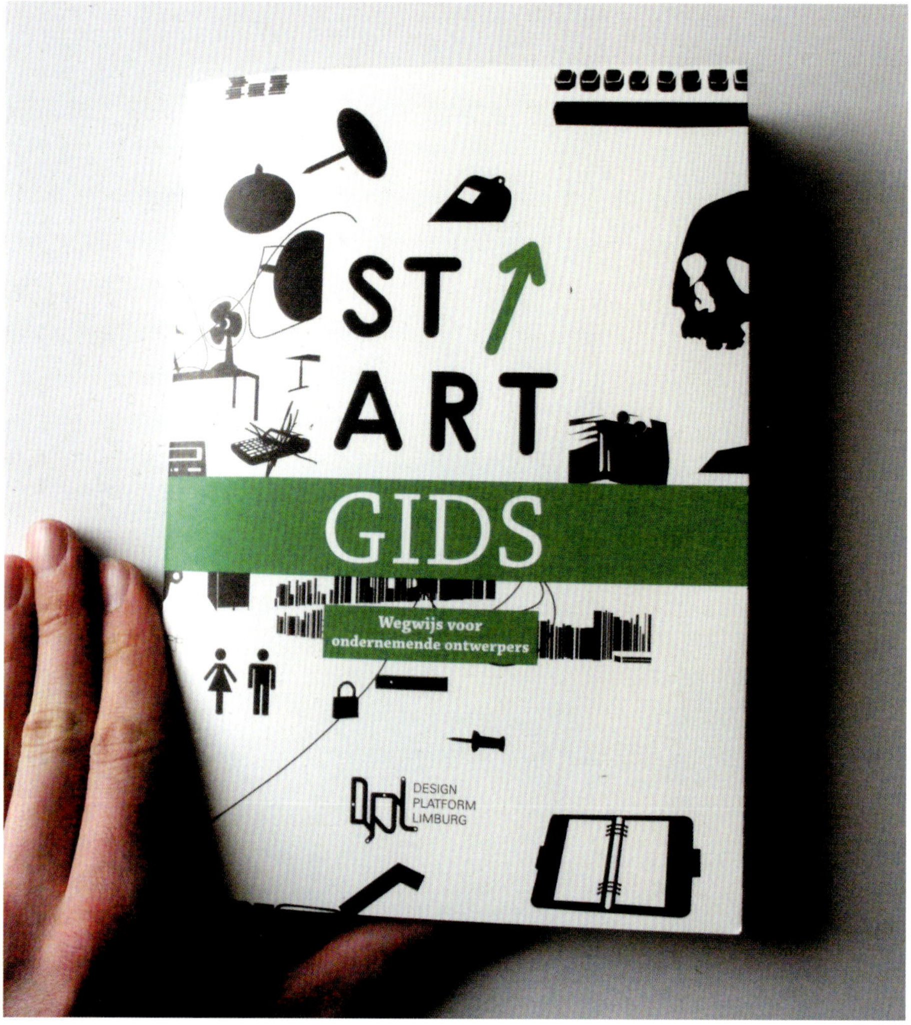

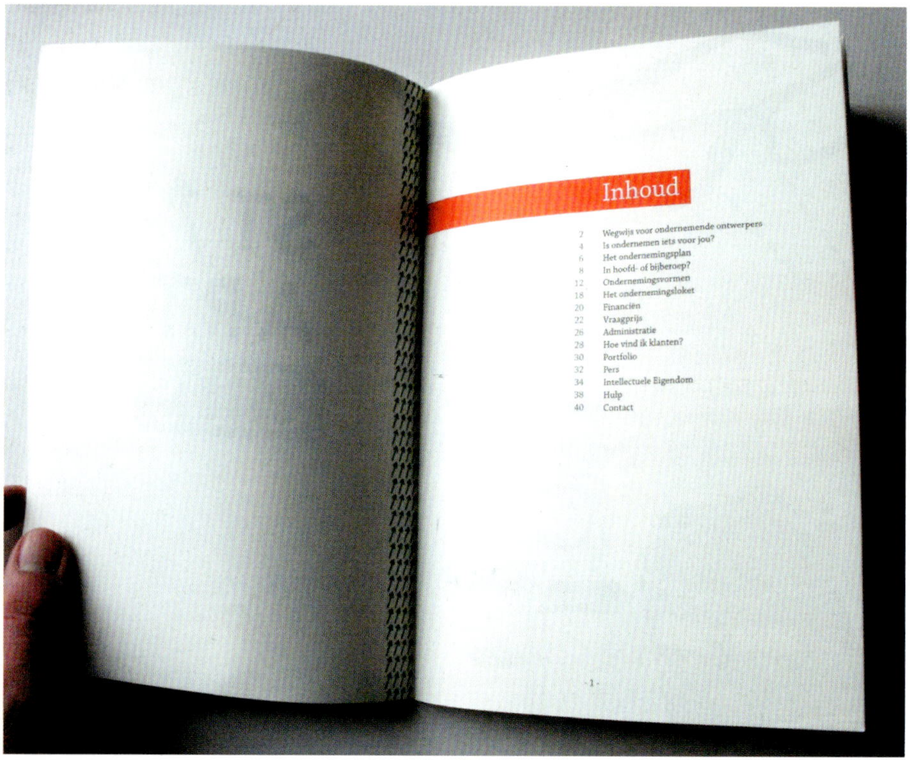

Design Agency:
Jens Dawn
Designer:
Jens Dawn
Client:
Design Platform Limburg
Production Date:
2009
Description:
The Startgids is a guide for college graduated designers in Belgium to give advice about starting a design practice.

This guide contains two changing colours and black throughout the book; this makes it cheaper to print (also cheaper for the client). Two colours are more relaxing for the eyes and therefore Jens Dawn think are beneficial in reading. The illustrations are a collection of wild subjective inspiration taken from the titles (topics) in the guide. The cover is the "work in progress" page of the illustrations that combine all the topics together.

The book got printed with 2,000 copies and got sent to the Dutch-speaking designers who finished their years in college. In March 2011, the guide got updated and had a new printing of another 2,000 copies.

Contact

Financiën

Het onder-
nemingsplan

Vraagprijs

Is ondernemen
iets voor jou ?

Het ondernem-
ingsloket

2009 Graduation Book

Design Agency:

Studio Boot

Client:

2009 Graduation Book

Production Date:

2009

Description:

It is the art direction photography and book design of graduation catalogue in 2009.

Zelf Geoogst

Design Agency:

Studio Boot

Client:

Zelfgeoogst

Production Date:

2010

Description:

After "The Netherlands to the Soup" received the bestseller soup calendar, its publisher Moustache now works with the book "Self Harvested" on super easy garden poultry in crates. The authors know the subject so well that you immediately rolled up sleeves to stabbing. The revolutionary method of vegetable garden boxes, the fifty original recipes for harvest Marian Flint and the beautiful design of Studio Boot guaranteed the success in the garden and even on the balcony.

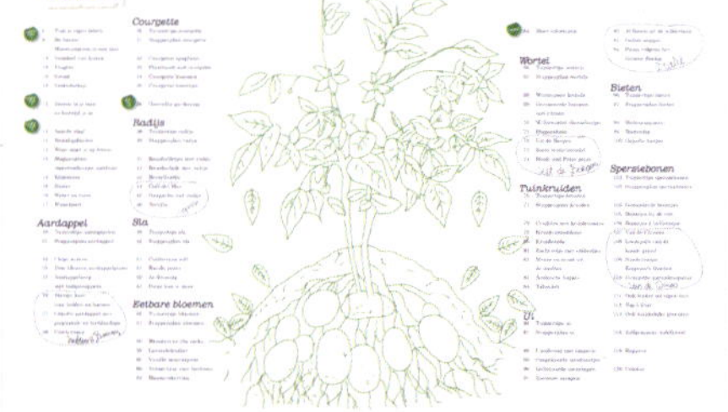

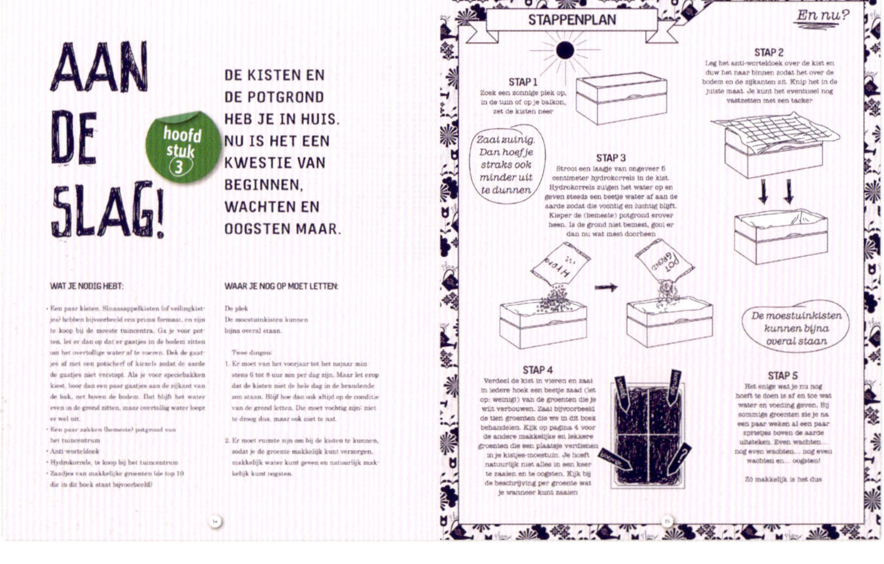

STEVIGE KOST VOOR HELDEN EN BOEVEN

Wie hard werkt in de buitenlucht, verdient een stevige maaltijd. Cowboysoep die smaakt alsof je hem op een houtvuurtje hebt gekookt. Eet 'm met pittige chilibroodjes. Enne... couchpotatoes vinden 'm ook lekker.

RECEPT

De tortillachips kun je als 'lepel' gebruiken om de aardappel leeg te eten

Gepofte aardappels met guacamole en zelfgemaakte tortillachips

xxxxxxxxxxxxxxxxxxxxxxxxxxxxxxxx

ZELFGEOOGST
- 4 aardappels
- 1 handje koriander, wassen, steeltjes eraf en fijnhakken
- 1/4 rode peper, zonder pitjes, fijnhakken
- 1 tomaat, wassen, zaden eruit, in heel kleine blokjes snijden

UIT HET KEUKENKASTJE
- aluminiumfolie
- zout en peper uit de molen

UIT DE WINKEL
- 1 rijpe avocado, pit eruit, leegscheppen, fijnprakken met limoensap
- crème fraîche
- 1 tortilla, in puntjes snijden en bakken in een beetje olie
- sap van limoen

xxxxxxxxxxxxxxxxxxxxxxxxxxxxxxxx

ZO MAAK JE HET

Verwarm de oven voor op 200°C (heteluchtoven 180°C).
Boen de aardappels met schil schoon en droog ze af. Vouw in aluminiumfolie en leg op een bakplaat in het midden van de oven. Ze hebben ± 50 minuten nodig om gaar te worden. Misschien zelfs wel langer. Controleer of de aardappels gaar zijn door erin te prikken. Haal ze uit de oven. Snij de aardappel van boven kruislings in en breek verder open met je handen. Pas op: heet!!!
Meng 1 eetlepel crème fraîche met de geprakte avocado, koriander, rode peper en tomaat.
Proef en voeg zout en peper naar smaak toe.
Vul de aardappel met een klodder guacamole.
Steek er een paar zelfgemaakte tortillachipjes in.

RECEPT

Cowboysoep

VOOR 4-6 PERSONEN

xxxxxxxxxxxxxxxxxxxxxxxxxxxxxxxx

ZELFGEOOGST
- 2 aardappels, schillen en in kleine stukjes snijden
- 1 ui, snipperen
- paar takjes koriander, wassen, blaadjes eraf

UIT HET KEUKENKASTJE
- 2 eetlepel olijfolie
- 2 bouillonblokjes (kip), voor 1 liter bouillon
- zout en peper uit de molen

UIT DE WINKEL
- 1 blik maïs
- 1 blik red kidneybeans
- paar eetlepels crème fraiche

EXTRA NODIG
- staafmixer

xxxxxxxxxxxxxxxxxxxxxxxxxxxxxxxx

ZO MAAK JE HET

Fruit de ui in de olie tot deze goudgeel en glazig is. Voeg de maïs en de bouillon toe. Breng tegen de kook aan en laat een tijdje zachtjes koken.
Pureer de soep grof. Voeg de aardappelblokjes toe. Laat zachtjes koken. Als de aardappels gaar zijn, voeg je de bonen toe. Die zijn al gaar, dus die kook je kort mee – tot ze goed warm zijn. Verdeel de soep over vier kommen en schep in elke kom een lepel crème fraiche. Bestrooi met korianderblaadjes.
Lekker met tortilla chips en (voor volwassenen of pittige kinderen): een eetlepel zoete chilisaus per kom.

Tip

xxxxxxxxxxxxxxx

Met kant-en-klare broodmix kun je chilibroodjes maken. Kneed door het deeg een halve fijngehakte rode peper mee. Kneed of wikkel het deeg om een stok en bak boven de vuurkorf.
Of maak er als je driehoog achter woont, langwerpige broodjes van. Die bak je in 20-30 min knapperig in een oven van 175°C.

Small Book

vrline
zapadne
civilizacije
Art Grabov

art grabov vrline zapadne civilizacije

vrline
zapadne
civilizacije

vrline
zapadne
civilizacije
Art Grabov

Art Grabov
VRLINE
ZAPADNE
CIVILIZACIJE

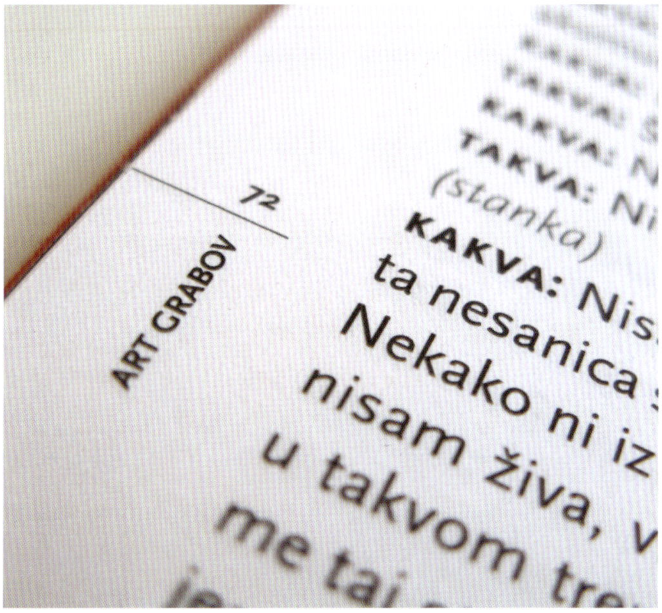

Design Agency:

Studio Revolucija

Designer:

Vladimir Končar

Client:

Kristalna Kocka Vedrine, Dom Kulture Sisak

Production Date:

2008

Description:

This book has a cover which is a poster on one side and a part of a big illustration on the other. When all four of those covers are put together, they make one big illustration. The fourth book is in the process of making. The entire books are done with the Scala Sans and cover titles are made with the Officina Serif. Paper used for press is Agripina / Maxioffset.

Szembeszélo

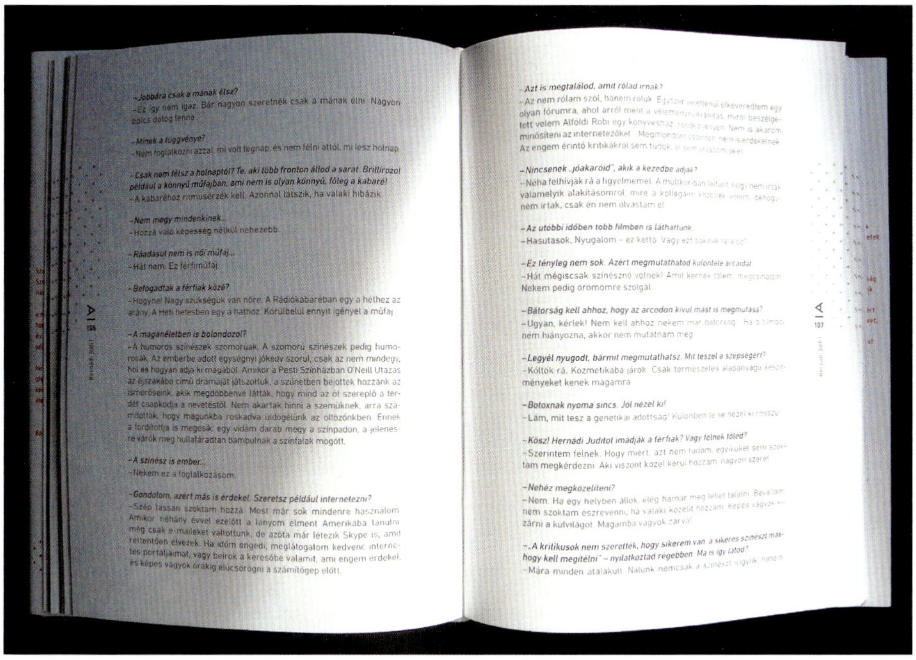

Designer:

Márton Borzák, Réka Diósi

Client:

BT-Press

Production Date:

2010

Description:

The book was designed to feature 30 interviews and stories with famous Hungarian people. Actors, writers and many other well-known people share unique and interesting stories about their lives. The cover was divided into several pieces using recursive tiling algorithm to represent the structure of the book: various stories in various lengths.

All Green, Let's Stay Together, Diary 2011

Design Agency:

Studio Beige

Designer:

Jens Dawn

Client:

Self promotion project in cooperation with Shop Around and PrintvisieWork

Production Date:

2010

Description:

Having difficulty keeping track of time? Keep forgetting your appointments? Desperate to live a greener life, but still in for a laugh? Have no fear, the answer is near: Studio Beige designed the instant must-have classic: "All Green, Let's Stay Together Diary 2011", in collaboration with Shop Around and Printvisie. The diary contains tons of helpful information on how to get your life into green mode, interesting interviews and lots of hilarious - as well as deep - green quotes.

#02
SUPER GREEN INVENTIONS THAT WILL HOPEFULLY SAVE THE EARTH!

YOUR PERSONAL DIARY FOR 2011 & VISUAL GUIDE TO BECOME GREENER

"SEX IS A PART OF NATURE."
"I GO ALONG WITH NATURE."

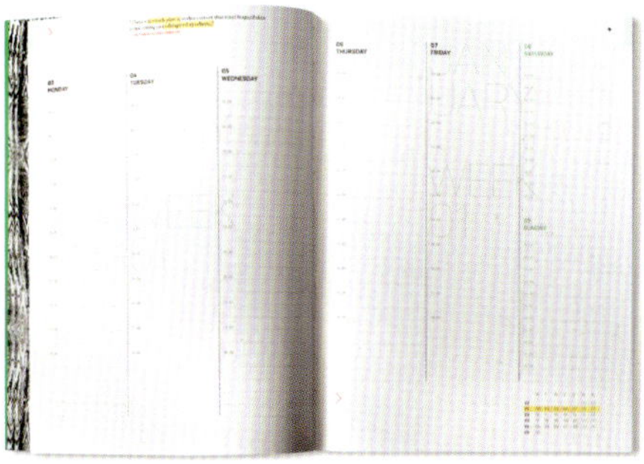

— DAVID LETTERMAN TELEVISION HOST/ COMEDIAN
"Fall is my favorite season in Los Angeles, watching the birds change color and fall from the trees."

Sweet Life, Anne Wenzel

Design Agency:
Studio Beige
Client:
Anne Wenzel
Production Date:
2008
Description:
Anne Wenzel's catalogue Sweet Life showcases her, often sizeable, black clay sculptures. Her works focus on "the aesthetics of darkness, the entrails of kitsch". Studio Beige designed a beautifully bound book with a hard cover coated with black paper. On this cover a negative photographic image was printed in white ink on which a silkscreen print was superimposed in shiny lacquer. It constitutes a smart link to the work itself. The title is foil printed in pink - the only colour Anne Wenzel embraces in her work.

ANNE WENZEL
SWEET LIFE

INTERVIEW

Olaf Mooij | 1189.81.237

Design Agency:
Studio Beige
Client:
Olaf Mooij
Production Date:
2010
Description:
Dutch artist Olaf Mooij focuses on redefining the meaning of existing objects. In the Netherlands he's well known for his car sculptures.

Mooij's work is firmly rooted in the sculptural tradition. At the basis of all his sculptures lies the artist's ability to suggest life using only dead matter.

Olaf Mooij's cars consist of nothing more than mere bodywork, yet he finds a way to shape them into personalities, into living objects.

Studio Beige designed a beautiful book inspired by vintage car manuals, using soft skincolours which Mooij frequently uses in his work as well as bold typography. The book aspires to be a one man exhibition in print.

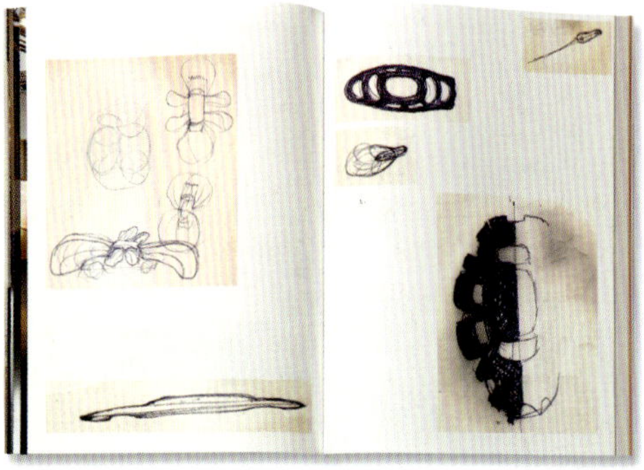

1189.81.237

BEFORE AND AFTER
_MARIETTE DÖLLE

De Rotterdamse kunstenaar Olaf Mooij heeft vooral bekendheid verworven met zijn autosculpturen in de openbare ruimte. Bijna iedereen kent zijn *Braincar*, een auto waarvan de bovenkap is omgevormd tot grote hersenpan. Overdag rijdt de auto door een wijk, stad of straat, en 's avonds droomt de auto van zijn dag door middel van videoprojecties op het matwitte hersenvlak.

Al vroeg in de jaren negentig zocht Mooij de straat als podium voor zijn werk. Kenmerkend voor zijn generatie, met kunstenaars als Joep van Lieshout en Jeroen Doorenweerd, was dat ze hun werk veel meer verbonden met de wereld buiten de muren van de tentoonstellingszalen. Dat leidde vaak tot verwarring: was het wel kunst dat ze maakten? Zo werd Mooij in 2001 genomineerd voor de Designprijs Rotterdam met zijn *DJ Mobiel* (1999), een verbouwde Ford Sierra met professionele geluidsinstallatie, veertien speakers en een DJ booth. Maar voor de goede beschouwer is het altijd duidelijk geweest: het werk van Mooij is stevig geworteld in de beeldhouwtraditie.

Aan de basis van de beeldhouwkunst ligt het vermogen van de kunstenaar om in dode materie leven te suggereren. De beroemde *Kus* van Rodin is in feite een brok steen, maar wij kunnen niets anders zien (en voelen) dan een hartstochtelijke omhelzing. De auto's van Olaf Mooij zijn niets meer dan carrosserie, maar worden door hem getransformeerd tot persoonlijkheid, tot levende materie. Door toevoeging van overdreven kappen, haarstukken of uitvergrotingen van onderdelen komen speelse, karikaturale beelden tot stand. De humoristische beelden relativeren de hedendaagse verhouding van de mens tot de machines en apparaten die hem omringen. Het universele fenomeen van de objectliefde wordt op speelse wijze geridiculiseerd, zoals in de *Chesterfield Car*, net zo uitnodigend als een echte Chesterfield bank (2004, collectie Museum Boijmans van Beuningen).

In zijn recente serie werken, die vrijwel volledig tijdens de tentoonstelling 'Before and After' in TENT Rotterdam (februari 2009) werden gepresenteerd, lijkt Mooij te willen terugkeren naar de volstrekte autonomie van de sculptuur. Zijn autobeelden hebben geen gebruiksfunctie meer, maar doen alleen nog herinneren aan het transportmiddel. De werken staan, liggen, hangen en leunen in de tentoonstellingsruimte. Ze zijn zonder sokkel op de grond geplaatst en hebben zonder hun gebruikswaarde een kwetsbare uitstraling. De huid, het oppervlak van de auto staat centraal. Het vel van wat een stationcar geweest zou kunnen zijn ligt geplooid op de grond. Een Volkswagenvorm ligt wankel op de vloer, zijn oppervlak bedekt met een zwarte steenachtige laag. Het werk presenteert zich als een fossiel overblijfsel van een ver verleden. Een kleine autovorm wordt omspannen door een geelachtig vlies waar het bijna uit lijkt los te breken; de suggestie van een geboorte is gewekt. In het spel tussen vorm en betekenis, tussen volume en oppervlak, tussen symboolfunctie en gebruiksfunctie zoekt Mooij precies het punt waarop ze samenvallen. Einde en begin, before and after: deze dode materie is biomorf, de verbeelding van levende wezens. De recente sculpturen van Mooij hebben een sterk tactiele uitstraling, ze nodigen uit om aan te raken en, ach waarom niet, om van te houden.

1189.81.237

BEFORE AND AFTER
_MARIETTE DÖLLE

The Rotterdam artist Olaf Mooij is especially known for his car sculptures in the open air. Almost everyone is familiar with his *Braincar*, a vehicle whose top has the shape of a human brain. During the day, the car drives through neighbourhoods or down city streets, while in the evening its dreams about the day's events are visualised through video projections on the matt white surface of its brain.
Already in the early nineties, Mooij looked to the street as a stage for his work. It was characteristic of artists of his generation – including the likes of Joep van Lieshout and Jeroen Doorenweerd – to connect their work much more with the world outside the walls of the exhibition halls. But people often found that confusing: was it really visual art? In 2001, for example, Mooij's *DJ Mobile* (1999) – a converted Ford Sierra with a professional sound system, fourteen speakers and a built-in DJ booth – was even nominated for the Rotterdam Design Prize. But to those with a keen eye it has always been clear: Mooij's work is firmly rooted in the sculptural tradition.

Sculpture has always been about the artist's ability to suggest life in inanimate matter. Rodin's famous *The Kiss* is simply a piece of rock, yet we cannot see (or feel) anything but a passionate embrace. Olaf Mooij's cars are nothing more than bodywork, yet he has transformed them into personalities, into living matter. With the addition of exaggerated hairstyles or hairpieces or the enlargement of certain parts, playful and caricatural images materialise. These humorous images put into perspective the relationship that contemporary human beings have with the various machines and gadgets that surround them. Mooij pokes fun at our universal infatuation with such objects with works like his *Chesterfield Car* (2004, Museum Boijmans van Beuningen collection), which looks just as inviting as any real chesterfield couch.

With his recent series of works – nearly all of which were exhibited in the show 'Before and After' at TENT Rotterdam (February 2009) – Mooij appears to want to return to the absolute autonomy of sculpture. His car pieces no longer have any practical function but are only reminiscent of the familiar mode of transport. The individual works stand, lie, hang or lean in the exhibition space. Placed on the ground without a pedestal, and lacking any functional value, they seem rather vulnerable. The car's surface forms the focal point. The 'skin' of what once could have been an estate car lies in folds on the ground. A Volkswagen form lies unsteady on the floor, its surface covered with a layer of black, stone-like material. The work presents itself as a fossilised remnant of a distant past. A tiny car form appears to be on the verge of breaking out of the yellowish membrane that envelops it, suggesting the notion of birth. Mooij seeks exactly that point within the interplay between form and meaning, between volume and surface, between symbolic function and practical use, where all those things converge. Beginning and end, before and after: this inanimate matter is biomorphic, a representation of living beings. Mooij's recent sculptures have a strongly tactile quality; they are practically asking to be touched and – indeed, why not? – to be loved.

1189.81.237

HAIRCARS _2000-2005

1 **Haircars, 2000-2004**
Scale model 1:18
Odapark, Venray, 2006
2 **Haircars, final series, 2004**
Scale model 1:18
30x11x13 cm
3 **Punk Trabant, 2005**
400x160x290 cm
Collection: Planet Art, Hengelo

HONG KONG _2006

4 Posters for Haircars exhibition in Hong Kong, 2006
5 Overview of Haircars at Festival Walk in Hong Kong, 2006

PIRATENWAGEN _1997

6 **Piratenwagen 4, 1997**
350x150x190 cm (On the road)
7 **Piratenwagen 4, 1997**
350x150x190 cm
Beeldenbiënnale Bearse, Belgium, 2005

SOUNDSYSTEM _2000-2002

8 **Soundsystem (large), 2002**
9 **Soundbike, 2000**
Collection: Veeger-van Heeswijck
10 **Soundshoe (m), 2001**
Size 42 | Collection: CBK Rotterdam
11 **Soundshoe (f), 2001**
Size 38 | Collection: CBK Rotterdam
12 **Soundsystem (medium), 2002**

DJ MOBILE _1999

13 **DJ Mobile, 1999**
470x195x195 cm
Heineken Nightlife at Ahoy, Rotterdam, 2001
14 **DJ Mobile, 1999**
Video still from a TV commercial for Studio Brussel, 2009
15 **DJ Mobile, 1999**
Collection: VRT TV Brussel

BRAINCAR _2005

16 **Braincar, 2005**
560x240x245 cm
Braincar, 2005 (During the day)
Braincar, 2005 (Dreaming)

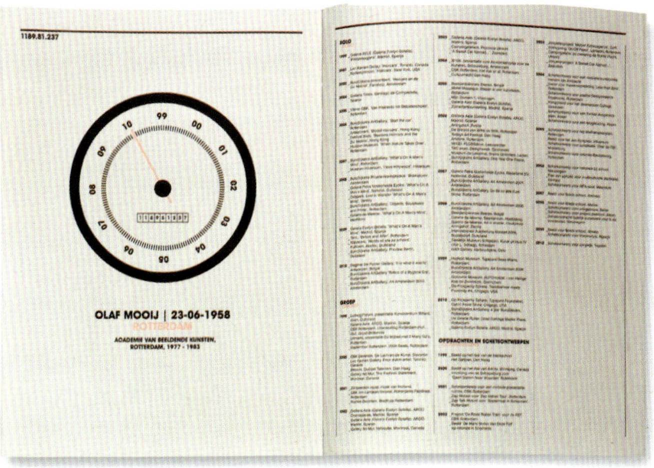

1189.81.237

OLAF MOOIJ | 23-06-1958
ROTTERDAM
ACADEMIE VAN BEELDENDE KUNSTEN, ROTTERDAM, 1977 - 1983

SOLO

GROEP

"WHEN I WAS A CHILD, MY FATHER ALWAYS SAID, 'WELL DONE BOY!' TO HIS CAR AFTER A LONG DRIVE, AND GAVE IT A FRIENDLY PUNCH."

Why Not, Otto Snoek

Design Agency:
Studio Beige
Client:
Otto Snoek
Production Date:
2010
Description:
For over a decade photographer Otto Snoek has been photographing the people of his hometown Rotterdam. Studio Beige designed a comprehensive book of his most compelling works. The designer tried to emphasise their theatrical quality by mounting the works onto full spreads, which enables the reader to almost physically enter the photographs. When closed the book - dull-grey on the outside - looks like a piece of pavement or a tile, referring to Otto Snoek's professional habitat: the streets of Rotterdam.
Award: Nominated for the Best Book Award at the Photofestival Photo Espana 2010.

WHY NOT/ OTTO SNOEK

De Kuip
HAL Cruise Terminal
Pretorialaan
Boompjes
Het Park
Coolsingel
Eendrachtsplein
Baja Beach Club
Groothandelsgebouw
Coolsingel
Ahoy
Maasboulevard
Pretorialaan
Baja Beach Club
Museum Boymans Van Beuningen
Las Palmas

Lijnbaan
Schouwburgplein
De Bijenkorf
Maashaven
Boompjes
De Doelen
Hoogstraat
Hofplein
De Kuip
Nieuwe Binnenweg
Aert van Nesstraat
Coolsingel
Lijnbaan
Baja Beach Club
Hoogstraat
Baja Beach Club

DE STAD HEEFT GEEN BOODSCHAP MEER AAN HAAR BEWONERS, WANT DEZE DOEN ALLEEN NOG MAAR BOODSCHAPPEN.

geeft onze exacte positie door en met een TomTom komen we overal zonder te weten waar we naartoe gaan. Misschien kunnen we de versnelling van het dagelijkse leven alleen maar bijhouden door ons in automobiele capsules op te sluiten. Zo kunnen we wrijvingsloos aan elkaar voorbij gaan. Wanneer de stem zich via de earphone verinnerlijkt en de blik zich achter de autovoorruit verschanst, bereikt de automobiele netwerkstad haar publieke grenzen. De openbare ruimte verinnerlijkt zich in dit automobiele bestaan.

We wonen in een decor, waar onze levens fysiek en digitaal, met auto en mobieltje globaal worden geënsceneerd en gemobiliseerd. Ook al kom je nauwelijks je buurt uit en speelt je leven zich grotendeels lokaal af, met auto's en vliegtuigen zijn we reëel, met mobiel en computer virtueel met de hele wereld verbonden. Het zijn verlengstukken van onze armen en benen, ogen en oren. Door deze media of middelen transformeren we van passanten naar buitenstaanders: we treden via auto en mobiel buiten onszelf. We zijn letterlijk ek(naar buiten)-statisch (staand), extatisch.

Glokaal-mediale extase: binnenstebuiten

In de media keren we onszelf binnenstebuiten. De 'personal computer' is zeker geen private aangelegenheid: elk bericht wordt opgeslagen, iedere aanslag op het toetsenboard geregistreerd. Ons privéverlangen is een publiek geheim. Die extase ervaren we vooral in genotvol rijden: rijden om het rijden. Of dat nu te langzaam gaat of te snel, maakt niet uit. Zondagsrijders verschillen niet veel van joyrijders, ook al denkt de politie daar anders over. De absolute vrijheid ligt in het afschaffen van de snelheidsbeperking. Ook onafgebroken chatten is genotvol. Het maakt ons gewichtsloos. We zweven extatisch door de wereld. De belofte van deze wrijvingsloze vrijheid ligt al besloten in louter de beschikbaarheid van auto of mobiel: we kunnen immers weg wanneer we willen. Zo zijn we thuis altijd alweer onderweg. Ons privéleven en publieke leven wordt in de automobiliteit kortgesloten.

Niets is zo lokaal als ons eigen huis. Wanneer we de voordeur achter ons dichttrekken lijken we ons af te sluiten in een fysieke capsule. Maar binnen zijn we ook alweer globaal. We staan op elk moment interfaciaal oog in oog met iedereen over de hele globe. Ook al slaat de voordeur dicht, we blijven browsend, MSN'end en SMSend interactief de planeet omcirkelen. Zelfs sporten is nu virtueel mogelijk met de Wii. Ons huis is een gerieflijke glokaal-mediale capsule.

Deze private publiciteit werkt ook omgekeerd. Op het moment dat we ons huis verlaten en de openbare ruimte betreden creëren we daarin met onze auto en ons mobieltje privécapsules. De auto is ons tweede huis. Inmiddels is deze volledig aangesloten op de globe. Ons mobieltje is de nieuwste privécapsule in het publieke domein. Met auto en mobieltje - de pijlers van de hedendaagse automobiliteit - zijn we fysiek en virtueel *urbi et orbi*. We zijn - vaak uit veiligheidsoverwegingen - zelfvoorzienende capsules die als informationele knooppunten ingelogd en aangesloten blijven. Kortom, ons privédomein blijft op het publieke domein aangesloten en de openbare ruimte is door auto's en mobieltjes geprivatiseerd. Ziedaar onze glokaal-mediale stadsextase.

De fysieke stad: face to face

Natuurlijk, de stadsmens was altijd al behept met een existentiële onrust. De huidige ADHD mentaliteit die voor het bijhouden van hypes, trends, flows en flexen vereist is om staande te blijven maakt het stadsleven amechtig. De arbeidersstad Rotterdam sprak nog in slogans als 'geen woorden maar daden' en 'niet lullen maar poetsen'. Zij baatte haar daadkrachtige aanpak uit via het beeld van opgestroopte mouwen. Deze tomeloze energie sluit naadloos aan op de jobhoppende, funshoppende en flexwerkende netwerkstad. Inmiddels heeft het ook het culturele leven gemobiliseerd. Dit leven speelt zich steeds meer in de buitenruimte af. In de stad als theater is de afstand tussen passanten stilzwijgend vastgelegd en probleemloos zolang zij zich routineus verplaatsen. Niemand betreedt de actieradius van anderen, zeker niet die van groepen. Dit verandert allemaal als de stad de teugels laat vieren.

Teugels vieren

De consumptiesamenleving met zijn hyperindividualisme kent zijn eigen extase. De erbij horende excessen zijn geïndividualiseerd en dienstbaar gemaakt aan de levensstilering. Maar op gezette tijden hernieuwt de stad haar openbare leven en neemt de extase weer een collectieve vorm aan. Als excessieve mobiliteit het grootstedelijke leven runt, als we via onze excessieve consumptiepatronen in toom worden gehouden, dan is ieder feest, ieder festival, elke festiviteit letterlijk een viering van de teugels. Wanneer voorbijgangers weer buitenstaanders worden, wordt het capsulaire bestaan van angstige individuen doorbroken. De grootstedelijke kwaliteit van de openbare ruimte wordt opgeladen en versterkt door een gevoel van saamhorigheid. We consumeren weliswaar overvloedig, maar doen even geen boodschappen.

We zijn vrij en vieren feest. Carnaval heeft door de eeuwen heen mensen de gelegenheid geboden de boel letterlijk op zijn kop te zetten: de gewone burger kon even prins zijn. De autoriteiten konden bespot worden zonder dat daar sancties op stonden. De teugels van de noeste arbeid werden voor een korte tijd gevierd en er werd oogluikend gedoogd wat op gewone dagen streng verboden is. In Zuid-Amerika is carnaval een levensstijl en treffen mensen haast het jaar rond voorbereidingen. Er wordt enorm veel geld en menskracht geïnvesteerd die in enkele dagen worden verspild. Overvloedig voedsel, drank, drugs en seks consumeren, het hoort er allemaal bij.

Eternally Yours, Time in Design

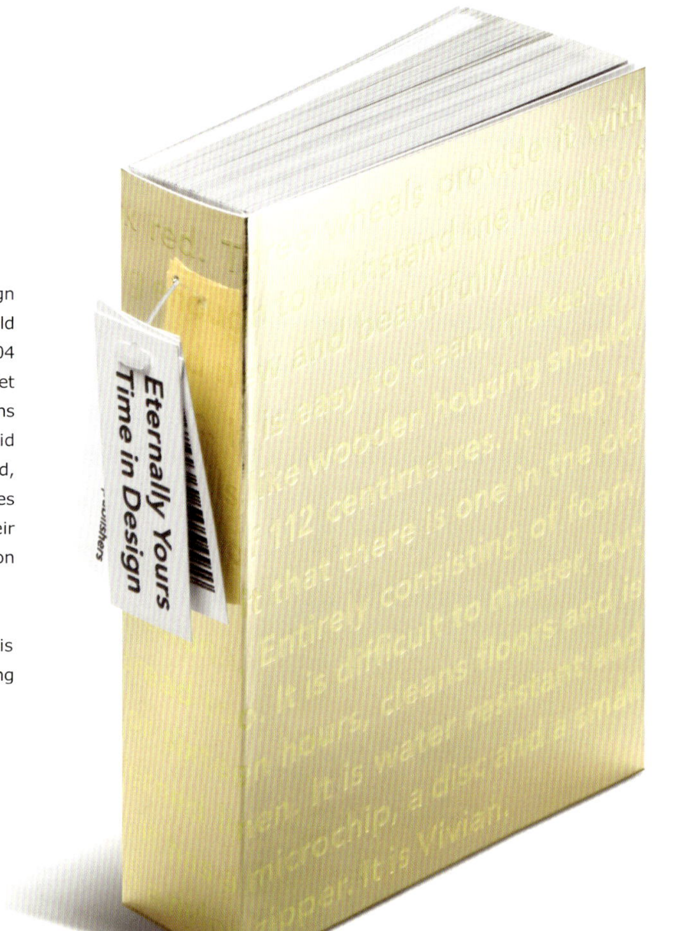

Design Agency:
Thonik
Designer:
Thonik
Client:
010 Publishers
Production Date:
2004
Description:

Eternally Yours wishes to prolong the lifetime of products by way of a new design mentality. The first conference in 1997 was accompanied by a publication, which sold out very quickly. It won an I.D. Best of Category 98. The second conference in 2004 was called "Time in Design". Because of this theme, and because the first booklet is reproduced on the last pages of the second, Thonik related some of the decisions in the design to the former publication. On the edge of the first booklet it said "eternally yours", now it says "Future Nostalgia". The former booklet was gilt-edged, now Gold has replaced yellow in the CMYK printing. The first booklet had pictures of the designers who had shortly fallen in love; the second has pictures of their children. To enhance the book as a product all information on the cover is printed on labels that hang from the spine.

Comment:

As a sample sheet of all possible considerations and views about this subject, this book is worth while. Bound in embossed gold foil, Time in Design's exquisite binding exudes care and preciousness. You'll want to keep it, which is exactly the point.

L.A. Lofts

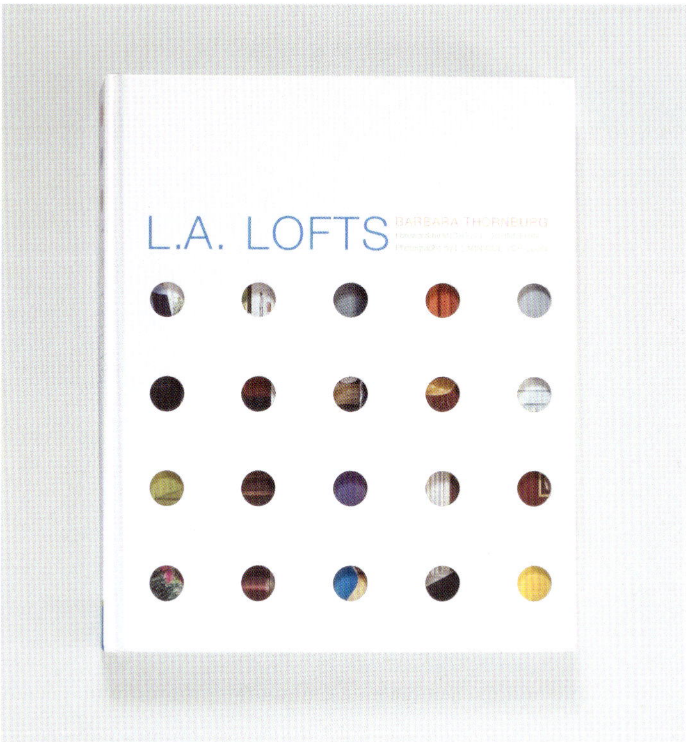

Design Agency:
Think Studio, NYC
Designer:
John Clifford
Client:
Chronicle Books
Production Date:
2006
Description:
There is such a variety of spaces in the book, that one image on the cover would not do the book justice. The thread that united all the lofts was the bold use of colour. So, the diecut cover hints at the varied colours and textures of the eclectic Los Angeles loft spaces featured within.

One Million

Design Agency:

Think Studio, NYC

Designer:

John Clifford, Herb Thornby

Client:

Abrams Image

Production Date:

2010

Description:

The plan of the book is simple: two hundred pages; five thousand dots to a page. Author and New Yorker editor Hendrik Hertzberg wants the reader to actually see, perhaps for the first time ever, exactly one million of something. To keep the simple design lively, the value of the dots were varied so they twinkle and animate a bit. The design won AIGA 50 Books/50 Covers; HOW Magazine International Design Award.

Comment:

A great example of humour intertwined with good information design.

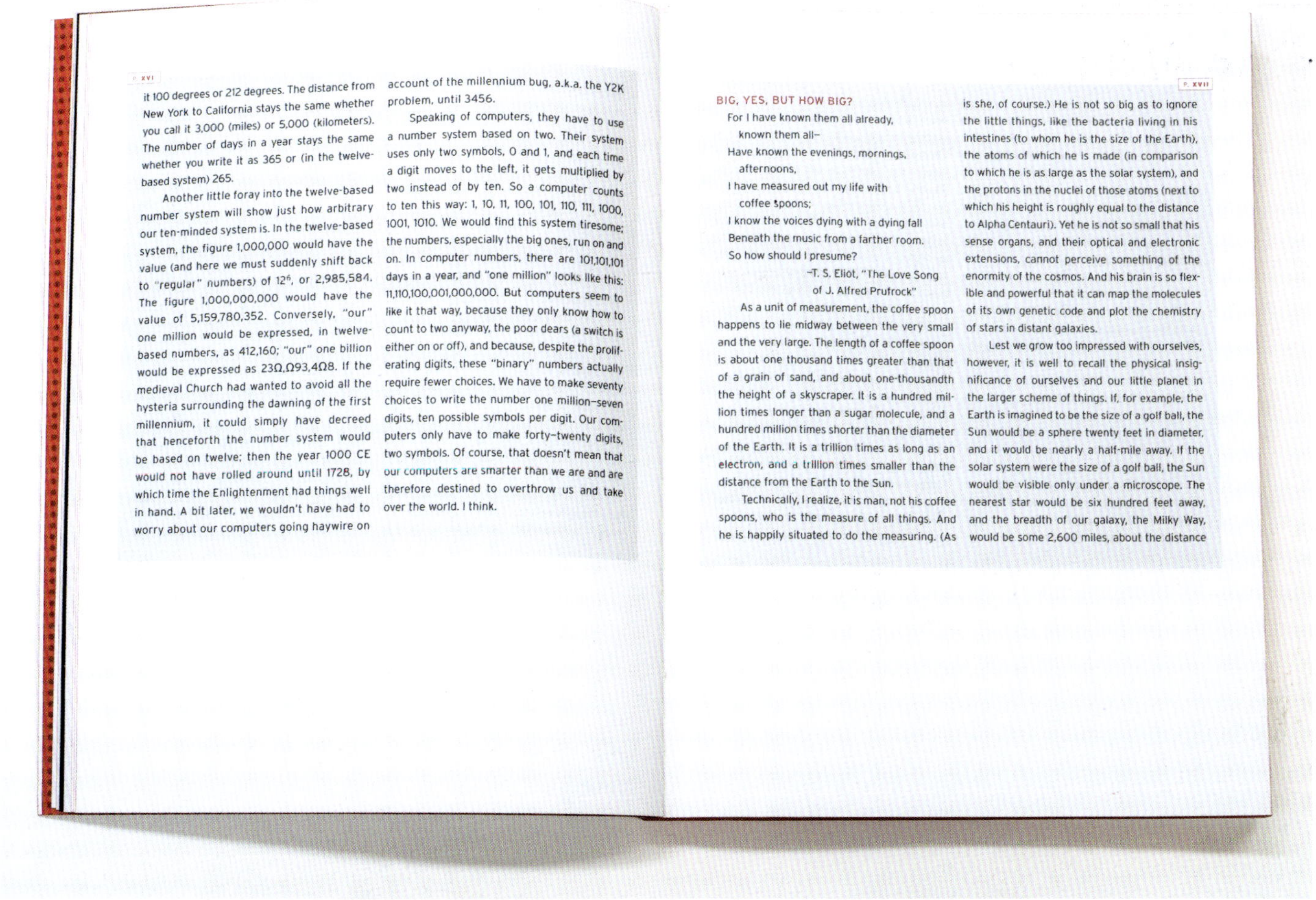
P. XVI
it 100 degrees or 212 degrees. The distance from New York to California stays the same whether you call it 3,000 (miles) or 5,000 (kilometers). The number of days in a year stays the same whether you write it as 365 or (in the twelve-based system) 265.
Another little foray into the twelve-based number system will show just how arbitrary our ten-minded system is. In the twelve-based system, the figure 1,000,000 would have the value (and here we must suddenly shift back to "regular" numbers) of 12⁶, or 2,985,584. The figure 1,000,000,000 would have the value of 5,159,780,352. Conversely, "our" one million would be expressed, in twelve-based numbers, as 412,160; "our" one billion would be expressed as 23Ω,Ω93,4Ω8. If the medieval Church had wanted to avoid all the hysteria surrounding the dawning of the first millennium, it could simply have decreed that henceforth the number system would be based on twelve; then the year 1000 CE would not have rolled around until 1728, by which time the Enlightenment had things well in hand. A bit later, we wouldn't have had to worry about our computers going haywire on account of the millennium bug, a.k.a. the Y2K problem, until 3456.
Speaking of computers, they have to use a number system based on two. Their system uses only two symbols, 0 and 1, and each time a digit moves to the left, it gets multiplied by two instead of by ten. So a computer counts to ten this way: 1, 10, 11, 100, 101, 110, 111, 1000, 1001, 1010. We would find this system tiresome; the numbers, especially the big ones, run on and on. In computer numbers, there are 101,101,101 days in a year, and "one million" looks like this: 11,110,100,001,000,000. But computers seem to like it that way, because they only know how to count to two anyway, the poor dears (a switch is either on or off), and because, despite the proliferating digits, these "binary" numbers actually require fewer choices. We have to make seventy choices to write the number one million—seven digits, ten possible symbols per digit. Our computers only have to make forty—twenty digits, two symbols. Of course, that doesn't mean that our computers are smarter than we are and are therefore destined to overthrow us and take over the world. I think.
P. XVII
BIG, YES, BUT HOW BIG?
For I have known them all already,
known them all—
Have known the evenings, mornings,
afternoons,
I have measured out my life with
coffee spoons;
I know the voices dying with a dying fall
Beneath the music from a farther room.
So how should I presume?
—T. S. Eliot, "The Love Song
of J. Alfred Prufrock"
As a unit of measurement, the coffee spoon happens to lie midway between the very small and the very large. The length of a coffee spoon is about one thousand times greater than that of a grain of sand, and about one-thousandth the height of a skyscraper. It is a hundred million times longer than a sugar molecule, and a hundred million times shorter than the diameter of the Earth. It is a trillion times as long as an electron, and a trillion times smaller than the distance from the Earth to the Sun.
Technically, I realize, it is man, not his coffee spoons, who is the measure of all things. And he is happily situated to do the measuring. (As is she, of course.) He is not so big as to ignore the little things, like the bacteria living in his intestines (to whom he is the size of the Earth), the atoms of which he is made (in comparison to which he is as large as the solar system), and the protons in the nuclei of those atoms (next to which his height is roughly equal to the distance to Alpha Centauri). Yet he is not so small that his sense organs, and their optical and electronic extensions, cannot perceive something of the enormity of the cosmos. And his brain is so flexible and powerful that it can map the molecules of its own genetic code and plot the chemistry of stars in distant galaxies.
Lest we grow too impressed with ourselves, however, it is well to recall the physical insignificance of ourselves and our little planet in the larger scheme of things. If, for example, the Earth is imagined to be the size of a golf ball, the Sun would be a sphere twenty feet in diameter, and it would be nearly a half-mile away. If the solar system were the size of a golf ball, the Sun would be visible only under a microscope. The nearest star would be six hundred feet away, and the breadth of our galaxy, the Milky Way, would be some 2,600 miles, about the distance

62,760
Beats per minute, the wing speed of the world's most frantic insect, a midge of the genus Forcipomyia
60,760
Miles of blood vessels in the average human body
63,360
Inches in a mile

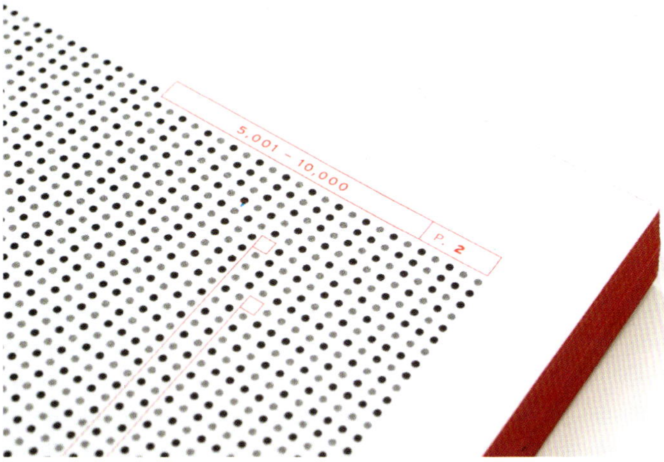
5,001 – 10,000
P. 2

Open Your Eyes

Design Agency:

Tiana Vasiljev

Client:

College Project

Production Date:

2008

Description:

Open Your Eyes was a final year college project that was designed to raise awareness of poverty and its effects. It is a collection of the third world stories and occurrences from around the globe. Bold typography was used as a powerful method of communication throughout the publication. The rough application of paint was created in combination with the imagery and colour, to portray the chaos contained in the stories. The final book has a rough and chaotic personality.

ARMS
OF AN
ANGEL
In late September 1968, I was blown out of a helicopter while we were attempting to land and pick up a small group of wounded soldiers at a remote base that was under attack.
We were apparently struck by a rocket fired from the ground nearby which severely damaged our ship throwing me clear.
I watched the ground rushing toward me 100 feet below and, just before impact, felt something squeeze me, then everything was black. I think this must have been my guardian angel protecting me – I was unconsciousness for several days and awoke to find I had lived with no permanent injury.
A few years later, in 1984 I quickly responded to a burglar alarm at a business with a great frequency of false alarms. It was almost 11pm, shift change, and I called off the backup unit assuming it to be another false alarm. I did not even unstrap my revolver when checking the building.
When I rounded the back corner of the building I saw all at the same time, a large hole knocked into the wall, a subject standing there with a car battery in his hand from the business and a gun on his waist that he was reaching for. Something behind me pushed me down while I was drawing my weapon and I heard two shots fired by the suspect. I later found
" My only fear is that someday my guardian angel might be busy with me and be needed by another" – Charles Carty

LOTS OF
MONEY = POV
ERTY
There is more to satisfaction than money, and public-policy programs aiming to tackle poverty need to move beyond simply raising people's income to also improving their quality of life in other areas.
These findings by Professor Mariano Rojas from Mexico's Facultad Latinoamericana de Ciencias Sociales are published online in Springer's journal, Applied Research in Quality Life.
The reduction of poverty is one of the main considerations in the design of both domestic and foreign-aid programs. To date, the focus of these programs has been to get people out of poverty by increasing their buying power.
Raising people's income will translate into greater well-being. Professor Rojas challenges this assumption and argues that measures of life satisfaction should also be taken into account when designing and evaluating poverty-abatement programs.
Professor Rojas used data from a yearly national survey run by the University of Costa Rica covering the years 2004-2006. In addition to questions about household income and the dependency on household income, he added more subjective questions about life satisfaction in general, as well as satisfaction with health, job, family relations and friendship

Fairly Unfair

Design Agency:

Toby Ng Design

Client:

Toby Ng

Production Date:

2007

Description:

This little game book contains games which are specially designed for lawyers. No, sorry, not everyone is given the opportunity to take the challenge. The rules are as set - simply the same as in all judicial courts and proceedings. Fair enough? This piece of work is inspired by the designer's experience of sitting in a few court sessions and listening to the discourse in them. Don't be fooled by the indication of trial language being your mother tongue; indeed, the conversations are filled with specialised terminology which bar common people from understanding. Last remark to players of these games: you should follow the instructions, but do not think about winning or completing the tasks.

game 01
A-maze-'n' term
HOW TO PLAY
The aim of the game is to find the way to the exit from the entrance.
PLAYER REQUIREMENT
The player should have graduated with an LLB.

start here
TERMINOLOGY

player 1
Judge
Witness
Barrister
Jury
Solicitor
Defendant
Journalist
Plaintiff

Who to listen to?
The plaintiff, having put her signature to the document, and not having been induced to do so by any fraud or misrepresentation, cannot be heard to say that she is not bound by the terms of the document because she did not read them.
The suing person had signed the document without being lied to or misled. As a result, she cannot say that she is not bound by the terms of the document.

Rediscover the Heritage of Hong Kong

Design Agency:
Toby Ng Design
Client:
Toby Ng
Production Date:
2006
Description:
The signature red-white-blue bag weighs with photos of some inconspicuous people, places and heritage of Hong Kong. To savour the beauty, the olde is captured on recycled newspaper.

皇后碼頭

Uncovered

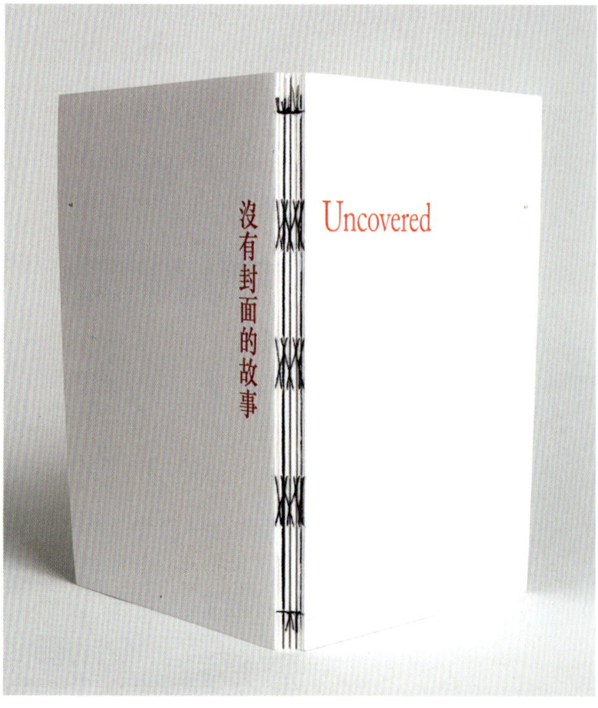

Design Agency:

Toby Ng Design

Client:

Uncovered

Production Date:

2008

Description:

If a book-cover is where people identify a book, no identity, like the ones in it, is offered to this book. Perspective is all that matters: read the book in any usual way and repeat the same in reverse – learn their stories in English, or in Chinese, or in both. The choice is upon you, but for the personages, they do not have one.

Concept Book & Kit for Prototype Typeface Experimental Work

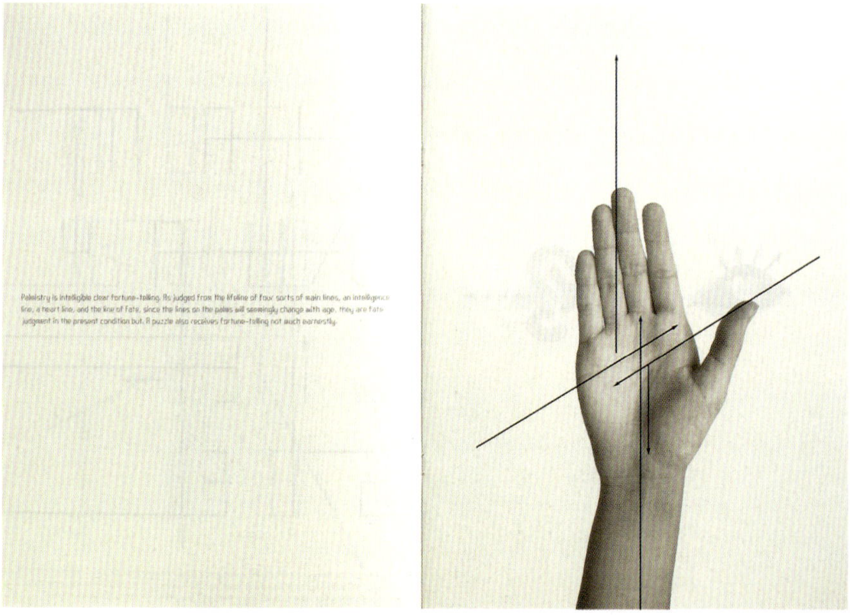

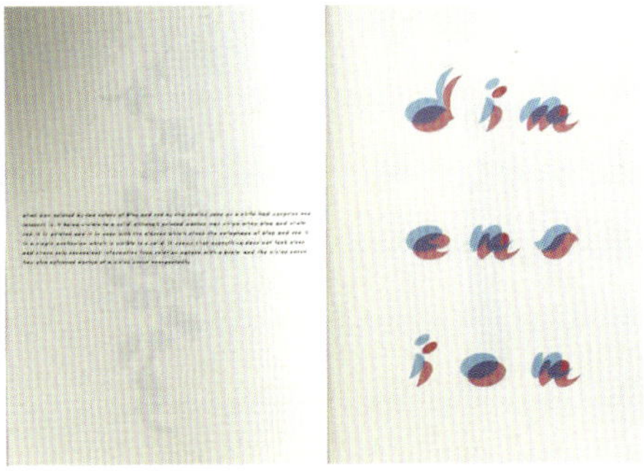

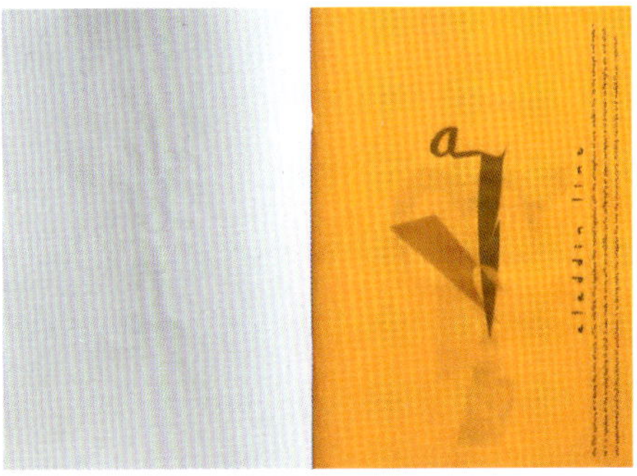

Designer:

Toshiyasu Nanbu

Client:

Taste Inc.

Production Date:

2010

Description:

In this Concept Book & Kit for Prototype Typeface Experimental Works, the Taste Inc. designed by art book form is an image book by an original font of production.

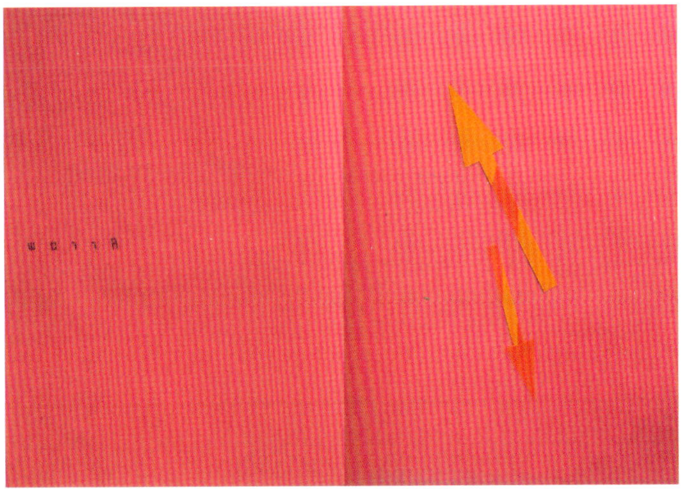

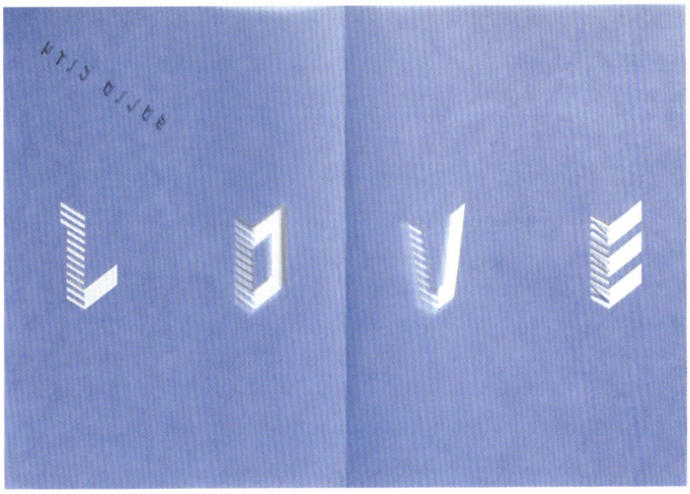

236—237

Publication Sound & Vision

Design Agency:

Trapped in Suburbia

Client:

Institute of Sound & Vision

Production Date:

2008

Description:

For the Institute of Sound and Vision the designer made a unique farewell present for their departing president. In the publication they've translated video and sound onto the 600 pages. The book contains David Bowies "Sound and Vision" (single version), pop-ups, a DVD, several flip booklets and a RFID tag.

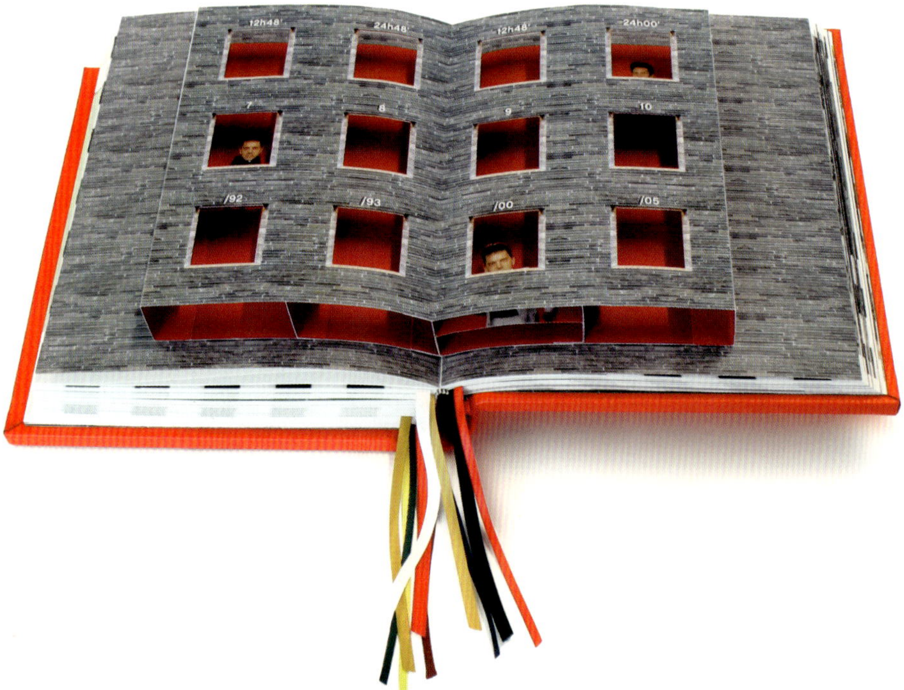

THE GIFT OF SOUND AND VISION

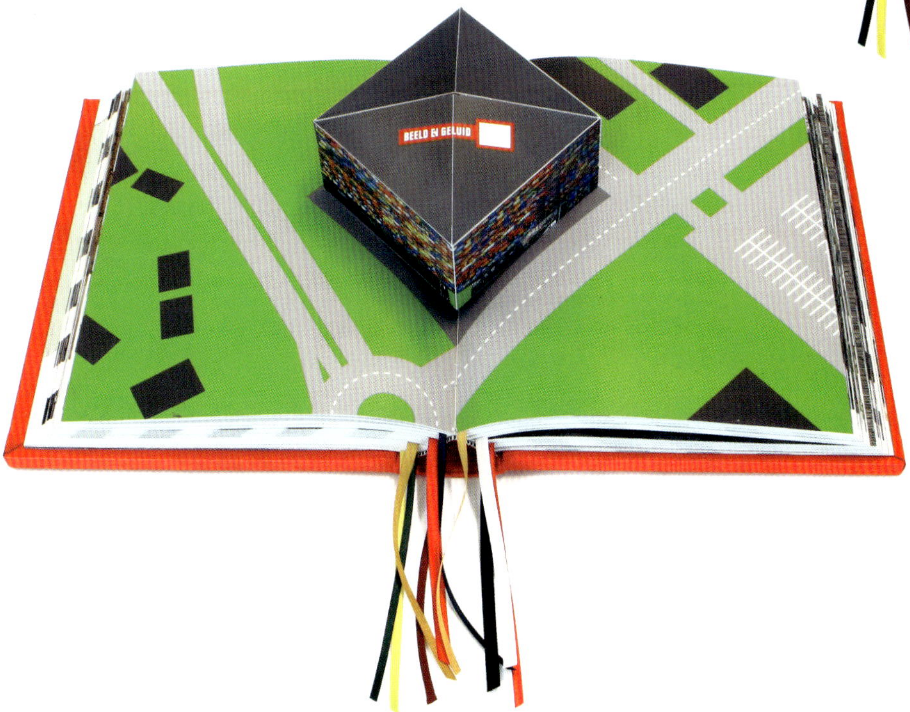
BEELD EN GELUID

Book VJ Movement

Design Agency:

Trapped in Suburbia

Client:

VJ Movement

Production Date:

2009

Description:

VJ Movement gives journalist around the world the opportunity to show their stories and tell their truths. Everyone can join the VJ Movement and pitch their story ideas to the journalists. If you want to hear more about a certain topic because you can't see this on the regular news, you can pitch your idea. If your idea get the most votes, a professional VJ journalist will report the story for you and it will be published online.

THE VJ MOVEMENT
CARTOONISTS

»THIS IS A HUGE GLOBAL CRISIS.
JUST UNDER A BILLION PEOPLE
LACK ACCESS TO WATER.«
JOHN SAUER
REPRESENTATIVE OF WATER ADVOCATES
AS TOLD TO KIRAN KHALID
[redacted]

Crisis

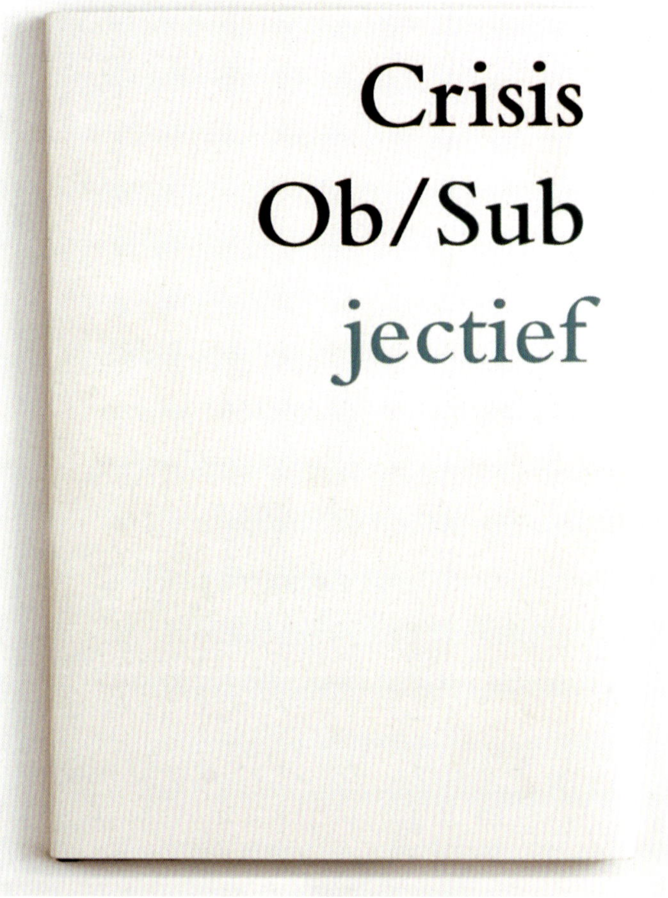

Designer:

Wilfred van der Weide

Client:

Crisis

Production Date:

2009

Description:

"Crisis" is a visual translation of the medium "newspaper" to "book". The designer picked a random article in the newspaper as a starting point for a change in form. The article is about how the worldwide economic crisis unfolds itself, first being only an undefinable banking issue but later surely effecting everyone. This observation is personalised into a poem that explains the issue at hand in clear language.

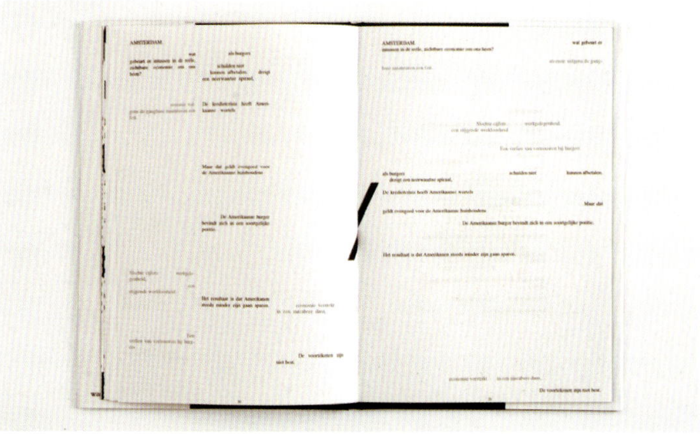

onder crisis

Ook echte econom lijdt onder crisis
De kredietcrisis woedt niet alleen in de financiële or. Ook Amerikaanse huishoudens zullen hun eigen
kredietbel moeten laten leeglopen. Dat trekt een zw wissel op de wereldeconomie.

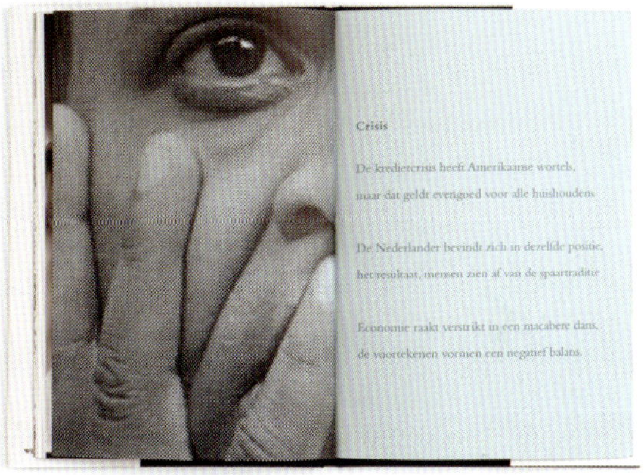
Crisis
De kredietcrisis heeft Amerikaanse wortels,
maar dat geldt evengoed voor alle huishoudens
De Nederlander bevindt zich in dezelfde positie,
het resultaat, mensen zien af van de spaartraditie
Economie raakt verstrikt in een macabere dans,
de voortekenen vormen een negatief balans.

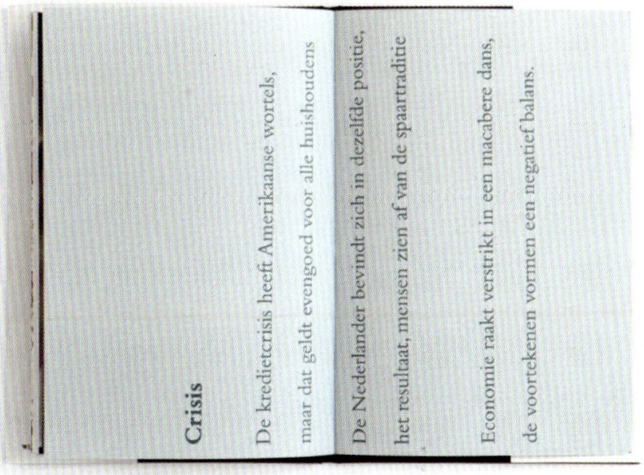
Crisis
De kredietcrisis heeft Amerikaanse wortels,
maar dat geldt evengoed voor alle huishoudens
De Nederlander bevindt zich in dezelfde positie,
het resultaat, mensen zien af van de spaartraditie
Economie raakt verstrikt in een macabere dans,
de voortekenen vormen een negatief balans.

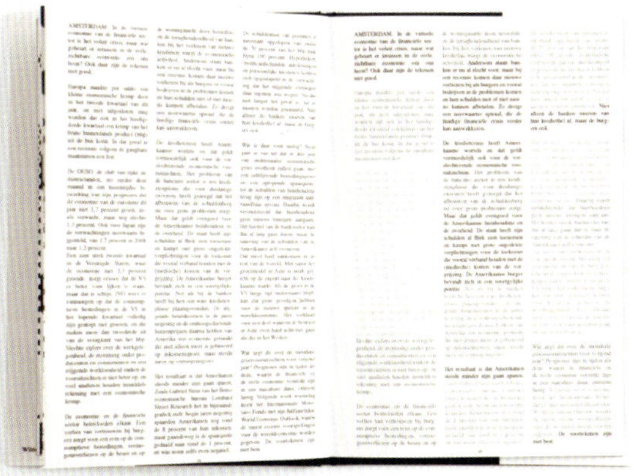

Vorming

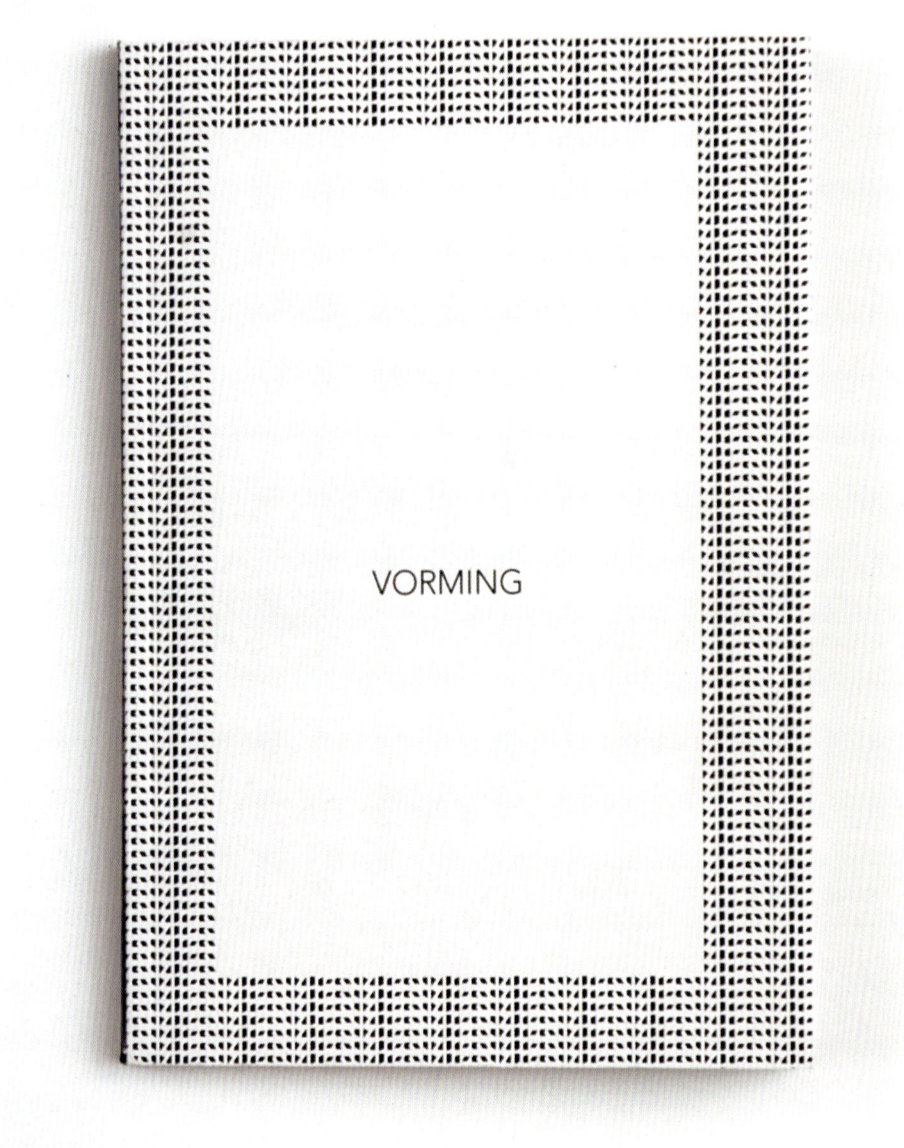

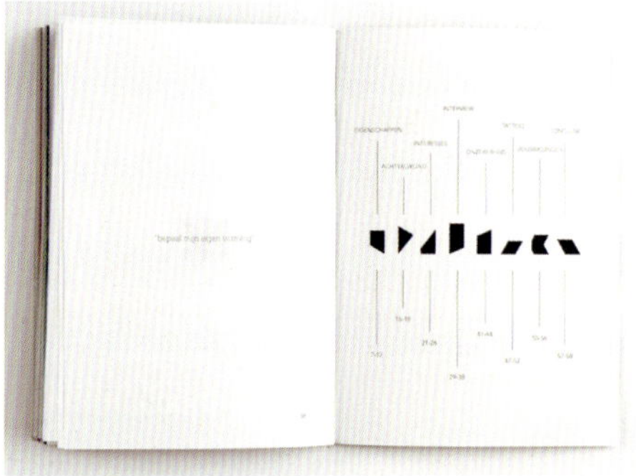

Designer:
Wilfred van der Weide
Client:
Vorming
Production Date:
2008
Description:
"Vorming" is a book revolving around the designer's classmate Janneke Smeets. A visual journey wherein the text and images about Janneke grow more personal by the page. This eventually leads to a portrait of her personal identity, for which the designer photographed Janneke in an expressive and full-frontal position. Her front and back are painted with the letters "I" and "K" ("ik" is dutch for "me"). The whole project was about the designer documenting Janneke's search for her own identity.

Film
Eternal sunshine of the spotless mind
Well, you d't know me,

TIVOLI
MASSIVE ATTACK
Stedelijk Museum
VIVE LA FETE

kleur ogen
blauw/
grijs

KAART

Moscow Style

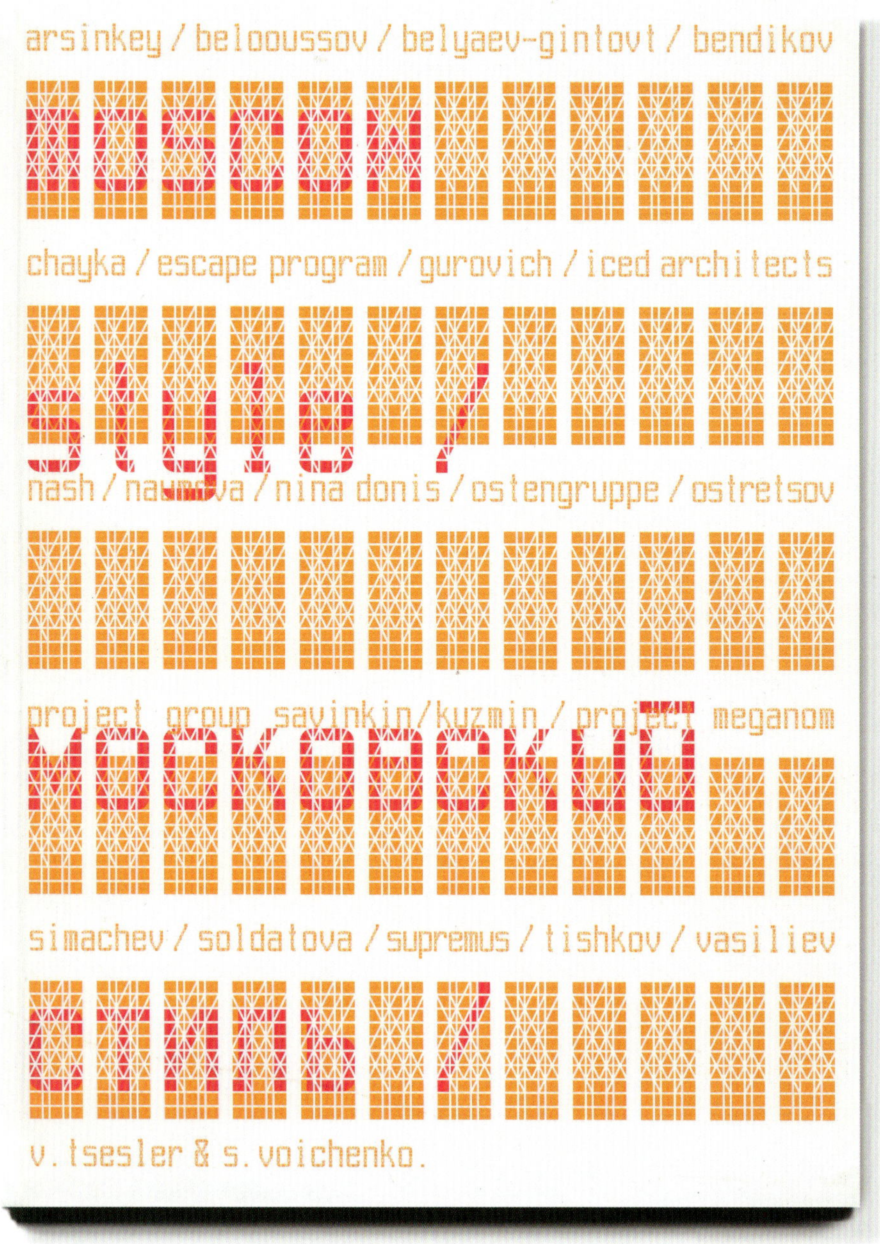

Design Agency:
Troika
Client:
Booth-Clibborn Editions
Production Date:
2005
Description:
Moscow Style was the first book Troika authored and is a compilation of the most exciting artists, designers and architects working in Moscow today. Troika compiled, edited and designed the book.

198,199 / credits / thank you /
copyright.

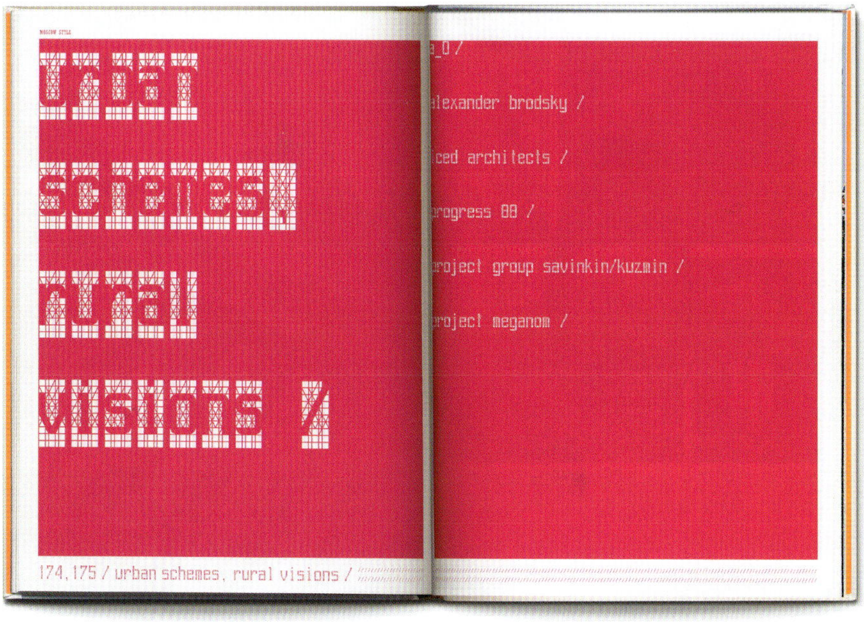
alexander brodsky /
iced architects /
progress 08 /
project group savinkin/kuzmin /
project meganom /
174,175 / urban schemes, rural visions /

24,25 / vladimir arkhipov /

MacroMicro

Design Agency:
Undoboy
Client:
MacroMicro
Production Date:
2005
Description:
The task is to design a book to hold two opposing texts together about postmodern design.

HONEST
Mobil
ON OVERCOMING MODERNISM
BY LORRAINE WILD
bitterness despite lifetimes of success, a lack of generosity towards
new work or new designers, defensiveness, the desire for control, and worst of all, the attempt to dictate the intellectually pathetic idea of a singular history.
Consider the recent spectacle of several of the most highly regarded names in graphic design excoriating the Walker Arts Center for daring to assemble an exhibition titled 'A History of Graphic Design' (note: not 'The History'), which, they thought, failed to

HONEST
Mobil
ON OVERCOMING MODERNISM
BY LORRAINE WI
pay suitable homage to their accomplishments. When graphic designers complain that their parents don't understand what they do, it used to sound like an innocent little joke, repeated to reinforce group identity; now it takes on a sinister tone, like a symptom of disease, grounds for professional counseling. Remember,
admitting that there is a problem is the first step to the road to recovery.
The only question is, who will be calling the shots?
A few competing ineffectual design organizations? The advertising-driven design press? Insular, pandering, academic institutions? Condescending cultural institutions? Commercially dependent design professionals? Or everyone else?

HELVETICA
ON OVERCOMING MODERNISM
BY LORRAINE WILD
art
Mobil
Mobil
Mobil
Mobil
Mobil

Man and Space

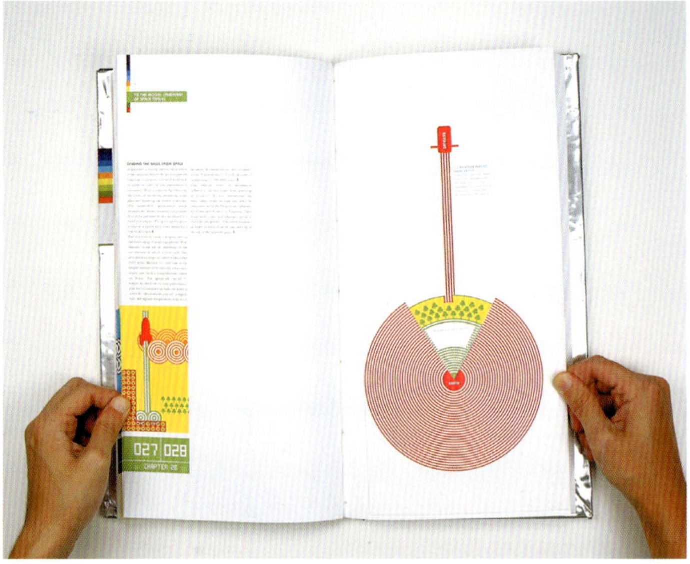

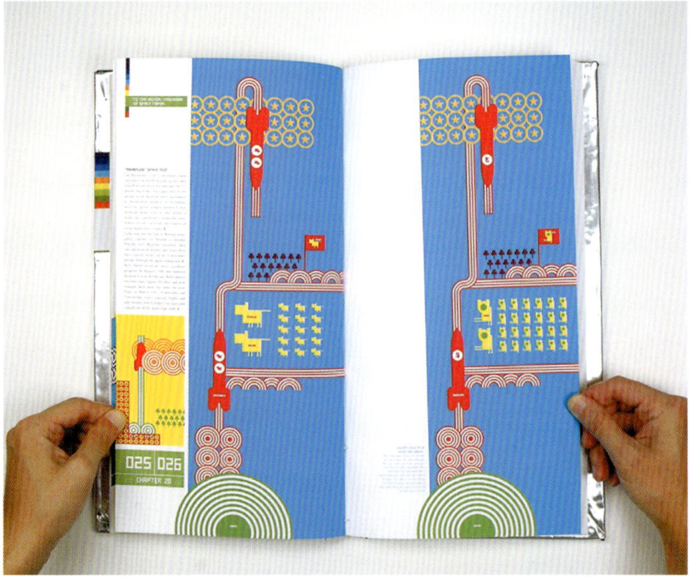

Design Agency:
Undoboy
Client:
Timelife Book
Production Date:
2005
Description:
The task is to redesign the 1960s' timelife book - Man and Space.

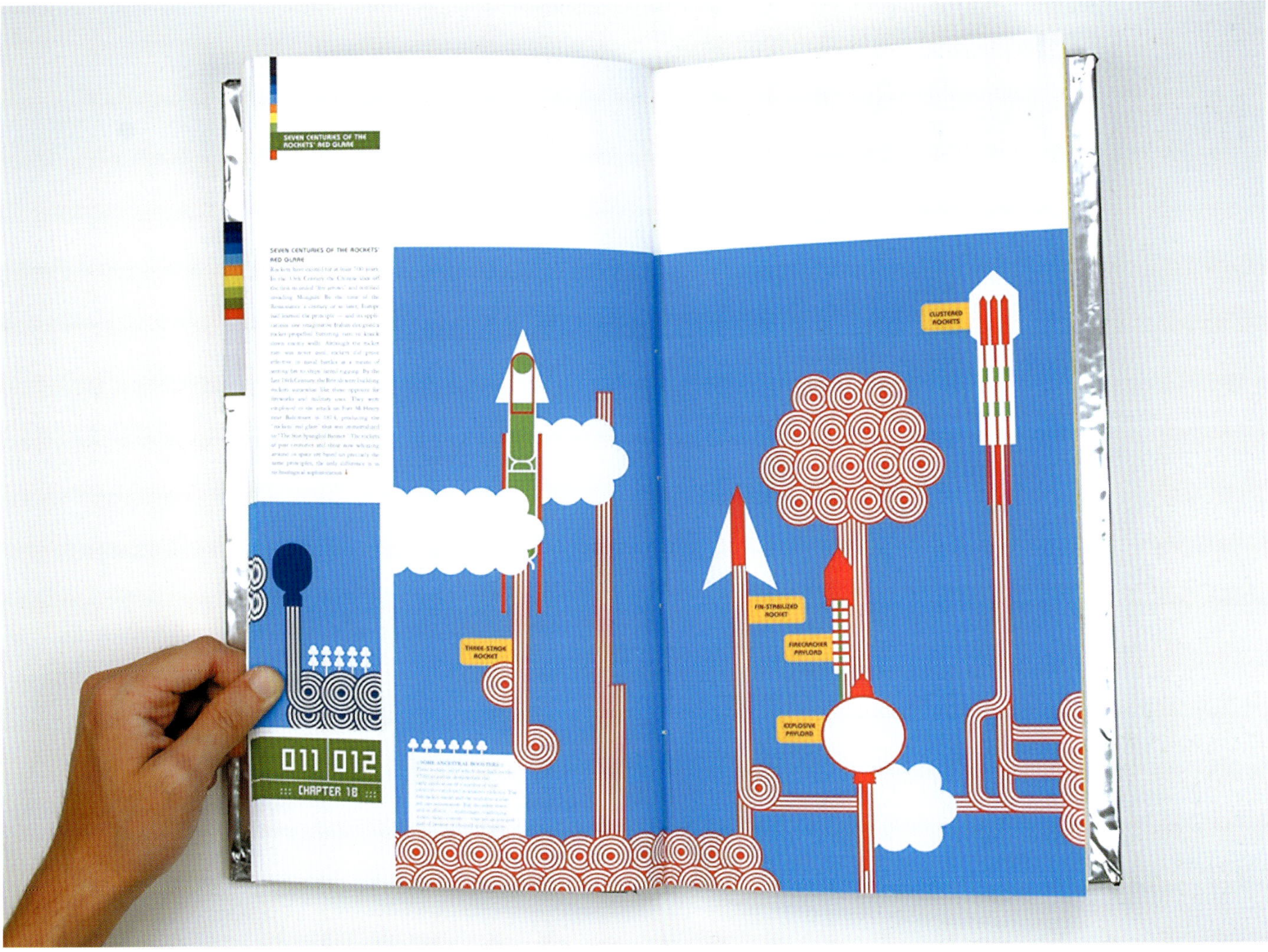
SEVEN CENTURIES OF THE ROCKETS' RED GLARE
CLUSTERED ROCKETS
THREE-STAGE ROCKET
FIN-STABILIZED ROCKET
FIRECRACKER PAYLOAD
EXPLOSIVE PAYLOAD
011 012
CHAPTER 18

019 020

005 006

The Art of Participation: 1950 to Now

Design Agency:
Volume Inc.
Creative Director:
Adam Brodsley, Eric Heiman
Designer:
Iran Narges
Client:
The San Francisco Museum of Modern Art
Production Date:
2008
Description:
Exhibition "The Art of Participation: 1950 to Now" presents an overview of participation-based art since the 1950s, reflecting on how artists create situations in which the public takes a collaborative role in the art-making process.

The exhibit catalogue's design demands similar participation on the audience's part by providing a space on the cover for a second, later book that will be a record of how visitor contributions change the form and content of the exhibition over its run at SFMOMA.

This theme is investigated further in the catalogue's interior through the "incomplete" nature of the headline typography and the empty spaces of the body text that are meant to be "filled in" (whether literally or mentally) by the reader.

specific social function for their proposals.[37] Despite an oft-proclaimed interest in social agendas associated with communal events (as seen in many Rirkrit Tiravanija projects) and in the creation of modular furniture that facilitates undefined gatherings (as in N55's *Hygiene System* [1997], Jorge Pardo's public pavilion for *Skulptur Projekte Münster 1997*, and c a l c's *DROPone* workspace for Michelangelo Pistoletto's Cittadellarte [1999; fig. 14]), most of these social spaces were confined to the art world. A second aspect is noteworthy: these updates on 1960s strategies rarely make use of today's networking technologies. They insist instead on a low-tech approach, stressing performative physical events and activities. Many refer back to the modular, precarious objects and installations of Clark and Oiticica, yet strangely ignore precedents such as the conceptual artist Tom Marioni or the activist collectives Ant Farm (see pls. 85–88) and Eventstructure Research Group (fig. 13).[38]

How, then, can an artwork include not only friends and peers, but also an undefined group of participants? How might the artist address a larger public without becoming simplistic, didactic, or compromised? Harrell Fletcher and Jon Rubin's *Pictures Collected from Museum Visitors' Wallets* (1998; pls. 123–24) started off with a participatory intervention in the museum space, which yielded the final artistic selection. Jochen Gerz, on the other hand, is no longer interested in exhibiting aesthetic choices made alone in the studio. The museum or the public space at large becomes his studio. His project *The Gift* (2000; pls. 147–50) does not question the "product" as such, but rather the way in which a work that is collaboratively produced, exhibited, and distributed can embody an actual representation of its coproducers. A community of museum visitors is documented in a temporary portrait gallery that is collected onsite but later dispersed throughout the city, region, or beyond. The museum unleashes its own products in a gesture of generosity toward those who were generous enough to contribute their portraits.

A great deal of critical attention has been directed at ways in which artists deal with institutional framing. The practice of institutional critique, as embodied by Haacke and Andrea Fraser (pl. 167), has worked to dissect the power regimes and ideological structures at work in the art world. It is equally interesting, though, to reflect on the public's use of the museum, whether prompted by an artist (Janet Cardiff's video walks [pls. 159–66]) or by the audience's own desires. Despite the structural conditions of the institutional setting—the need to obey the rules of quiet contemplation, not touch the artwork, respect the laws of ownership, etc.—visitors are constantly adopting tactical ways of using the museum. The French critic Michel de Certeau described a range of subjective counterpractices (cunning, tricks, maneuvers) as "weak." In the museum context, weak tactics might include drifting through an exhibition, simulating contemplation, or secretly taking pictures: a "fleeting and massive reality of a social activity at play with the order that contains it."[39] It is only through these personalized actions that the museum becomes what de Certeau would call "habitable"—a "space borrowed for a moment by a transient."[40] Artists such as Erwin Wurm (pls. 141–44) and Martin Walde (fig. 15), far from criticizing strong institutional ties, have successfully developed accessible yet also absurd or even obscure practices involving collaborative, performative actions. In their best moments, these actions transcend readability to posit a profound ambiguity, provoking "weak" responses toward the institution and the production process. By refusing to control such engagement through ubiquitous surveillance policies or, more subtly, to channel specific readings through didactic exhibition paths, a museum that offers open spaces for undefined interactions could radically change our general perception of the institution as an inflexible, deadening container.

Once again, artists have come to consider the museum a terrain for potentially transformative experiences, as Dorner envisioned in the 1920s. They openly address its codified spaces as social sites for singular visitors as well as for communities.[41] Without adhering to a specific political or activist agenda, artists and curators are exploring ways to address social relations beyond the ideological readings of Marxism and critical theory that dominated the discourse of the 1960s and 1970s, most notably expressed in the radical positions of Debord and the Situationists. But it is still an open question whether these practices actually constitute what Bourriaud calls "a social interstice [that] updates Situationism and reconciles it, as far as it is possible, with the

fig. 15
Martin Walde
***The Web*, 2006**
Installation view at Kunsthaus Baselland, Muttenz/Basel, Switzerland, 2006 / Strings, carbon rods, and springs / Courtesy Galerie Krinzinger, Vienna

37 Nicolas Bourriaud's *Relational Aesthetics* (Dijon, France: Les presses du réel, 2002) provoked numerous critical responses, most notably by Claire Bishop (to whom Liam Gillick and Grant Kester responded in turn). For a comprehensive study of their research, see Bishop's reader *Participation* (Cambridge, MA: MIT Press, 2006) and Kester's essays in *Conversation Pieces* (Berkeley: University of California Press, 2004). Whereas Bishop argues that the participatory experience needs to be acknowledged on a much broader scale, Kester—harking back to Eco's seminal *Open Work*—criticizes the lack of social responsibility and political impact from which relational aesthetics suffers even as it stakes a claim for microutopian concepts. Neither author, however, shows any interest in specifically media-related forms of participation. 38 "We propose the precarious as a new concept of existence against all the static crystallisation in the duration," Clark stated in 1983. *Lygia Clark* (Barcelona: Fundació Tàpies, 1994), 221.

39 Michel de Certeau, *The Practice of Everyday Life*, trans. Steven Rendall (Berkeley: University of California Press, 1984), xxiv. 40 Ibid., xxi. 41 In 2002, for example, Lee Mingwei addressed the museum as a living environment and involved the museum staff as hosts of *The Living Room*. Each host, including the artist, initiated discussions about the objects and personal belongings that they had brought into the "living room." The artist also worked with students and a kindergarten community on the importance of everyday objects. "I believe that the essence of this Museum does not reside merely in its architecture and objects, but also in its staff and extended family, who make this place function as a living organism on a day-to-day basis." http://gardnermuseum.org/education/airlee_text.html.

46

FRIELING 47

Zoo 09

ZOO
Idees
fresques de
Zoo
—
Ideas fres-
cas de
Zoo

ZOO
Idees
fresques de
Zoo
—
Ideas fres-
cas de
Zoo

ZOO

Design Agency:

Zoo Studio

Client:

Zoo Studio

Production Date:

2009

Description:

It is a book of self-promotion that contains some of the projects realised during year 2009.

INDEX

This edition published in June 2012

Design Media Publishing Limited
20/F Manulife Tower
169 Electric Rd, North Point
Hong Kong
Tel: 00852-28672587
Fax: 00852-25050411
E-mail: Kevinchoy@designmediahk.com
www.designmediahk.com

Editing: Andrea GUAN, Ryszard BIENERT
Proofreading: Qian YIN
Design/Layout: Jie ZHOU
Cover Design: Lin LIN

ISBN 978-988-15070-3-7

Printed in China